Praise for A GUEST IN MY OWN COUNTRY

"An East European might say that George Konrád's adventures through two terror regimes and a major revolution have been what one would expect from someone unfortunate enough to have been born in that part of Europe. In reality, Konrád's autobiography reveals much more than that: great tragedies, fabulous escapes, a complex personality, a great writer and beyond that, dignity and courage in the worst of circumstances." —István Deák, Professor Emeritus of history at Columbia University; author of *The Lawful Revolution: Louis Kossuth and the Hungarians, 1848–1849*

"Konrád takes you into another country. Another world. His words allow you to feel his world. In intimate and luxuriant detail. The world of childhood, the world of war, of politics, of hatreds. The world of words and of longing. In illuminating his country, his world, Konrád illuminates our world." —Lily Brett, author of *Too Many Men*

"Konrád's prose was never so luminous as in these moving yet clear-eyed and forthright recollections of his wartime childhood, his youth and early manhood under Communism, and of his life as a writer in the 'soft dictatorship' and after." —Ivan Sanders, translator, literary critic, and Adjunct Professor at Columbia University

"Emerging from the pen of a premier Hungarian intellectual, and spanning several turbulent decades, this vivid, unsentimental, candidly intimate memoir gives us an invaluable view of a complex history, and of a very Eastern European fate. Konrád's affectionate recollections of his childhood; his astonishing account of growing up precociously at war; and his sharply etched vignettes of repression and dissidence, poverty and pleasures thereafter, are marked by grace amidst turbulence, honesty without bitterness, and by an admirable balance between skepticism and deep attachments. An important, illuminating, and ultimately hopeful book." —Eva Hoffman, author of *Lost in Translation* and *After Such Knowledge*

A GUEST IN MY OWN COUNTRY

A Hungarian Life

George Konrád

Translated from the Hungarian by Jim Tucker

Edited by Michael Henry Heim

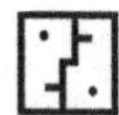

Other Press · New York

Originally published in Hungarian by Noran, Budapest, 2002, as *Elutazás és hazatérés*.

Originally published in Hungarian by Noran, Budapest, 2003, as *Fenn a hegyen napfogyatkozáskor*.
The author has approved the abridgment of Part II.

Production Editor: Mira S. Park
Text design: Kaoru Tamura

This book was set in 11 pt. ACaslon Regular by Alpha Graphics in Pittsfield, NH.

 Printed in the United States of America on acid-free paper. For information write to Other Press LLC, 2 Park Avenue, 24th Floor, New York, NY 10016. Or visit our Web site: www.otherpress.com.

Library of Congress Cataloging-in-Publication Data

Konrád, György.
[Elutazás és Hazatérés. English]
A guest in my own country : a Hungarian life / by George Konrád ;
translated by Jim Tucker ; edited by Michael Henry Heim.
p. cm.
Pt. 1. Originally published in 2001 as Elutazás és Hazatérés. Pt. 2. Originally published in 2003 as Fenn a hegyen napfogyatkozáskor.
ISBN-13: 978-1-59051-139-8
ISBN-10: 1-59051-139-5
1. Konrád, György. 2. Authors, Hungarian–20th century–Biography. I. Konrád, György. Fenn a hegyen napfogyatkozáskor. English. II. Tucker, Jim. III. Heim, Michael Henry. IV. Title.
PH3281.K7558Z46 2007
894'.51133—dc22
[B] 2006024280

I

Departure and Return

FEBRUARY 1945. WE ARE SITTING ON a bench in a motionless cattle car. I can't pull myself away from the open door and the wind whipping in off the snowy plains. I didn't want to be a constant guest in Budapest; I wanted to go home—a weeklong trip—to Berettyóújfalu, the town our parents had been abducted from, the town we had managed to leave a day before the deportations. Had we stayed one more day we would have ended up in Auschwitz. My sister, who was fourteen, might have survived, but I was eleven, and Dr. Mengele sent all my classmates, every last one, to the gas chambers.

Of our parents we knew nothing. I had given up on the idea of going from the staircase to the vestibule to the light-blue living room and finding everything as it had been. I had a feeling I would find nothing there at all. But if I closed my eyes, I could go through the old motions: walk downstairs, step through the iron gate, painted yellow, and see my father next to the tile oven, rubbing his hands, smiling, chatting, turning his blue eyes to everyone with a trusting but impish gaze, as if to ask, "We understand each other, don't we?" In a postprandial mood he would have gone onto the balcony and stretched out on his deck chair, lighting up a long Memphis cigarette in its gold mouthpiece, looking over the papers, then nodding off.

For as long as I can remember, I had a secret suspicion that everyone around me acted like children. I realized it applied to my parents as well when, not suspecting us of eavesdropping, they would banter playfully in the family bed: they were exactly like my sister and me.

From the age of five I knew I would be killed if Hitler won. One morning in my mother's lap I asked who Hitler was and why he said so many terrible things about the Jews. She replied that she herself didn't know. Maybe he was insane, maybe just cruel. Here was a man who said the Jews should disappear. But why should we disappear from our own house, and even if we did, where would we go? Just because this Hitler, whom my nanny followed with such enthusiasm, came up with crazy ideas like packing us off to somewhere else.

And how did Hilda feel about all this? How could she possibly be happy about my disappearing, yet go on bathing me with such kindness every morning, playing with me, letting me snuggle up to her, and even occasionally slipping into the tub with me? How could Hilda, who was so good to me, wish me ill? She was pretty, Hilda was, but obviously stupid. I decided quite early that anything threatening me was idiotic, since I was a threat to no one. I was unwilling to allow that anything bad for me could possibly be an intelligent idea.

For as long as I can remember, I have felt like the five-year-old who ventured all the way out to the Berettyó Bridge on his bicycle and stared into the river, a mere eight or ten meters wide in summer, twisting yellow and muddy through its grassy channel, pretending to be docile but in fact riddled with whirlpools. That boy was no different, no more or less a child than I am today. In spring I watched from the bridge as the swollen river swept away entire houses and uprooted large trees, watched it washing over the dike, watched animal carcasses floating by. You could row a boat between the houses: all the streets near the bank were under water.

I felt that you could not count on anything entirely, that danger was lurking everywhere. The air inside the Broken Tower was cool, moldy, bat-infested. I was frightened by the rats. The Turks had once laid siege to it and finally taken it. This is a wild region, a region of occupations: myriad armies have passed through it; myriad outlaws, marauders, haiduks, and bounty hunters have galloped over its plains. The townspeople take refuge in the swamps.

My childhood recollection is that people had a slow way of talking that was expansive and quite cordial. They took their time about communicating and expected no haste in return. The herdsmen cracked the whip every afternoon as they brought the cows home. Then there were the Bihar knifemen: cutting in on a Saturday-night dance could mean a stabbing.

With my long hair curling at the sides and suspenders holding up my trousers, I step into the living room. The upholstery is blue, blue the tablecloth. The living room opens onto a sunlit balcony, where cheese pastries and hot cocoa stand waiting. I am well disposed to everyone and aware of the many who have been working for me that day, making my entrance possible. The bathroom heater and the living-room tile stove have been lit, the cleaning done. Sounds of food being prepared travel in from the kitchen.

I cock an ear: it might be the diminutive Mr. Tóth, bringing buffalo milk and buffalo butter. On my way to Várad in summer I would see his herd from the train window lolling in a big puddle, barely lifting their heads above water. Mr. Tóth wasn't much larger than I. He was very graceful when he unrolled the bordered handkerchief he used for carrying money, including our monthly payment for the milk, curd cheese, and sour cream he brought, all as white as the buffalo were black.

I would have liked to be big and strong and gave our driver's biceps a hopeful squeeze. They had a nice bulge to them, and I wanted mine to be just as tan and thick. András and his horse Gyurka would bring water from the artesian well in the gray tank-cart. Women waited their turn with two pitchers apiece. I remember András and Gyula, and Vilma, Irma, Juliska, and Regina from the kitchen, and Annie, Hilda, and Lívia from the nursery.

The fire is still crackling in the tile oven. There is no need to close the oven door until the embers start crumbling. I rub its side and take my seat at the table, where a booster pillow rests on the chair. It is nine o'clock. My father went down to the store at eight; his assistants and errand boys awaited him at the door. I will have to eat breakfast without him in the company of my sister Éva and my nanny. Mother will join us later if she can spare the time. She will set her keys down on the blue tablecloth. Opening and closing the various doors and drawers takes a long time.

This is perhaps my third birthday, a Saturday. The play of bright light off the synagogue's yellow wall behind our house is dazzling. The chestnut and sour cherry trees in the garden are already in bud. The living room is quiet, but I hear rustlings coming from the dining room. I'm not looking forward to the door opening, because as soon as it does I will have to express my happiness openly. Once you have your gifts, you must play with them. How long can you sit on a rocking horse?

The big news is that the storks have taken their place on the tower next to the Tablets of the Covenant on the synagogue: the winter has not destroyed their nest. One tower is the family home, the other the sanctum of the paterfamilias, where, towards evening, having supplied his charges with treasures from the hunt, he would retire for meditation, leg up, bill tucked in.

A special smell emanates from the chest where the logs for the fire are kept. It mingles with the aroma of burning oak. From here we may proceed to my parents' bedroom, where the scent of Mother's dresser predominates, the ever-present scent of lavender, a moth repellent. Another exciting symphony of scents calls me to the kitchen, but can't we put off eating for the moment (well, maybe just a cheese pastry to go with my café au lait): the smell of onions and bloody meat is just too much, nor am I ready for the sight of a fowl lying on a stone, the blood spurting from its neck onto a white enameled plate. (The servants let it coagulate, then cook it with fried onions for their morning snack.)

The breakfast is splendid. Now let's make some serious plans for the day. We'll go down to my father's hardware store, a space ten meters by twenty, with a cellar below that serves as a warehouse. If it was made of iron, you could find it there—anything the people of Csonka-Bihar County could need. The reason it was called Csonka-Bihar, "Rum Bihar," was that neighboring Transylvania, including its capital Nagyvárad (together with most of my family, Hungarian-speaking middle-class Jews), had been uncoupled from Hungary after the First World War and Berettyóújfalu had become the seat of what was left of Bihar County. Everyone came here to do the weekly shopping on market Thursdays, even from outlying villages.

On that day things would bustle starting early in the morning: bells chiming on horses' necks, carts on runners in winter. Even closed windows in the children's room could not seal out the beating of hoofs, the whinnying, the rumble of carts, the mooing. My father's hardware store was filled with customers bargaining for goods, punctuated by bouts of hearty conviviality. His assistants, who knew most of them, followed suit, and old Aunt Mari and Uncle János held up their end as well. My father's employees had all started out with him; they were trained by him from the age of thirteen. Before opening they would sweep the greasy floor and sprinkle it down in figure-eights. The assistants wore blue smocks, the bookkeeper a black silk jacket, my father a dark gray suit. The smell of iron and wood shavings wafted over me, then the oil used to grease the cart axles, then the oily paper used to wrap hunting arms. I could have told nails from wire with my eyes shut, by smell alone. The room smelled of men, of boots, of the mid-morning snack: bread, raw bacon, and chunks of onion inserted under mustaches on the tip of a knife.

Lajos Üveges can wait on three customers at a time, tossing pleasantries and encouragement this way and that, yet find time to ask me "How's tricks?" He knows exactly what you need for your cart; there is no artisan in Berettyóújfalu whose craft is a mystery to Lajos Üveges. "Just watch how it's done," is his advice to me in life. I watch him rolling a cigarette with one hand, building a seesaw, repairing a bicycle. So that's how you do it. He loves to work: smelting iron, fixing circuits, extracting honey from a beehive—for Lajos it is all sheer entertainment. He jokes with the old peasants in a way that does not exclude respect. His mustache exudes a pleasant smell of pomade, like my grandfather's, the old man having given him some of his. If there is such a thing as an ideal mustache wax scent, this is it.

When my father's business was taken over by the state in 1950, Lajos Üveges was named manager. By then it had twenty-two employees, had expanded into the second-floor apartment, and used the neighboring synagogue as a warehouse. Among the assistants he was the best man for the job, though not quite so good as my father.

The town crier shouts out public announcements to the festive sound of a drumbeat. A military band marches past. The drum major, generally fat, swings his long, striped staff in the ritual manner. Bringing up the rear, a diminutive Gypsy boy pounds his drum. The lyrics grow ever more unpleasant: "Jew, Jew, dirty Jew!" is how one begins. My father simply closes the door.

The smell of horse and cow manure fills the streets. No matter how much the main street is swept, the horse- and ox-carts leave their muck clinging to the cobblestones. Herds too file by, morning and evening, resourcefully splitting up to fill the small side streets. Cows and geese find their way home as skillfully as people.

To this day I can smell the pool, filled by slow bubblings from the artesian spring. Every Sunday night it was drained; only after it had been cleaned did the refilling, which lasted until Wednesday evening, begin. The well-water, with its aroma of iron and sulfur, surged up several hundred meters to lend the walls of the pool a rust-brown hue. It was our drinking water, arriving at the house in an enameled can and at the table in a glass pitcher. Water for washing was hauled from the well on a horse-drawn tank cart, poured into the cellar, then pumped to the attic. From there it came through the tap to the bathtub. It took the work of many to keep a middle-class household going. I can still hear the servant girls singing. We had an old woman cook, Regina, a gentle soul. When she lost her temper, her curse was, "May a quiet rain fall on him!"

I can hear the congregation singing "The Lord Is One." The synagogue had a sour smell from the prayer shawls, and voices at prayer sometimes melted into a background of rumbling and muttering. I might have a scuffle with a goat in the temple courtyard, grabbing it by the horns and trying to push it back. It would yield to a point, then butt, and down I would fall on my behind.

My family was rural, mainly from Bihar County; some came from Nagyvárad, others from Berettyóújfalu, Debrecen, Miskolc, Brassó, and Kolozsvár. They were Hungarian-speaking Jews. Almost all are dead today. Five of my cousins were killed at Auschwitz and Mauthausen. My father's three older sisters and both of my mother's met the same end. One of my maternal uncles was shot in the head in the street by the Arrow Cross, the Hungarian Fascist party.

My father's generation had a *gimnázium* education, while my own—including a textile engineer, a biologist, a chemist, an economist, a mathematician, and a writer—graduated from the university. The previous generation had been businessmen, factory owners, a doctor, a banker, a pharmacist, and an optician, all respectable members of the middle class until they were deported; my generation became intellectuals and critical spirits: a leftist engineer who organized a strike against his father, a medic expelled from school who organized a group of partisans, and rebellious humanists.

My mother's family was more well-to-do, a result of the practicality and business sense not so much of my grandfather as of my grandmother. My maternal grandfather was more reader than businessman, but he had a son-in-law with a great flair for commerce, and through him the family was involved in a furniture factory, a bitumen and lime plant, and logging tracts. He was a religious man, if not strictly Orthodox, and read widely in Judaica. He belonged to the boards of both the Reform and Orthodox congregations in Nagyvárad. He had a taste for elaborate rituals, but also for the good life: working from nine to twelve was enough for him. Then came the family lunch, the afternoon café session, and, after dinner, reading—this in his own separate apartment, since by then he had had enough of the children and the commotion of family life.

For the Passover Seder dinner he would come to Berettyóújfalu from Nagyvárad. He was the one who read the answers to the Haggadah questions that I, as the youngest present, asked. Our Haggadah—the book containing the readings for the holiday, the memorial of exile—was bound in cedar and ornamented with mosaics. It had drawings as well, four in particular: the wise son, the wicked son, the merchant son, and the son so simple he does not know how to ask. I was particularly delighted by the one who does not know how to ask, but my grandfather said the role did not suit me as I was constantly pestering him with questions.

During the evening ceremony a glass of wine was set out between the two windows for the prophet Elijah. By morning it was gone. I was intrigued by the prospect of the prophet Elijah's visit. Once, in the nursery, I heard rustlings from the adjoining dining room. I darted from my bed and peeped out through the door. I saw my grandfather in a full-length white nightshirt take the glass and drink it. He remarried ten years after my grandmother's death. He was eighty.

We also had a Christmas tree with gifts beneath it, and my sister would play "Silent Night," which we knew as "Stille Nacht, heilige Nacht," on the piano. My parents did not mention Jesus, but my nanny said he came bringing gifts and even decorating the tree. I pictured him as a flying, birdlike creature in contrast to Elijah, who thundered across the sky in a chariot of fire. But in the end I suspected that neither came at all.

My great-grandfather Salamon Gottfried was the first Jew to settle in Berettyóújfalu. He arrived at the end of the eighteenth century and opened a pub, which he left to his son Sámuel. Sámuel, who eventually held seventy acres, was a strong man who commanded respect and kept order, brooking neither crude speech nor boisterousness in an establishment whose clientele included the local toughs. His photograph shows a man with focused and probably blue eyes wearing a wide-brimmed black hat and a white shirt buttoned to the neck—a determined, strong-boned man, browned by the sun, full of endurance, and sporting a bifurcated beard. He too remarried as a widower, at seventy-seven. The only letters on their waist-high marble tombstones in the Jewish cemetery at Berettyóújfalu are Hebrew.

My paternal grandmother Karolina Gottfried was by all reports a kindly, good-humored, plump old woman. She had three girls, then a boy, my father József. She spoiled her only son, and when she looked in on her father in the pub at Szentmárton across the river, she would dress little Józsi up in a sailor suit and patent leather shoes and take him in a fiacre, which inspired sarcastic remarks. It was the same when Karolina took Józsi in a hired carriage to his grandfather. She wore the trousers in that house, at least at table, where the helpers and servants ate together with the master.

The master, my grandfather Ignác Kohn, was a tinsmith, and he and his men produced the buckets, cans, tubs, and other goods of galvanized sheet-iron for the local artisans. He was not happy when factory-produced goods swamped the market, and had no choice but to switch to retailing. By the turn of the century his hardware business, established in 1878, was the largest in the region.

My grandmother was somewhat embarrassed to find herself pregnant again at the age of forty-three. (Apparently in those days it would have been fitting to conceal the fact that Karolina and Ignác were still making love at such an advanced age.) The outcome was my father's youngest and favorite sister, the pretty Mariska, the most spoiled of all the siblings.

Both of their black-granite, life-size gravestones are still standing in the abandoned, weed-infested Jewish cemetery at Berettyóújfalu, where no one has been interred for decades, that is, since the entire Jewish community, some one thousand people, disappeared from the village, which has since become a small city. Ignác, who outlived his wife Karolina, had the following carved on her gravestone: "You were my happiness, my pride." Despite heavy battles in the cemetery at the end of the Second World War their granite pillars were not so much as scratched by the bullets, and they will long continue to stand—if no one sees fit to knock them down, that is.

When I read out my father's particulars to the officials in charge of granting gravesites at the Síp Street congregation in Budapest, the old gentleman who kept the enormous register slapped his forehead and said, "I remember him. Fine reputation. Solid, solvent." Apparently he had once visited us as a traveling salesman. My father tended to buy from factories and had reservations about these wanderers with samples in their bags, but he also had a feeling for people and a sense of humor that made his company quite pleasant. He was a guileless man who never thought his debtors might run off on him, as they generally did not. To his poorer customers he granted credit if they could not pay, certain as he was that sooner or later they would come up with what they owed him. He never bought or sold wares that were less than reliable. Everything associated with him was thoroughly sturdy, be it a kettle, a bicycle, or his word.

My father read several newspapers and started listening to the BBC's Hungarian-language broadcasts at the beginning of the war. I was intimately familiar with the BBC's four knocks, since I would crouch behind my father as he tried to hear the news amidst all the jamming. From the middle of the war he listened to Moscow as well. We had to close the doors and windows: by turning the knob this way and that with great concentration over the forty-nine, forty-one, thirty-one, and twenty-five meter bands of the shortwave we were committing a subversive act.

An old photo from the family album (lost at the end of the war) comes to mind: my grandfather, my aunts, and my father are leaning over a white-enameled basin, their heads cocked to one side, which would be rather odd were it not for the wire hanging out of the basin: it signaled they were gathered around a single headphone to hear the first radio broadcast in the twenties. An uncomfortable setup, yet worth the trouble.

I was not yet in a position to take part in the scene, but by the time of the war I would perch behind my father on the couch every day at a quarter to two listening to the news, the real news, amidst the static. The sound would come and go; you really had to keep your ears pricked. My nine-year-old ears filled the intermittent gaps in my father's hearing. I became so attached to "This Is London" that when the Gestapo arrested my father in May

1944 on the charge of sending news to the BBC from his secret radio transmitter in the attic I was proud he was the object of such a noble accusation. Not a word of it was true.

My Bavarian nanny, the beautiful blonde Hilda, left us for Hitler: her father forbade her to work for Jews no matter how comfortable she felt with us. Then came the warm-hearted Hungarian Lívia, who not only spoke German and French well but played the piano. She wore her waist-length blonde hair braided; I never tired of watching her comb it. The Catholic Lívia fell in love with my father's accountant, Ernő Vashegyi, a quiet, lanky, well-read man, and center on the local soccer team. Ernő Vashegyi was handsome, but a Jew, which gave Lívia some pause. We often went to the soccer field with our nanny and sat in the small, wooden riser; everyone else either stood on the hill or perched on the fence. Whenever Ernő Vashegyi kicked a goal, Lívia and I would squeeze hands. Once in a while the earnest fellow would join us at the family table for lunch, but before long he was called up for forced labor and never returned.

Every Monday the local tradesmen would gather in my father's store to evaluate the previous day's performance of our team, the county champions. Other topics of long conversations included rain (precious), drought (worrisome), the price of wheat, and what that lunatic was after anyway. Politics was a theme to be discussed mainly with other Jews; otherwise it was prudent to hold one's tongue: fascism had crept into the heads of some intelligent people, for whom regaining the Hungarian-speaking territories lost after World War I at the Trianon Conference was conceivable only with Hitler's support.

My ancestors lived out their lives as Jewish middle-class Hungarians. My father was the primary taxpayer in the town's ambit of some twelve thousand people. As such, he was given membership at the gentleman's club, the "casino," though he never went there. Nailed to the right side of the street entrance to his business was a mezuzah, a parchment roll in a mother-of-pearl case containing a handwritten text of the "Sh'ma," the central Sabbath prayer: "Hear O Israel, the Lord our God, the Lord is one." Only He, and no other: no pagan godhead in animal or human form.

On the doorpost below the mezuzah was a small metal plaque showing the outline of the historical borders of Hungary in 1914 and within it, painted in solid black, the 1920 territory, chopped to thirty percent of its original size and the slogan "No, no, never!"—meaning that we would never accept the loss. The members of my family thought of themselves as good Hungarians and good Jews. The two did not come to be viewed as separate until World War II.

The Hungarian government took up arms on the German side with the aim of recovering part of the lost territories, and it was willing to send half a million Jews to German camps in exchange. It was a bad bargain, because in the end they lost not only the Jews but the territory as well, and were left with the shame of it all. True, not everyone feels this way: there are those who feel that while many Hungarian Jews were killed in Auschwitz the number was too small.

The Hungarian flag in the middle of the village flew at half mast, and as one piece of territory or another rejoined Hungary it was raised a bit higher. On 15 March, the holiday of the 1848 War of Independence, the children of the Jewish elementary school would march before it in ceremonial step sporting white shirts and dark blue shorts.

My father took part in the reoccupation of Ruthenia and its principal cities, Ungvár and Munkács. He had an artilleryman's uniform with a single white star on it, signifying the rank of private first class, but with the red arm braid that marked those who had graduated from the *gimnázium*. On weekends he would don his uniform and boots and meet my mother at the hotel in Ungvár.

I advanced one rank higher in the military order, becoming a corporal. (My son Miklós did not carry on the tradition, never advancing past private in the French Army; in fact, they tossed him in the clink for talking back to his commander.) I was interested in military events from the age of seven and prayed for General Montgomery to defeat General Rommel in Africa and for the Allies to take Tunis and Bizerta. I was a patriot who could be moved to tears for Hungary, but at the same time I was for an Allied victory. Based on what I heard and saw in the newsreels, I tried to imagine the battles of Stalingrad, Smolensk, and Kursk as well. Lying prone in the dark under the net of my brass bed, I would press my thumbs lightly to my eyes and on would come the newsreels, my own versions of the Hungarian and German products, all tanks and heavy artillery and air battles fading into the starry night.

The sky is bigger beyond the Tisza, the roads muddier than west of the Danube. This is the eastern end of the country, where you would once have found the highest concentration of people going barefoot and old men standing before their house doors in dark blue burlap aprons. It was a picture as constant as the buffaloes grazing in their lake.

Coming to Berettyóújfalu by train, I make my way over red slag between the tracks, then pass the green iron-tube railing onto the platform with its yellow-brick paving. The red-hatted signalman salutes me with his signal disk, the telegraph machine jingling away behind him. It is some time in the seventies, and I am lying in a room at the Bihar Hotel, a few steps from my childhood home. There is no hot water, and the door to the W.C. does not close: you have to hold the handle. Even though the flies land all over me, I do not swipe at them. I have drunk a lot of *pálinka* in the heat. The bus motors at the station produce a constant rumble. In the cinema across the road the Gypsy kids make the same smacking sound when kissing as they did before the war, but nowadays it is no longer permitted to spit pumpkin and sunflower husks onto the floor.

I take a close look at our house, ambling over the cracked sidewalk by the hapless shacks that seem to survive all events. A couple emerges from the courtyard that was one of my old haunts. The little girls who used to play with dolls are old now; they look like their mothers, the boys like their fathers. Faces peering through the fence. The indifference of the stares.

I go to the marketplace too. Nearly everything is different there now: trucks and tractors stirring up dust, the young scooting around on motorcycles. What has not changed is the rumpus of the women, the clamor of geese and ducks, the long baying of the oxen, the fresh scent of horse manure, the mounds of apricots and new potatoes. The merry-go-round is still there, as are the cotton-candy vendor and the table covered with jackknives. You can still get a little wooden rooster that clacks its wings. All but gone by now, though, is the bench in front of a house where one or two old men would pass the hours smoking a pipe, and the bright light unwrapping all the objects to reveal their slow decay.

I think I wanted to make up my mind about something. One hot afternoon, after lolling for a while on a sweaty bed in a hotel room the size of a coffin, I wandered down the main street and through the soccer field. No one said a word to me. Sometimes I had the feeling I was being watched. In a side-street bar, smelly and raucous, a drunkard launched into a song, then gave up and stared out of the window.

An old man, wearing nothing but a jacket over his bronze, tattooed torso, told me of a time when I liked to sit with him on the coach-box and he would pass me the whip. It was András, our former coachman, he of the large, reverie-inspiring biceps. András was the one who polished the linoleum in my room by skating on waxed brushes, the one who brought the firewood upstairs, who lit the fire in the cast-iron stove in the bathroom so I could have warm water for my bath when I got up. His horse Gyurka pulled the water tank, and András filled it, bucket by bucket, at the slow-gurgling artesian well in front of the post office and behind the national flag in the park. As likely as not, András had never had the experience of lounging in a bathtub. The servants bathed once a week in the galvanized tin tub in the laundry room. Just so I could step in the tub, the servant girl would have to keep the fire going while my nanny set out my ironed whites. The washing-soap smell was part of a larger picture: the servant girl had a servant smell, the valet a valet smell.

The servant girl would not simply take her pay from my mother's hand; she would seize her hand and kiss it. My father would shake hands with his employees when handing them their pay envelopes. I don't remember the coachman or the woman who was our cook ever sitting down in any of our rooms—in the kitchen, yes: András would sit there on the stool, stirring the thick soup the cook ladled straight from the kettle into his bowl with an enameled spoon. No kettle was ever put on the dining table, only a porcelain soup server and a silver spoon for serving. The servants would spend whole afternoons polishing the silverware.

Was I religious? Since I prayed, I was religious. But children are hedonists and enjoy some aspects of a religion while rejecting those that deprive them of pleasure. The wine I enjoyed, though I got it only on Seder evening, when I was allowed to dip my little finger into the wineglass and lick it. The horseradish on the table represented bitterness, the bread dipped in honey good fortune. After presiding over the ritual, my grandfather would listen to my doubts and say that there are many images of God, but that He is greater than any image, for God always transcends what is portrayed.

We were Cohanites, Cohens, that is, descendants of Aaron and the priests who guarded the Ark of the Covenant. My maternal grandfather was also a Cohen, though the designation passed from father to son. Only Cohanites are entitled to remove the Torah scrolls from the tabernacle and carry them around the temple, blessing the congregation. Special regulations of cleanliness forbid them to marry a divorced woman or enter a cemetery: whoever touches Holy Scripture may have no contact with the dead. For my part, I have married two divorcées and enjoy strolling through cemeteries.

My father was comfortable with the positions of responsibility he held, and had no desire to take a leading role in either the town or the congregation. He was who he was. My parents were no more assimilated than other Jews; they simply went a little further into the world at large, where all religions and nationalities learn new ways of life, with mixed feelings perhaps, but slowly and surely, where Jews and Christians alike are assimilants, adapting to the age and to life beyond national borders. But my cousin István and I were the only ones at the Jewish school who did not attend afternoon Talmud lessons in the whitewashed one-story building where one day half a brick tumbled through the dusty courtyard's fence and landed on my head. The others would arrive home from school at one, but had to go to the *cheder*, the religious school, at three, where they would immerse themselves in the study of Jewish law and its interpretation. Since they stayed in the classroom until six, they tended to be sickly. I was stronger. Ugly fights were the fashion. All the kids would stand around the enemies and spur them on. We fought on a floor regularly sprinkled with oil. The winner was the one who pinned the other's shoulders to the ground and held him there. Success was sweeter if a little blood flowed from the loser's nose and mouth.

Even in childhood the pen was my favorite tool, though I also assembled model airplanes and even soldered one from steel wire. Fixing the hubs on my bike or patching an inner tube was no trickier for me than scratching the tip of my nose. The screwdriver and the saw took gladly to my hand. There was nothing I enjoyed more than observing master craftsmen: I loved watching the locksmith, the blacksmith, the radio repairman at work—

my father's customers all. Nagy, the hospital's chief engineer, I considered a superior being, and the fact that he never could wash the oil entirely from his hands met with my reverential approval.

Actually I was preparing an enterprise similar to his, an airplane factory, which was to be located just behind the lake where we skated (and bathed the geese in the summertime). All it would take was a little land from the pasture. Obviously I would first have to study at the English *gimnázium* in Sárospatak, then at Oxford or Cambridge. Having returned with my diploma, I would inherit—or simply run—my father's hardware business and thence take the step into production. Though why not manufacture planes from the outset? Start small but quickly move on to passenger planes, so one day all of Berettyóújfalu would ride out to the airport in their oxcarts and take a pleasure flight free of charge, experience Derecske, Mikepércs, Zsáka, Furta, Csökmő, and maybe even Bakonszeg from the air. Such was the plan.

My cousin István Zádor was a month younger then I: He was a Taurus, I an Aries. We entered the world in the same birthing room. He was a nice pink color and quiet, while I (a breech birth, with the umbilical cord wrapped around my neck) came out red, bald, and in agony. My mother, ashamed of my pointed head, kept it a secret by covering it with a crocheted cap before my father came to visit. To this day I have to laugh when I think of my father's face as I plagued him with questions about our first meeting. "You were quite an ugly little runt," he would say, and then add reassuringly, "but you managed to outgrow it."

Both István and I were born at the university clinic in Debrecen, though we lived in Berettyóújfalu. Ours were the two most affluent Jewish families in the Alföld region. József Konrád, my father, was generally considered wealthier, since he had a multistory house on the main street, but actually his cousin Béla Zádor had more money and a college degree to boot.

My father had only a commercial high school education, which he received in Késmárk, an ancient town in the Tatra Mountains, home to a significant Saxon—that is, German—community. Although our family's native tongue was Hungarian, it made sense at the time of the Austro-Hungarian Monarchy to board the boys with a family where German was spoken at table. My father ended up in the house of a mathematics teacher. He would take the young lady of the family walking on the castle walls or skating in the Dobsina ice cave, where the snow lingered into summer. This cave occupied my imagination intensely. Several times I asked my father about it as he reclined on a chaise longue on the balcony after dinner and his words flowed freely. All I learned was that the young lady had a red skating outfit and that my father also turned a few figures with the girl on his arm.

István and I took our first steps with a walker while our mothers chatted. They were sisters-in-law and friends. István's mother was my father's younger sister, his father my father's cousin. Mariska, the young beauty, was noticed early by Béla Zádor, her cousin.

During my first days at school my governess Lívia sat with me at my desk. Whenever she stood, I sobbed at the thought of her leaving me there alone. On the fourth day she managed to tear herself from my side. I cried, and the others made fun of me, so I got angry and beat up every single one of them. At home I announced that I did not want to go to school, and repeated this regularly over the course of a month. My parents finally accepted the situation, and I became a home student. So did István. As our instructor did not come until the afternoon, we were free all morning out in their large garden among the sour-cherry trees on the banks of Kálló Creek. We would finish the lesson quickly and go back to playing soccer or cutting cattails or catching frogs.

When Aunt Mariska allowed it, little István would watch his mother stretch out in the tub. He would feel her clothes and smell her colognes. The governess, who answered to the name of Nene, would shout for him to come out immediately and stop bothering his mother, but István would just stand there, watching through fogged-up glasses as his mother turned her beautiful legs.

We sat together in school and were reluctant to part company. István would walk me home and come up the stairs. "You understand, Gyuri, don't you?" he would ask at intervals, standing in the front doorway. "I understand, I understand," I would answer after a considered pause. No one was as good to talk to as István, and I never talked to anyone else as much. With our arms on each other's shoulders we would walk round and round the courtyard at school. Having failed to shut us up, they tried to separate us, but ended up leaving us in the same row. István was not beyond a few pranks, but was bored by childish rowdiness. I know a number of people who admit that István was smarter than they; I am one.

István Zádor's brother Pál was three years younger than he and followed in his footsteps. A mathematician, he has been living in Washington for about forty years now. Pali could beat both of us in ping-pong: he was bent on making up for those three years. He had no tolerance for an affront. If a salesman happened to say anything out of line, Pali would answer with a single compound noun: "Curcowstupidpig!" In the time it would have taken for his father to come out of the house and set him straight, we were all down on the bank of the creek amid the sour-cherry trees and raspberry bushes.

They lived in a spacious house just opposite ours. It incorporated a large clothing and shoe store. The salesmen cut fine figures in well-tailored suits of English cloth and liked to wave fabrics in the air with a flourish. They had a pleasant way about them, complimenting the women as they pivoted in front of the mirror.

Stepping into my father's hardware store, you inhaled the reliable iron smell of nails, wire, cart-axles, ploughs, harrows, stoves, pots, bicycles, and hunting weapons. You could check the sharpness of a scythe with the tip of a finger, and should you wish to verify whether it was made of well-tempered steel, you would use a twenty-kilo iron weight that had done service since the beginning of human memory: you would knock the head of the scythe (without the handle) hard against the weight a few times and raise it to your ear to hear it ring.

It was an event for me whenever a load of goods arrived at the Berettyóújfalu station, the fruit of one of Father's Budapest trips. András and Gyurka would cart the crates home, and I would sit up on the box, where I had permission to give Gyurka the commands to go (*Ne!*) and stop (*Ho!*). It was exciting to help unload the large crates of flame-red enameled pots nested amid thick beds of fragrant wood shavings.

These pleasures were alien to István, who paid little attention to his father's business and rarely set foot in the store. He was none too comfortable playing the little son, hearing how much he had grown, suffering a pinch on the cheek. After one or two hellos he would retire to the innards of the house. Aunt Mariska, too, observed the store's activity from a distance, leaving things to Aunt Etelka, her untiring mother-in-law, who—small, thin, and deeply wrinkled—kept an eye on everything from the most natural place, her perch at the cash register.

Uncle Béla would pace the store, dealing personally with a few preferred customers, but bilious and impatient as he was he soon retreated into the apartment, which opened onto the garden, and settled into his heavy leather armchair in the half-darkness of the study next to Aunt Mariska's room. There he would read the ever-worsening news, later to discuss it with my father in our living room with concern, though not without hope.

Most ladies from the town's upper stratum found items to their liking in Uncle Béla's store. Aunt Mariska, though, did not—meaning that my mother, her friend, was under no obligation to buy her wardrobe from him either. The two would occasionally travel to Budapest.

Such a trip was inconceivable without a trunk and a hatbox, and they would be dutifully installed in a first-class compartment by András and the fiacre driver and the red-capped railway porter. At the Nyugati Station in Budapest the process was repeated in reverse, except that a taxi took my mother and Aunt Mariska to the Hotel Hungária on the Danube. They spent mornings at the finest tailors and evenings at the theater. When they returned, I would interrogate my mother about the best places to buy fabrics, whites, and shoes, just as I interrogated my father about the strengths and weaknesses of Budapest ironworks and Budapest wholesalers: everything in life had its place.

We all knew who the prettiest girl in the classroom was, who the biggest shrew. I will take this occasion to reveal that it was a true pleasure to grab the thick braids of Baba Blau, who sat in front of me, and give them a tug. Baba would laugh in a deep voice, then squeal on me. I would have to leave the room with the lid to my pen-case, which the teacher would use to slap my hand a few times. Once I had come back, Baba would stroke my hand and gaze up at the ceiling with a little sneer on her large, dark mouth. Then she would position her braids back within reach.

Aunt Mariska prepared all her life for something that never came. She loved clothes and dressed with originality and at great cost. She bought a great many books: modern novels for herself, Indian stories for the boys. But one day she went into the garden to rest under a camel-hair blanket in the whitewashed, rose-covered arbor and emerged all yellow, and yellow she remained. Only her gravestone is white, white marble.

István was left on his own at the age of five: after his mother died, his father grew melancholic. When Aunt Etelka died as well, Nene took over the household. Nene was unshakable in her knowledge of what constituted a proper diet: she was committed to whole-grain bread, creamed spinach, and boiled breast of chicken. Anyone who so much as cleared his throat at this fare was put to bed on the spot. She was a conscientious woman and a devout Catholic, but neither pretty nor happy. There were few signs of joy in István's house.

We would walk up and down the main street wearing jackets, caps, and gloves. We needed to ask permission to take off our gloves or open the top button of the jacket. We were watched by peasant boys wearing poor-quality boots.

When we cranked the arm of the telephone, a young lady answered, "Operator." "Give me 11," I would say. "Give me 60," said István. We did this many times a day. "Why don't you just walk across the street?" the girl would ask. "Just connect me, please," we said coolly, even at the age of seven.

Our fathers would hold onto our shoulders at the edge of the sidewalk until they felt we were old enough to cross the street on our own. An automobile was a rare and wondrous event, but there was no end of horse-drawn carriages.

We received one another in jackets, shook hands, showed our guests to their seats, and proceeded to speak of important issues. If we didn't want others to hear us, we left the house for the autumn garden. It was a pleasure to feel the leaf-bed crunching under our feet.

István never uttered a word lightly, and his face would show irritation at any idle remark; I was interested in all sorts of things that seemed to bore the often distant István, and I tried to amuse him with my clowning. Coming from him, a *yes* or *no* had a real edge to it. He liked to draw the most extreme conclusions from his observations; I followed the path of his logic guardedly: I might see it differently tomorrow, by which time the now devastating train of his thought would have lost some of its force.

When the Germans occupied Hungary on 19 March 1944, I was eleven years old. What around the table we had merely feared had now come to pass: our island of exception was no more; something new was afoot. How simple it had all been! How comical everything that had happened now seemed! I thought back on the evenings I had spent listening to the men's dinner-table strategizing about how the English would move in from

Italy and Greece and initiate the western invasion, thereby giving our leader, Admiral Horthy, more room to maneuver and enabling him to jump ship and Hungary to begin its evolution into a neutral, Anglo-Saxon form of democracy. Until then our fathers could still run their businesses, medical practices, and law offices in peace. Jewish children could attend school in that sad, little one-story building with its dusty courtyard and beautiful prayer room without being humiliated by their teacher for being Jewish. On Friday evenings we could hear the shuffle of footsteps on the walkway by our house, where men dressed in black would make their way to temple under their broad-brimmed black hats accompanied by my wide-eyed schoolmates holding their fathers' hands.

On the day of the occupation I sat with my father at the radio in his bedroom. There was no news of resistance: the Hungarian troops did not put up a fight. The regent, the government, and the country as a whole simply lay down before the mighty Germans. I did not much trust Horthy. I had had a lead soldier of him from my earliest boyhood. I surrounded him with officers and an entire leaden infantry. They were all in green, while Horthy sported a cornflower-blue admiral's coat with gold tassels. I had a cannon as well. It could shoot miniature cannonballs a meter or so. The battlefield was the large, brown linoleum surface, where I would divide the armies and materiel in two. In the early days the winning army was always the one led by His Excellency the Regent. After we entered the war, cannonballs started knocking His Highness over, and from that point on, Horthy's army was the loser. I would shoot him with the cannon; he would fall on his back.

That evening all my uncles and cousins sat around the radio. According to a piece of stray news a local garrison commander had exhibited displeasure at the German invasion, and I immediately decided it would be the Újfalu regiment, under the command of Lieutenant Colonel Egyed, that would push the Germans back. After all, we had a large barracks on the edge of town, a powerful garrison with cannons drawn by giant artillery horses. If the Regent called on the people to fight for their freedom, he would find a foothold here in Bihar County.

"Him, of all people? Here?" István's smile was more than acerbic. Yes, the Lieutenant Colonel was a good man and no friend to the Germans. For years I had been formulating political prayers in bed after the lights were out. At school I discussed the war only with István, between classes, out in the corridors. We looked around to make sure others could not hear us. We soon learned we were individuals to be avoided. On the very eve of the occupation we had to concede that not only Horthy but also the commander of the local garrison had offered no resistance. The next day German tanks stood before the town hall and the Calvinist church manned by soldiers in pike-gray uniforms. Civilians avoided contact with them, avoided even looking in their direction. To the strains of a vigorous march, in rows so tight they practically touched, the Germans demonstrated how a military review was meant to look. They put our cockeyed Hungarian sad sacks to shame.

Before long there were patrols moving through the town commandeering living quarters. As my uncle's house was occupied in its entirety, my cousins moved in with us. Friends and relatives visited my parents to exchange news and share their bewilderment. My father sat out in the sunshine of the balcony with his eyes shut. He had had to close down the business, it being no longer his: there was a lock with a seal on the door. All valuables had to be turned in, the radio included. We three boys slept in the living room or, rather, pretended to sleep, then turned on a low lamp and availed ourselves of the walnut brandy in the sideboard to keep us awake through a night of talking politics.

New decrees appeared daily, so we knew that each day would be worse than the one before. We played ping-pong until dusk and fortunately did not have to part in the evening. Lacking the patience for board games, we discussed the chaotic current events. István thought the Russians would get here first and we would have communism. We did not know much about that. People returning from Ukraine said it was quite poor: goats slept in houses in the countryside; many families shared one apartment in the city. In our high-backed leather chairs we opined that poverty was tolerable as long as there was justice.

Ukraine held dark associations for the Jews of Berettyóújfalu. The younger men had been taken off to forced labor there in 1942. They had been forced to run naked through the halls of a Ukrainian school strewn with boot-nails. Hungarian police standing along the walls would hit them with the butts of their rifles. Something had got them worked up: they must have been drinking rum. Once the men's bundles had been inspected, they were allowed to dress outside in the snow. Watches, rings, and other valuables were confiscated. If they had concealed something, they were sent back to dance in the hall.

As the army retreated, they were moved westward. The sick were delivered to infirmary barracks; those who could not walk were carried on their comrades' backs. One night tongues of flame shot into the sky beyond the field of snow: soldiers had doused the infirmary in gasoline and set it afire, burning the sick Jews of the forced-labor patrol to death. Bandi Svéd rushed back through the snow, hallucinating that his brother at the barracks was walking towards him. His comrades ran after him and brought him back before the guards could shoot. The survivors were released in 1943, went back to Újfalu, and took up their previous lives. Everything was as in the old days, except they didn't talk much.

Our classmates were not particularly hostile to us, nor did they rejoice in our situation. They were uninformed and indifferent. They would look at the tanks and say nothing. "Now you're gonna have a peck of trouble," scornfully remarked a scraggly little boy, the poorest of us all and the worst pupil. His father had joined the Arrow Cross as a road worker. There were only two Jews at the school: István and myself. The poorer ones were not accepted.

István liked to establish bitter truths, the kind that got you absolutely nowhere. "We are the richest in our class and the best pupils: of course they don't like us. How many people are free of envy? Some like one or two Jews but not the rest. There are few good people and few truly bad ones; the rest are neither one nor the other. If they let the Jews live, all well and good; if they kill them, that's fine too. Everyone agrees to everything."

We were still heating the living room, and the atmosphere was familial: my mother was sewing yellow stars onto everyone's coats and jackets. Homemade stars were acceptable, though private industry was flexible in responding to the new needs. Everyone knew the specifications: canary yellow, machine-hemmed, six-by-six centimeters. You had to sew it on tightly enough to keep a pencil from going under the threads: those clever Jews were capable of putting it on just for show and taking it off whenever they felt like it. The Jewish newspaper encouraged its readers to follow the authorities' instructions to the letter.

One day István and I decided that the yellow star was nothing to be ashamed of, and walked all over town. It was spring, and since the school year had ended in April we had time on our hands. We stomped through the mud-covered unpaved side streets in heavy boots. Women stared down at us from tile-roofed, white-colonnaded porticoes.

I took to drinking from the lids of water barrels like a peasant boy. I went to the artesian well in front of the post office, where my good suit and shoes provoked pleasure at our misfortune from the constant semicircle of its users. But even with the yellow star I made new acquaintances: women occasionally greeted me warmly on the street; I would exchange a few words while waiting for the well. The village idiot, who once managed to eat an entire bucket of cooked beans on a bet, asked me for my yellow star. The onlookers laughed: still crazy as ever.

Then one morning they came, a loud pounding at the garden gate. I looked down from the balcony and saw five German officers, as many Hungarian gendarmes, and the ridiculous policeman Csontos, who had previously threatened to inform on everyone, but would let it slide for a few pengős. There were black caps too, but we did not yet know that they were the Gestapo. My father donned his tweed jacket, regulation yellow star and all, and went down to open the gate.

The Gestapo officer informed him in German that he had received a report accusing him of being an English spy and keeping a radio transmitter hidden in the attic. The house was searched from cellar to roof. I knew he had no transmitter, but it felt good to think he had been accused of having one. I very much wanted to look up to him. Had they searched him for a weapon I would have respected him even more.

My father was rather fearful and sensitive to pain, so my mother, the stronger of the two, led the Germans and gendarmes through the house, moving among them without any show of nerves and providing succinct information. They collected a few things—money, jewelry, a camera—but made no major finds. They appeared dissatisfied and ordered my father and uncle to go with them to the gendarmerie barracks and divulge where they had hidden the radio transmitter and, in general, what was hidden where. "Or, madam, would you *truly* have us believe that you are hiding nothing?"

Starting 15 May my father was no longer mine but the Gestapo's. He departed through the garden gate accompanied by gendarmes and German officers. I watched his slightly bent back from the upstairs balcony. I had never seen him escorted by bayonets before. After he and my uncle had been led off, we went to the dining room, where we could follow them through the window facing the street. In front were the Gestapo officers, behind them a couple of gendarmes in their sickle-feathered caps, then my father and uncle, then more gendarmes with bayonets at the ready, and the ridiculous Csontos policeman drawing up the rear. Everything else was as it always was: the cow pats drying in threes on the hot cobblestones, it being mid-May, the yellow light falling on the thick spire of the Calvinist church, the indifferent row of locust trees lining the main street.

My father looked neither right nor left: he greeted no one, nor did anyone greet him. It is instructive to observe the faces of acquaintances approaching from the opposite direction when one is being escorted by armed men. Although my father knew everyone he passed, he walked like an actor making an entrance on stage. The scene was not outrageous, just unusual. At first the faces showed puzzlement; then, slowly, things fell into place: Well, of course, it's the next step, they're taking the Jews. Only my mother and we children remained in the house.

Mother felt something had to be done. How could Hungarian gendarmes take her husband away at the command of some Germans in black uniforms? And what of the Hungarian leadership in the local administration? Had those gentlemen, whom we knew, contributed to the situation?

Mother put on a good dress and went to report the incident to the chief constable and lodge a complaint. As she was leaving the constable's office, a black car pulled up alongside her and a voice in German called out, "Step in, Mrs. Konrád, or do you want me to lock you up with your husband?" He was the chief Gestapo officer. My mother nodded. They did her the favor of putting her in the same jail as my father, though in another section. The gendarmes had rounded up a number of wealthier and better known Jews as hostages. Their wives had stayed at home. Only my mother went with her husband.

That saved our lives. I later found out it was an Arrow Cross pastry-maker who had turned us in. I have him to thank that I am alive today. Perhaps he bore us a grudge for avoiding his shop, though the entrance was pretty spectacular: polar bears—cut from planks with jigsaws and painted in oils—licking raspberry and vanilla ice cream. But the fare was worse than at Petrik's, where two little bird-faced old ladies with buns of gray hair served cream pastries and ice cream against a backdrop of butter-colored tile walls. They used eggs, sugar, vanilla—the proper ingredients—and eschewed experimentation. They were not Arrow Cross, and they went to church every Sunday morning, arm in arm, in white silk blouses and dark gray veiled hats. They opened their shop only after Mass, still redolent of church, selling cream pastries still warm from having been baked at dawn.

But they did not determine history. Providence had placed my fate in the hands of their rival, the one who compensated for poor quality with painted icebergs and seals. By finding an appropriate outlet for his flights of fancy in the genre of the denunciation letter and thereby landing my parents in a Gestapo internment camp, he bestowed a great fortune upon us, for the result was that we all, each in his own way, avoided the common fate of the Jews of Újfalu: Auschwitz.

Four of us children were left: myself, my sister, and my two cousins. They still had their Jewish governess Ibi, who, what with the fear and uncertain prospects of the times, exuded a less than pleasant smell. She was an awkward, weak-spined girl who had trouble with the cooking and cleaning: everything ended up jumbled and more or less dirty.

It was disturbing to see a way of life disintegrate, and I watched it crumble day by day. The absence of our parents and the worry were bad enough, but the nausea of helplessness was worse. István and I decided that our parents had made a mistake: we should have abandoned everything and departed earlier, because now we would have to abandon the house and garden anyway.

It was hot, a beautiful early summer, the cranes occupying their usual spot by the Tables of the Covenant. We played ping-pong like maniacs. The small market on Mondays, the large one on Thursdays, and on Friday afternoons, yellow stars on their jackets, a prayer shawl under their arms, the Jewish men plying their usual route past our house to the synagogue. Every evening we followed the regulations for the blackout, putting slat frames covered with black paper in the windows.

Though no longer allowed into the pool, we would peek through the fence and watch the boys imitating Stukas, the German dive-bombers, as they dived screeching from the trampoline into the twenty-five meter basin fed by the lazy, quiet flow of the artesian water. As usual it was drained on Sunday and would refill by Wednesday afternoon. The previous year István, Pali, and I had swum eighty lengths and were given money for chicken paprikás and noodles at the pool restaurant.

Taking walks with the yellow star gradually grew less pleasant. The message in the faces of the passersby did not generally leave a good feeling. The crudest would communicate, "Well, now you'll get what's been coming to you!"; the majority, "Aha. So that's how it is. So they're taking you away. Well, let them!" Even the warm looks, looks of sympathy, were combined with a quickened pace: solidarity in a hurry. We preferred to stay in the garden. I would swing for hours, until my head spun.

One day at noon a squadron of English and American bombers flashed their silver over the town. They dropped nothing on us, just sparkled in the light on the way to bomb the Debrecen railway station. The church bells tolled; a siren bleated. Gendarmes checked to see that everyone was down in the cellar. But we did not hide; we put our heads back and scoured the sky: Good. Up there at least *they* are in charge.

We got a postcard from my parents in Debrecen saying they were well, nothing more. Although the radio had been confiscated, we had other things to conceal: a sack of flour obtained without a permit, a few sides of bacon. They were in the cellar in a very clever spot that the house's architect (Mr. Berger, who ended up in the same transport and same camp as my parents) had shown my father in 1933, saying that a hiding place might come in handy some day. It was a tiny nook in total darkness on the far side of the concrete water tank and under the basement stair, a place only the most meticulous searcher would find. Our searchers were not so meticulous as all that.

There was also some money concealed behind the drawer in my father's desk: three packs of hundreds, thirty thousand pengős, the price of a large house. Even more serious was a cache of two iron boxes buried in the pipe shed and containing gold jewelry, for which my father had regularly traded a portion of his inventory. One box was buried in the corner and was later discovered, but they never found the other one because it was in the asymmetrical center of the area, where a gray-enamel kettle holding oats for the angora rabbits hung from a ceiling beam.

In those days we kept a dozen rabbits in a warren in the yard. Along the sides of the uppermost two cages were little wooden birthing-boxes, their doors open to the mother's large compartment. Bunnies are pink and hairless at birth and cuddle together, shivering, under their mother's belly. I would have liked to stroke them with at least the tip of my finger, but was told that the mother smells the scent of the human hand on her young and either pushes the human-scented young away or eats it. We were allowed to touch them only after their fur began to grow. Then we could take a few bunnies on our beds and play with them.

It was a joy to spin the soft, white shearings into yarn on a wheel. The line tended to break unless I was careful, in which case the foot-powered spinning wheel, jerry-built from bicycle wheels, could turn it unbroken for minutes on end, gently winding the line onto the spindle. The line that was unwinding from the ball of wool I held in my left hand, regulating its thickness between my right thumb and index finger. On winter afternoons, when the stove gave off more than enough heat even with its doors closed, we would transfer the yarn onto reels. We would listen to war news and classical music over the radio while my mother knitted us warm hats and skating sweaters from a Norwegian pattern.

Anyway, the kettle in the pipe shed hung there to keep the mice from fouling the oats for the rabbits. Though it was suspended from a wire attached to a hook on the ceiling, the mice managed to reach the oats by climbing along the ceiling beams and plopping down into Canaan, which turned out to be their vale of tears, because they were unable to clamber up the enameled walls of the kettle with their little claws and would scramble round and round, just above the endless bounty until a gruesome hand grabbed them by the tail and slammed them down on the cornerstone.

Night after night with admirable foresight Mother showed us exactly what she and Father had buried. "In case we are separated or never meet again, you children need to know what we have." Both my sister and I noted everything precisely. We spoke to no one about it. Even children can keep a secret. Our mother also sewed a few thin gold chains into our overcoats in case we needed them wherever we ended up. We had to prepare to be parted. The tone of the conversation was quite objective.

In May 1944 it was rumored that Jews outside the capital would be resettled in a work camp in what had been Polish territory. Cities were being built for them amidst lakes and forests. They would be set off from the population at large, but their lot would otherwise be decent. From this point on, Jews and Christians could not live together or even have contact with one another. The source of the problem—we, that is—had to be isolated.

The authorities relied on our understanding: Of course we can't live together; how could we ever think such a thing? The Hungarian Jewish newspaper was still exhorting everyone to respect the laws and follow regulations to the letter: Now, in this difficult hour, in this time of trial we must hold our own and show we are good Hungarians; only then can we hope for relief.

The national solidarity behind segregation was all well and good, but how complicated the process was to organize and execute, how much meticulous work was required on the authorities' part, how many Interior Ministry functionaries, high and low, had to curtail their hard-earned sleep and beg their wives' forgiveness. And this deportation took a great deal of work. Every bureau had to play its part, from the gendarmerie to the Commissioner for Abandoned Possessions. Worthy of special praise was the railway workers' model cooperation during enemy bombing: in a matter of weeks they had packed the Jews into freight trains and rolled them out of the country. Collecting six hundred thousand Jews, fencing them in, then transporting them with an armed patrol to freight cars—now *that* was something to drink to. The daily papers of the provincial cities announced with a sigh of relief that the air was clear, the region *judenfrei*, Jew-free.

We received a letter from relatives in Budapest inviting us to stay with them. We needed to decide quickly whether to go. Jews were no longer allowed to travel on trains, and papers were checked constantly: denunciation was a responsibility generally accepted. To travel to our relatives' in Budapest would require special permission from the gendarmerie, an exception, a one-time suspension of the regulations. And why go, anyway? Why not stay behind with the others? We had aunts and uncles and cousins here in town; we were still in our own house. Maybe they wouldn't come for us. Maybe some higher power would intervene. Swinging on my swing, I felt the joy of our ever-present swallows unalloyed. I was an Újfalu boy to the marrow of my bones. I would live here and die here.

But if they did come? It was easier to hide in Budapest, harder to find a needle in that haystack. I cast spells on the garden gate, still foolishly hoping my parents would simply return. I'd hear a knock, open the gate, and there they'd be, smiling in the gateway. I heard a knock. Jumping off the swing, I ran to the gate and slid back the bolt. There was no one standing there. Only German soldiers sauntering along the street with local girls.

I gave myself a good shake: we must leave the house after all. I went up to the apartment to make sure the cache of thirty thousand pengős was in its place. It was. I crossed the street to the house of a Christian lawyer, a good customer of my father's, rightist, yes, but not excessively anti-Semitic. I asked him to arrange transit permits for us. "It will cost a lot," he said. "Do you have money?" I said we did. "How much?" I told him. He said it was enough and I should give him half in advance. I went home and took him the fifteen thousand. He said he would let us know the next day what he had arranged. The whole matter was to remain between ourselves. Not a word about the money.

All of us discussed the issue. I was the most intent on going. That the others were hesitant was understandable: none of us relished the idea of being lodgers. Besides, we still had enough to eat and could curl up in our own armchairs. Our nearest relatives came and told us not to leave: they might deport only the residents of Nagyvárad, not us. Hungarian Jews had long since been reassuring themselves that what had happened to the Polish Jews could never happen to them.

By now every Jew had been registered. Under orders from the county registrar the congregation itself drew up the list, organizing it by street and number. As a result the gendarmes had no trouble rounding everyone up in the wee hours. Absolutely no one in town would risk hiding us. Since it would be harder to round up the Budapest Jews—they outnumbered us by far—they would go last. At least we could gain time.

The lawyer came the next day for the other fifteen thousand and told me I could pick up the papers. But first, he said, I should go to see Somody, the headmaster at the Civic Boys' School, a good man who had a high opinion of my abilities. I should thank him for being receptive to our petition. I went to the headmaster, thanked him for his kindness, and clicked my heels. He smiled at me, stroked my head, and said that I should continue to study hard and be a good Magyar. Now I could go to the gendarmerie for the transit papers.

A staff sergeant at the gendarmerie formulated the permit and knocked it out on a typewriter with his large hands. It took him some time to extract the information from the birth records and police registration papers and integrate it into the text. Rifles in the corner stand, hats with sickle-feathers on the hat stand, the smell of boots, an old desk, a green table lamp, an ink pad, separate permits for each of us four, eight thumps with the seal. A corporal eating bacon at the other desk looked over at me.

"So you're leaving?"

"Yes we are."

The staff sergeant handed me the four sheets of paper. He had worked hard and was satisfied with himself. And with me because I smiled at him deferentially. He wished me a pleasant journey, for which I thanked him. The papers fit into the inner pocket of my linen suit jacket. I had something in my pocket that other Jews lacked. The town leadership had given its blessing to our departure.

Laló Kádár offered to accompany us to our relatives' in Budapest. We were glad: Christians would no longer set foot in our garden; segregation was practically total. He was an assistant in my uncle's textile factory, a tall and elegant young man, center-half on the town's soccer team. His younger sister Katalin was my sister's classmate and friend and often came to our place to play board games. She had a black ponytail, very white teeth, and large brown eyes. I used to stare at her when she visited, and when it was time to say hello or goodbye I never neglected to kiss her on the cheek. She was three years older than I and therefore taller as well. She would come up to me to say goodbye. We would stand in silence before she let me kiss her.

My cousin Vera, who was my age, also came to see us. She wanted to know if I would write to her and where. It was still unclear which of us should feel sorry for the other. I kissed her on the cheek too, at dusk on 5 June 1944. We then set to packing. The question was how much to take and for what? What should we leave behind? Come to think of it, we wouldn't need this, we wouldn't need that either. Beyond the weight limit prescribed by railway regulations we had to keep in mind that once we arrived we could keep only what we could carry.

The next morning we got up at three-thirty. Standing in the bathtub, the cold water having gushed over my head, I opened my eyes and saw myself in the mirror. Laló Kádár came for us at five in a light, gray suit. He had bought the tickets the previous day. The stork couple stood motionless in the growing light by the Tablets of the Covenant.

Our parents' house closed behind us. Whoever comes may have whatever remains. We took a fiacre to the station. There was little traffic. Whoever looked at us looked at us with indifference. No one said anything. We were shadows, irregular shadows at that, on a road of our own, without bayonet escort for the time being. We waited at the station for the Budapest express from Nagyvárad. We leaned against the platform's green railing. It was growing warm. People stared at the yellow stars on our chests. How could *we* be *there*?

I was glad to see the train come. By the time I began looking back from the train window, I could make out only the steam mill and the Calvinist church tower. Soon nothing at all. Something had ended. Today I would say it was childhood. I saw that István too was clenching his teeth: we both felt the finality of it. We stood wordlessly by the window: German military trains with cannons and tanks on flatbed cars, someone playing a harmonica, gray uniforms, rubber mackintoshes.

There were people at work in the fields. The wheat was high and turning yellow in spots: a good harvest. The previous day the Szolnok railway station had been bombed. The control tower had toppled, the overpass been struck. Burned out, blackened ruins. We stood there for some time, giving priority to German military trains. Another train also went by. Women's eyes behind a cattle-car window screened with barbed wire, Jewish women's eyes most likely.

People on the platforms looked serious and frightened. The train made long stops. Everything was slow, but ordinary. Announcements often spoke of track repairs. Inspectors came twice during the journey to examine papers. The first time the chief inspector, a chubby, red-faced mustachioed man, wearing a small round feathered cap, snarled at Laló Kádár and said, "How come you're meddling in Jew business if you're a real Hungarian? How come you're escorting Jew brats?" Laló paled and did not respond.

There was no problem with the papers themselves, but I had a feeling that this inspector had the power to kick us off the train under some pretense or other. He looked us over, not yet sure whether he felt like it; we looked back, unsmiling, serious. We were children of privilege, and he was clearly not a member of the gentry, but I could not tell whether this would tip the scales in our favor or vice versa. He moved on.

Our stars and this little incident made us unusual passengers. Our fellow passengers said not a word either to us or to Laló. At times like this it is better to say nothing. The second inspection was almost lackadaisical and went more smoothly. The papers were in order, the inspector nodded coolly.

I was afraid of Budapest though I had traveled there with my mother for a week the previous year to partake of its pleasures. In the glass gallery of Nyugati Station we had entrusted ourselves to the care of a pink-capped porter, then taken a cab to the Hungária Hotel, where a bellboy opened the door to our anteroom and pulled back the floor-length cambric lace curtain so I could step out onto the balcony and view the Danube, the bridges, the green row of chestnut trees on the far bank, and the Royal Castle in all their radiance. I could hardly breathe I was so happy; I grew weak, as one does when the curtain rises at the opera and a fabulous ballroom emerges from the darkness. Then my mother stood behind me; now she might have been in that cattle car. Then we had a porter; now we carried our own bags. Yet now as then the glassed-in gallery was beautiful, untouched by bombs. "The invasion has begun!" shouted the newspaper hawker. "British and American troops land on the beaches of Normandy!" People pressed around the leather bag holding the papers, but made no comment. István and I set down our bags and shook hands. Then we looked around at the people. They were just like the people back in Újfalu: they acted as if nothing had happened.

We bade Laló Kádár a heavy-hearted farewell. He could return home now. How I would have liked to go back with him.

We later found out that the next day all Berettyóújfalu Jews were rounded up. Accompanied by gendarmes, they dragged their bags through the streets. The rest of the population watched them from the sidelines, some with greetings, others with insults, but most were silent. Thus just one day after our departure the Újfalu Jews were taken in cattle cars to the ghetto in Nagyvárad and from there to Auschwitz.

Two weeks later I was strolling along the Danube, and Vera had been gassed and burned. I did not know at the time that of the two hundred Jewish children in the town the only ones still alive were the four of us who had left, two quiet twins with freckles, who became the subjects of testicular experiments, and my cousin Zsófi, fourteen at the time, who was waved by Doctor Mengele's baton into the group of those capable of work. She endured the ordeal and came home. All the others ended up as ashes.

I spent the summer of 1944 mainly on the balcony of my Aunt Gizella's Budapest apartment on the fourth floor of 36 Ernő Hollán Street. I could see the corner from there and would wait for my parents to appear, coming up from Saint Stephen Ring. They never did.

Aunt Gizu's husband, Uncle Andor, had served his country as a first lieutenant in the First World War. A glass case housing porcelain and silver knickknacks also contained a small burgundy cushion for his war decorations: a *signum laudis*, iron crosses, and various other medals of honor. Having failed to gain special status in light of his war record, he would haunt the Budapest Jewish Council during the hours Jews were permitted to circulate, and bring back reassuring news.

Uncle Andor was far from the pride of the family, but he did save our lives: when the Gestapo took our parents off, it was Uncle Andor who sent the letter of invitation. That he would later abandon us was the result of duress, but rescue us he did. Not a handsome man, he carried himself as dashingly as he could, holding his chin high and pulling his shoulders back. Always the "gentleman," he ate corn on the cob and peaches with a knife and fork. There was something cloyingly condescending in his manner: he would give me encouraging pats on the back. But he also indulged in surprising and graceless outbursts of emotion.

Back in the twenties Andor had sent twenty-one red roses to Gizella, my mother's older sister, to win her dowry and settle his debts. After they said their vows, he asked my grandfather—proudly at first, though ultimately on his knees—to keep his money in his, Andor's, bank, because how would it look for the young man if even his wife's father had no faith in his institution. Grandfather acceded and transferred his accounts. The next day Andor's bank declared bankruptcy and my grandfather went broke through the good offices of his son-in-law. With the family's support Andor rented an apartment in Budapest, opening a glove shop nearby and securing them a comfortable bourgeois existence.

Uncle Andor was the air-raid captain in his five-story building and would make his way with a squeaky lamp up and down between the shelter and the ground floor. He wore a shiny helmet that barely revealed his prideful, jutting chin and pink dewlap. By September the Jews were required to squeeze together into a smaller space, and we had to move, because he, Aunt Gizi, and our two cousins Ági and Jancsi got so small a room that it barely held their four cots. I remember the heavy smell of the friendly but unfamiliar woman and children. There was no place for us.

Aunt Zsófi lived in the next building. She was not a blood relative but the wife of Dr. Gyula Zádor, my father's cousin. By then my two cousins, István and Pál Zádor, were living there, along with Aunt Zsófi's son, Péter Polonyi, who was nearly our age. The face of a man with close-cropped graying hair emerges from the fog of memory. I liked his family name: Mandula, "Almond." I also recall a child a little older than me. Since we were forbidden to go out into the street, we played in the hallway. Aunt Zsófi was willing to let us live there as long as Uncle Andor's family took care of feeding us. For the first few days we still went back to our relatives' room for lunch.

Then came 15 October, the day Regent Horthy announced on the radio that he had requested a cease-fire. It was a bright autumn Sunday morning. People flowed out into the street. We too were giddy with the news. Everyone in the building—women and children, old and young—was Jewish. The old men climbed a ladder to take down the yellow paper star on the plank over the entrance. Some ripped off the yellow stars from their coats right there in the street. We might go on living after all, go home, find our parents; everything might again be as it had been in the days of a peacetime that perhaps never was. We waited for news of confirmation; the radio broadcast nothing but some incomprehensible public announcements: the Regent's address was not followed up by official substantiation.

We walked around our block. Not everyone in the neighborhood had dared to remove the emblem from the doorways of Jewish buildings, but one of the children had set fire to the yellow cardboard star and we stood around watching it burn. A couple not wearing yellow stars strolled past arm in arm. "See how insolent they've become," said a man in a hat to the woman in a hat. The new armed command was nowhere in evidence, but German military vehicles and trucks full of green-shirted men with Arrow Cross armbands raced along the Ring wearing looks of agitated determination.

A Jew asked a policeman whether there were any new regulations, whether we could now go outside after curfew. Officially we had the right to be in public areas only from eleven in the morning until five in the afternoon. Uncertainty was everywhere. What were we to do now that things had taken a 180-degree turn and official talk was of peace, not heroic battle, when the old rules seemed no longer to apply and Jews were not partitioned off from the Aryan "national organism"? What should we Jews be doing once the law no longer permitted persecution? That day we had no idea what to do on our own behalf.

By that night we had: the cease-fire had merely been a clumsy move by a clumsy regent, who had informed the German ambassador of his intention before telling his own troops! Szálasi, the leader of the Arrow Cross, announced the regent's removal, declaring that we would now fight even more resolutely at the side of our great German allies to win the war and cleanse our fatherland —of me. Extermination was next. Vermin, cockroach, Jew—you're done for! The will of steel was there; the rest was merely a matter of execution. It was important to remain discreet, since there were still about one hundred thousand Jews in Budapest and the open murder of so many people might create a mood of defeatism among the Christian population, but slaughter was on the way, a St. Bartholomew's night. Stay away from your home, hide if you can, or blend into the crowd, fade into the background, don't be conspicuous or you'll get yourself popped off.

We looked down through the open roof at the cinema screen: the Jew-baiting propaganda film *I Came from Tarnopol* was still playing. We trotted up and down the hallways of our building and even dared to go outside, where we excitedly discussed developments. We were wild game and fearful of the hunters, who, though little people like us, had been supplied by politics with weapons and the authorization to kill even children and the aged for as long as the yellow star was legal.

My view was that since I was innocent the laws that ordered my extermination were themselves illegal. I had seen little snots go around killing as easily as one shoots a hare or swats a fly, all in the name of our state, our fatherland. We were dealing with the ultimate enemy, the one who claims your life, and for want of a better method he was prepared to shoot you into the Danube and let the water carry you off.

We *took a powder*, as people used to say. Uncle Andor laid out his plan to us with sober self-confidence: we were to hide in the basement workshop they called the glove factory, three blocks away. We couldn't take much, as the Arrow Cross was patrolling the area and we had to be inconspicuous. We could sleep on the cutting table and wash at the basin in the toilet. We couldn't turn on the lights, but when the sun was shining enough light came into the room at midday to read by. Not hearing any shooting outside, we hoped the worst would not come. By the second day certain comforts made their absence felt in the dark workshop, particularly to Uncle Andor, who noticed in the morning that he had left his shaving brush at home. A painful loss. Though you could rub up a little rudimentary foam with the tip of your finger after wetting the skin and applying soap, neither the operation nor its result was aesthetically satisfactory. Uncle Andor felt it was inadvisable to return home (though the St.

Bartholomew's night had not materialized), but he did want that shaving brush. The simplest solution in Uncle Andor's eyes (after excluding the draconian options of brushless shaving and not shaving at all) was for me to fetch the brush.

I set off. There were soldiers wearing armbands standing at the gate of the third building down. It was drizzling. Perhaps they didn't know what they were supposed to be doing. They called me over.

"Hey kid, come over here. Are you a Jew?"

"What makes you ask?"

"Well, you could be," they said.

"I could," said I.

"Well, are you?"

"What makes you ask?" I said, returning to my original question.

"Hey, that's the way Jews talk."

"Are *you* a Jew?" I asked.

"What makes you ask?" he said.

"You know how they talk."

"Drop your pants."

I didn't move. We stared at each other.

"Well?"

"It's raining."

"All right. Get going."

He and I both knew the score. He just didn't feel like killing me.

The rest of the way was incident-free. When I got to the apartment, the elderly ladies asked me excitedly where the family had spent the night. I no longer remember what I came up with—something about being guests somewhere—but they got a peek of me slipping the shaving brush into my pocket from the shelf below the bathroom mirror. "You came for *that*?" asked one of the ladies.

"Good-bye," I said.

On the corner I saw Arrow Cross men coming up Hollán Street at a run. I took a quick turn to the left, hoping to get back to my family via a Pozsonyi Avenue detour, but I didn't realize they would be making parallel runs, and in large numbers, and that they would not only be coming down Pozsonyi Avenue in a row that spanned the entire street, but also from behind, from the Saint Stephen Ring, to sweep up everyone in sight. In those days it was not unusual to find Jews at midday in the New Leopold Town district. Those they detained were dispatched to a brick factory in Old Buda, and from there they would be sent westward, on foot. There were still a few spots where Jews could be packed off onto railroad cars. It would be a few weeks before the authorities adopted the simplified procedure of fencing in an area and shooting people into the Danube.

I saw a thin man wearing glasses and a white armband trying to explain his exceptional status: he had once risked his life fighting Béla Kun's commune. The Arrow Cross man was silent for a moment, then spit a cigarette butt into his face and led him off to the side. People stood in line to have their papers checked. It wasn't enough to have a document with an official seal; you had to answer questions.

I picked a line where a man in a leather coat and a hat with a flipped-up visor, hands on hips, was putting people through the questions. When there were only two people in front of me, I slipped down on my hands and knees and crawled off past his brown hunting boots: there was no way he could keep track of what was going on with all the people milling around. I was careful to amble my way back to the workshop, going around the block and making sure no one saw me enter.

"So you're back," said Uncle Andor, kindly patting my head. He immediately had a shave using plenty of cologne, then paced up and down stroking his chin. The lunch hour was approaching. Uncle Andor said the workshop was not a good hiding place, so one by one we should all go back to where we had been staying. As for my sister and me, we could go to his place for lunch after four, until which time we were to wait "with that woman," meaning Aunt Zsófi. He liked to speak disparagingly of her. But when we rang the bell at 9 Hollán Street at four o'clock, the door was opened by the same elderly lady who had noticed my little maneuver with the shaving brush that morning. When I asked where the family was, she said that my uncle, his wife, and their two children had departed with their luggage. Where they had gone she did not know.

There we stood, Éva and I, at a loss what to do. It took a little time for us to grasp that our relatives had left for a hiding place, that Uncle Andor had procured them false papers with which they would register as a Christian family of Transylvanian refugees under a new name and stay with acquaintances who had agreed to take them in for money. We went back the next day and the day after, but there was no news.

Half a year later, in April of 1945, I caught a glimpse of Aunt Gizu on a street corner in Nagyvárad. I did a double take, but she went her way on the other side of the street. A week later we met face to face. She invited me to walk with her, but I demurred. She told me their new address. It was the address of relatives from Várad who had disappeared into thin air and whose apartment she and her family had taken over. I quickly took my leave with a shaky promise to visit.

On that night, 15 October, Aunt Zsófi also went into hiding with the boys, Péter, István, and Pali. They took very few bags and went to the Margaret Ring, where an acquaintance had given them his apartment. They entered without yellow stars. They had only just set down their bags when a resident phoned and told them to make a quick getaway because the concierge had reported them as possible Jews. Rushing down the stairs, they saw the elevator moving up with armed Arrow Cross men inside. They heard the pounding on the door upstairs and scurried back to their wonted place of fear.

Aunt Zsófi not only gave us lodging; she gave us food and care as well. After taking in my sister and me, she had five children in the two rooms of a good-sized temporary apartment. She sold her things to feed us. Meanwhile, we children thought up ways to escape—climbing down a rope from the bathroom window onto a garage roof—should the Arrow Cross come to take us away.

Every morning, when we were permitted outside, Aunt Zsófi set out to procure papers. One or another neutral embassy took apartment buildings under its wing, hanging signs over the main entrance indicating that a given house was under the protection of the Swiss, Swedish, Spanish, or Vatican mission. Papal protection was said to be the best. If you couldn't make it into a safe house, you went to the ghetto, where they had started dismantling the high fence and gates. Owing to Aunt Zsófi's secret morning trips we had a good chance of getting letters of protection from the Swiss.

I did not grieve over the loss of Uncle Andor's supervision, as I felt more at home with Aunt Zsófi and my cousins from Berettyóújfalu. We were a natural "we" again, a branch of my father's family. Dr. Gyula Zádor, Zsófia's husband and István and Pali's paternal uncle, was interned in a work camp. A neurologist and psychiatrist, he had studied in Heidelberg and practiced in Zurich, and returned home in 1938. He had been the personification of irony in my childhood mythology. For some inner reason a chilly element would infiltrate his otherwise warm, heartfelt smile. It gave me pause: he seemed to be making fun at my expense.

Here is an example. When I was five, I had a hernia operation, after which I screamed at the top of my lungs for them to remove my bonds: I had just come around from the anesthesia and could not tolerate being tied down. It was outrageous not to be trusted with my own decisions, as if my five-year-old self lacked the brains to lie motionless and rest after the operation without being humiliatingly strapped to the bed. Besides, the white gauze they used, the white bed, the staff all in white, the white room—it offended my sense of color.

My governess Lívia's camel-hair housecoat was of a warm beige. Whenever she touched me—to give me a spoonful of medicine or hold my left arm down and take my temperature—she did so with kindness. But the nurse —that unfamiliar, middle-aged excuse for a woman—had no right to lay a hand on me just because she happened to be disguised in a white shell. I wanted her out of there, her and her energetic, aggressive benevolence! I had stiffened my body into a girder and was screaming bloody murder—No! I won't give in! Unbind me!—when a familiar face appeared at the foot of my bed. Thick, graying hair, a high forehead, and that cheeky smile, incredulous at my rage, certain I was playacting. Where did that white-gowned figure get off looking into my soul? Even if he was Uncle Gyula behind the white mask.

Our family doctor, Dr. Spernáth, would come and see us in civilian clothes, a gray suit. Éva and I would hide behind the dining-room curtains so he wouldn't be able to "stick us" or so we wouldn't have to take that disgusting cod liver oil or just for the sake of hiding, so we could later appear, forcing back giggles of complicity. Uncle Spinach (for that was what we called him) would talk politics with my father even as he listened to our chests. This tickled unpleasantly, because Dr. Spernáth was bald and his cold pate had a medicinal smell that turned our stomachs. We shuddered when that head pressed against our bare skin. Yet despite his white gown Uncle Gyula said he would recommend that they untie my straps if I stopped squirming. The pact was made and kept.

Some thirty years later I asked another ironist, the psychologist Ferenc Mérei, whether he had known Uncle Gyula. He said something to the effect that he had been considered half-crazy. In 1941 Dr. Gyula Zádor had rented a large apartment in the middle of town, at 5 Szép Street, furnished it in his wife's Bauhaus taste, and opened a private practice with his Heidelberg and Zurich diplomas and his reputation as chief neurologist at the Jewish Hospital. There might have been no Second World War; he had simply followed the logical path for a man of his standing. His beautiful wife, whom he wooed away from a respected and successful journalist, was a friend to poets, painters, and all kinds of revolutionaries.

Uncle Gyula himself came from a more modest background. His family in Berettyóújfalu gave him his portion of the inheritance early to get him started. Their house served as both shop and workshop. They were their own bosses and enjoyed looking in on the warm, private side of life whenever they felt so inclined. The shop and workshop gave onto the street, the world, while the back and upstairs room belonged to the Biedermeier zone, the realm of passions, quick successions of joy and despair, passion and resentment. Their life was beautiful one moment, unbearable the next.

So this Berettyóújfalu citizen of the world, who had the temerity to look down on us, natives of the same town, had taken up residence in the capital as if everything were perfectly normal, as if the number one business of the day were to build his patient base and publish his findings in domestic and international professional journals. As he sat under the arbor in his Újfalu garden I would stare at his white cord trousers, yellow shoes, and bluish-pink silk shirt. He would let us villagers turn our finest phrases, but even as he listened he was forming his own big-city opinions about us. We were naive; irony was something we had no experience of; we did not realize that existence is ambiguous and even love jaundiced. Uncle Gyula's village optimism was tainted with the city-dweller's ability to see through things. The city slicker pokes his nose into everything and always seems to know what cards you've got. As if people didn't reveal their true selves the very first time they shake hands! When Uncle Gyula first gave me that look of his, he was not yet forty. Now that I could be his father, I feel that had he not been killed his true, naive nature would have won out. (Actually, it did win out, though in a self-destructive way: through his village burgher's respect for the law he voluntarily returned to a labor camp, leaving his wife behind.)

Aunt Zsófi was a delicate, thin figure of a woman. Everything about her was silvery: her voice, her eyes, and the few graying locks in her thick, black hair. I often had the feeling that we little wild creatures amused her. She had a son, Péter Polonyi, and acted as guardian for my two cousins, István and Pál Zádor. And by the good graces of fate and Uncle Andor my sister Éva and I added two more to her charge. Four boys make a lot of noise, and Aunt Zsófi would occasionally get a headache and ask us to disappear—for a while at least.

In the fall of 1944 Aunt Zsófi must have been thirty. She sometimes had a sardonic glint in her eye, but her voice had a delicacy to it that came from a distant shore. Never one to hesitate about doing what her taste dictated, she treated us as her very own, a single mother to five children. She even managed to see to it that we got through those abominable times with our souls intact.

Her husband would have been able to skip out on the forced-labor camp: he was granted a day's leave to visit his family at Christmas of 1944. Despite Zsófi's entreaties the doctor returned to the camp: he had no desire to get his family into trouble, he had his sick comrades to treat, and what is more he had promised his charitable commander to return. But while he was away, the charitable commander had been replaced, and the honest Doctor Zádor and his patients—poets and scholars all—ended up in a mass grave.

Jews were still being deported to Auschwitz from Budapest's outer districts of Újpest and Kispest as late as the summer. They could have come into the city on foot or by tram, but they followed orders and went to the railway station. The communists among them—the Zionists, the resistors, the bold—got hold of false papers and went into hiding. The more resigned and perhaps fearful middle class tried to ride out the dangerous times in safe houses. The safe houses were inhabited by better-off, secular Jews who had managed to contact one of the neutral diplomatic embassies. The poorer, orthodox Jews, who had black beards and hats, wives wrapped in shawls, sons with side-locks, and daughters with big eyes, went to the ghetto. That was their place: it had the greatest concentration of synagogues. Both they and the neutral diplomats must have felt this. But it was open season in the ghetto: drunken Arrow Cross men would go in and shoot at will.

Swiss letters of protection, *Schützpässe*, were distributed in an operation organized by the Swiss consul, Carl Lutz. His name comes up less often than that of his Swedish colleague Raoul Wallenberg, though Lutz saved as many people as Wallenberg. Under the protection of the Helvetic Confederation we moved to 49 Pozsonyi Avenue, a building where my greatest respect went to three or four young men hiding out in the cellar, about whom people whispered that they were resistors and had defected from the military. There were perhaps eighty of us living in a three-room apartment on the fourth floor. At night we would stack up any furniture that could not be slept on. Not everyone got a bed or mattress, but everyone had at least a rug. The four of us boys slept on mattresses on the floor by the window behind a pile of furniture. It was like an ongoing house party. There was always someone to talk to. For two hours every morning we could leave the building, five children clinging to a beautiful young woman. Aunt Zsófi protected us, as perhaps we did her. Whoever asked for her papers was astounded. "Are they all yours?" The crush diminished as time passed: some people moved down to hiding places, while others were abducted during spur-of-the-moment raids and shot into the Danube.

In the winter of 1944–45 I saw any number of dead bodies. I could picture myself among them, but the tasks of day-to-day existence obscured most of my imaginings. Danger makes you practical. Only at isolated moments do you face the possibility of death—when someone holds a pistol to your head, for example. Then you feel: yes, it could happen. You become an adult from the moment you face your own death, which means I have been an adult from the age of eleven. For some people it happens earlier, for others later, and there are those for whom the moment never comes.

Death is hardly pleasant, nor is mortal danger. But you can be standing on a rooftop terrace with fighter planes machine-gunning above and feel the whole scene is not all that serious. So let's just slide around in our hobnailed boots on the ice rink we have made with a few buckets of water. *Not all that serious* later saved me from succumbing to melodramatic moods.

I owe my life to a benevolent chain of coincidences. It has proved an enduring gift to recognize, at the age of eleven, the bald fact that I could be killed at any time, and to have learned how to act in such a situation. In the winter of 1944–45 I thought of death as I might have thought of, say, firewood: there was nothing unusual about it. It was outside my control, like drawing the wrong card.

Beautiful young women in ski boots and Norwegian sweaters were smoking cigarettes, their abundant hair combed smooth into a bun, their long legs crossed in ski pants. They laughed at all kinds of things I did not understand. They were different from the small-town beauties I had known: more malicious, more enigmatic, radical yet refined. They spoke of the French surrealists, German expressionists, and Russian abstractionists like old friends. They were artists, dancers, left-wingers—and they stretched so beautifully. They would sing for us children, sing the "Internationale" and "Dubinushka" in Hungarian.

But none amazed me more than Aunt Zsófi. I would have loved to perform some heroic act for her and did not dare to so much as scratch myself in her sight. Her slightly indolent voice would ask, "My knight in shining armor, will you accompany me?" I would have accompanied her to the gates of hell. For Aunt Zsófi's sake I was willing to hold thick novels under my arms to keep my elbows in while eating. The more fearful moved down into the cellar, but Aunt Zsófi was unable to separate cleanliness from human dignity. She would have found it repulsive for us to hide from the explosive and incendiary bombs, the cannonballs and artillery mines, down in the bomb shelter, the putrid darkness, the chaotically congested company of so many ill-washed bodies. What if it did raise the level of risk a notch.

"Dignity means more than security," she would say. "We are not going to let the lice take us over." We did not go down to the cellar even when the sirens started. The most sensible choice was the rooftop terrace, where the winter sun shone brightly every morning even in January, though at temperatures of twenty degrees below freezing. We would pour out a few buckets of water and make a fabulous skating rink for ourselves. With a running start you could slide from one end to the other. Machine-gun rounds from Ratas, Soviet fighter planes, landed on the ice with a pop. We always looked up to see where the bombs pouring from their bellies would fall. A cloud of dust or smoke indicated whether the bomb was explosive or incendiary.

From the street below came the rumble of trams carrying trunks of ammunition to the front, now just a few blocks away, and the voices of Germans shouting to one another. The Russians were getting close, but the Arrow Cross was still goring Jews and Christian defectors in the neighborhood. The word "gore" was on every public poster; it meant kill on the spot and leave the body behind. With weapons exploding in the street, documents meant nothing: only drunkenness and fear had meaning—and the sympathy or antipathy of the moment. The armed men in armbands had plenty of people to shoot, though they had begun to sense they couldn't execute every single Jew. They may even have had trouble getting into the man-hunting mood day in and day out. Filling the ice-flow-congested Danube with old ladies and young girls was an art whose charm was intermittent. Even the defenseless people they killed—and they could have killed as many as they pleased—even they expressed a modicum of resistance in their eyes, reinforced by the gaze of passersby, who watched the quiet winter coats being led down to the riverbank with some degree of empathy. Of course you needed to make time for other things too, like drinking and getting warm. It must also have occurred to the men in armbands that if the Russians were at the outskirts of the city—and with plenty of artillery too, judging from the din—they would hardly stop but forge on into the center. If they occupied the entire city, Arrow Cross troops could expect anything but decorations, not a pleasant thought by any means. The mood for murder flared up and flagged by turns.

Shooting at Russians was dangerous; Jews were fish in a barrel. Life is a matter of luck, and death bad luck. You can do something for yourself, but not much, and sometimes pride keeps you from doing even that. Several people had been taken from the apartment the previous night. From the next room, not ours.

I watch the Germans. Can they really believe they will drive back the Russians, just five blocks away? Intelligent as they are, they have no idea what they are and are not allowed to do. The Arrow Cross, on the other hand, are the bottom of the barrel, the school dropouts. Their only talent is for torturing cats. A child has to grow up to understand just how underdeveloped adults can be. A fourteen-year-old kid with a gun accompanies unarmed people down to the bank of the Danube. Instead of grabbing the gun from his hand, they go where he orders them. Most victims call it fate, but fate should cause fear and stir them to self-defense whether the threat be sleet falling on their garden or death at the hands of an enemy. Yet people much like pets get used to seeing their companions cut down around them. You can't feel outrage and empathy every half hour. Standing out on the roof terrace, we hear the occasional sputter of shots. Someone (armed) checks the papers of someone else (unarmed). The former doesn't like the latter's face or papers, stands him against the wall, and shoots him dead. The people taken down to the Danube have to stand in a row, their faces to the river. The shots come from behind.

Even so abundant a variety of violent deaths could not obscure the beauty of those dazzling winter mornings. In the shadow of our mortality bread became more like bread, jam more like jam. I gladly chopped all kinds of furniture into firewood. We even ventured down to the riverbank, where we chopped up a small pier. It was good dry pine that burned wonderfully with its white paint.

We knew that the Russians had come in great numbers with tanks and heavy artillery. They had relatively fewer planes than the English and Americans, whose bombers arrived mostly later, in the summer of 1944; in the winter it was still the Ratas that thundered though the sky.

Klára often stood out on the roof terrace, adjusting her black ponytail, tying and untying it. I would give it an occasional yank. She had a little birthmark at the base of her nose and a mole at the tip. In exchange for my services I was granted permission on that very terrace to plant a quick kiss on that mole. It was forbidden to tarry on the nose. Klára liked to speak of parts of her body without possessive pronouns, as if they were independent beings: "The nose has had enough," she informed me. We spent a lot of time wrestling. It was no easy task to pin Klára down: one of us, then the other would end up on top. Once in a while I managed to pin her shoulders to the horsehair mattress on the floor and lie on her belly, but I would get such a bite on the wrist that the rows of teeth left a lasting mark. "Do you have what it takes to hold your hand over the candle?" asked Klára. I did, and got a burn mark on my palm. Klára kissed it. I carefully slid my fist into my pocket, as if holding a sparrow.

Klára could not stand being shut in and was incapable of spending the entire day in the safe house. The curfew for Jews did not apply to her. I would try to detain her. I was worried, but did not dog her heels. She would make the rounds of the neighborhood, then boast of what she had seen. When an officer asked for her papers, she lacked the nerve to answer his skeptical questions; she merely held her peace. They led Klára down to the Danube together with a long line of Jews. There she recognized one of her aunts and squeezed in next to her. The were all told to empty their pockets and stand with their hands up, facing the bare trees of Margaret Island, the freestanding piers of the bombed-out Margaret Bridge. Her aunt pitched forward into the river, but Klára was not hit. "You're lucky my magazine ran out," said the machine-gunner with a friendly laugh. "Now move it—and be good at home!" Thus did the junior (though no longer all that young) officer send her on her way.

I opened the street door for Klára, having recognized the sound of her footsteps through the planked-up door. "Let's stand here a minute," she said. "Hold my hand. And don't let me out tomorrow. Stay with me all day. Don't tell Mother they shot Sári dead right at my side."

The next morning I squatted in the courtyard in front of a stove—three bricks and an iron grill—on which bean soup was cooking painfully slowly. My duty was to keep it well stirred, taste it from time to time to see if it was softening up, and stoke the embers with pieces of sawed-up chair legs. Klára stood next to me and talked about her first two years in school, when she couldn't bring herself to say a word. She would do her work, but not utter a single syllable. She would have liked to say at least hello to the other children, but could not open her mouth. I was more interested in whether the soup was ready. I lifted the cover and stuck in a wooden spoon.

The roar of a Russian fighter plane. Klára pressed against the wall. When she screamed "Come here!" there was such rage in her voice that I spun around in astonishment. The fighter sprinkled the interior flagstone courtyards of the block with machine-gun rounds, hitting no one. The reason Klára was so angry was that I was always playing the hero, which was a decided exaggeration. Suddenly I heard the embers sizzling and looked down to see soup pouring out of a hole in the pot: a bullet had passed through the bottom of the large red enameled vessel. Had I not turned around, it would also have passed through my head, which had been bent over the soup. Finding another pot was no easy task.

"Why did you scream at me?" I asked Klára that evening.

"I don't know," she answered, unsure of herself by then.

We stood on the rooftop and heard a famous actress singing. Coming from the Russian military's speakers, her voice took on a deep, threatening thrum. The goal was to plant fear in the faltering hearts of the Hungarian soldiers pointlessly defending themselves alongside the Germans: "You cannot run, you cannot hide. Your fate, it cannot be denied." The Russians had entered the city and advanced all the way to the Angyalföld district. The speakers were just a few blocks away. A Stalin-candle shot up, illuminating the rooftops. Hand in hand, we watched, squinting. "It's beautiful," whispered Klára. We both laughed at her whisper.

We had an unexpected visitor at the safe house: Nene. She brought a small aluminum medallion of Mary on a chain. Nene asked us to wear it around our necks. She wanted us to convert to Catholicism. If we did—or merely declared our willingness to do—she would take us to a convent where they protected and hid converted Jewish children. We thanked Nene for her offer, but told her we would rather not.

We children had agreed on a plan in case we were driven out in a large group, which would most likely end with our being shot into the Danube: we would drop our knapsacks at the corner of the park and run off in different directions. Even if they shot at us—and plenty of guards would be on hand if hundreds of Jews were turned out of their building—some might make it.

The next morning four or five Arrow Cross men and gendarmes burst into the room, screaming at us to get dressed and turn over all weapons, including kitchen knives and pocketknives, plus anything of value, and then line up obediently and quietly on the sidewalk in front of the building. They had a rabbi with them, who gently counseled us to obey and specifically recommended that we hand over all necklaces, mementoes, and engagement rings. I took my time putting my socks on.

Down in front of the building Rebenyák's red hat stood out. Rebenyák was the house's bad boy. He would have liked to belong to our gang, but we never let him in. He speculated that the rabbi would get his cut of the items, assuming they didn't shoot him. We looked at one another inquisitively, wondering whether this was the time to implement the plan and whether we should let Rebenyák in on it, when two loud-voiced men came along, one wearing a gendarme's uniform, the other a German officer's. They were shouting—not at us but at the Arrow Cross men and the two gendarmes with us—and ordered us back into the building. They might have been communists in disguise or two Jewish actors. The better actor played his role less effectively; the worse actor was more convincing. Soon we were back in our room again, still in our overcoats, clueless.

The lobby was our clubhouse. Kids would alternate looking out while the rest of us slid down the marble ramp along the bottom flight of stairs. Rebenyák showed up in his red cap. He was fourteen or so and was always pestering me with his stamps, knowing I had brought my stamp album from Újfalu. I always traded smaller, more valuable stamps for larger, nicer-looking ones. I had trouble understanding him: his language was full of city-tough words. Instead of "piss" he would say "drimple," or "wankle," or "slash." He spoke obscurely of some pussy or other, by which I finally realized he meant the sexual organ of one of the older girls. He would punctuate his sentences with "You dig, buddy? No? Then suck my dick!" Klára said he was just throwing his weight around; she had more brains in her shoelaces than Rebenyák under that red hat of his. He liked to boast he could no longer even look at the broads, the tomatoes, the merchandise—in short, at women—who were supposedly all over him down in the cellar. Klára reviewed my trades, checking the stamps' value in a catalogue. "That lying bastard is constantly getting the better of you. Don't you mind?" I didn't really. Ultimately I gave Rebenyák my entire stamp album for a hunk of bacon which, when roasted with onion atop a dish of peas, became the envy of the apartment house. Rebenyák had pinched the bacon from under his mother's bed in the cellar and crept back with it, weasel-like. He slept in the same bed as his mother, a strong-smelling corpulent woman with hair sprouting from her chin.

I ran into Rebenyák decades later. He was lame and living in a cellar again: he had ceded three apartments to three wives, who would come home with lovers more muscular than he and announce that for the time being Rebenyák would be sleeping in the next room. In his basement flat Rebenyák bought and sold girls from orphanages to rich tourists, instructing the former to steal the latter's passports. Rebenyák delighted in the possibilities: Swedish, Brazilian, Australian . . .

In the safe house Rebenyák would venture upstairs despite his mother's warning that fire was more likely to hit the building there: he was attracted by our cosmopolitan ways. Longingly, he would study the Rosenthal soup cups we ate beans from at the long black table, holding them up to the light: translucent. He stole one.

"Don't be a creep," I said. "They might shoot you tomorrow."

Rebenyák was superstitious, and my remark got to him. "Know who they're going to shoot tomorrow? *You*, you wooden-dicked Újfalu crybaby!"

Klára twisted his arm. "You take that back!" She was superstitious herself.

"Just see if your wooden pussy ever gets my jism!" But after whimpering a while in his agony, he brought it back.

More shots penetrated the apartment. Shards of glass made the beans in the Rosenthal cups inedible. The iron stove, whose exhaust pipe we had aimed out of the window, was buckled over like a man kicked in the stomach. Machine gun fire ricocheted off the outside wall. Klára suddenly turned childlike, sitting underneath the table and directing a sumptuous wedding of a clay lamb and a wooden mouse. Rebenyák crouched under the table next to her. I made him nervous.

"Are you really in love with that dodo? I mean, he doesn't even know the difference between allegory and paregoric."

"What's . . . allegory?" I asked suspiciously.

Rebenyák changed the subject to the pot with the hole: "You saved that hick's life. Isn't that enough? Now fall in love with me."

A depraved smile appeared on Klára's face.

"Fine. Just give me your stamp collection and fill my hat with sugar cubes."

Rebenyák blushed, but did not reach for the hat, whose wheat-blue tassel had dangled before my eyes from morning to night.

That night a young fellow named Mário, who lived in the next room, came back from the Danube. The shot had hit him in the arm, and he'd managed to swim out. The only hard part was to free himself from his father, to whom he had been tied. His father had been hit in the chest and held him fast for a while, but finally let go. Clinging to a block of ice, Mário had drifted down the Danube under the bridges. He was afraid of being crushed between blocks of ice. Ultimately he had climbed out onto the stairs at the foot of the Elisabeth Bridge and made his way home, wet and bloody. He was stopped on the way, but was by then indifferent to everything.

"Shoot me into the Danube again if you want."

"Jews are like cats," said an old Arrow Cross man. "They keep coming back to life." He sees it all the time. That's why they're so dangerous. Here he's hardly out of the river and he gets cheeky. When it's all over, they'll have the nerve to blame it all on us. "Hey, weren't you our guest once?"

Yes, he had been—he and his father. They had grilled him about his younger brother, who had taken part in a weapons heist. His father didn't know anything. They said that if he didn't tell them they would take care of his other son, Mário. The father gave a false address. The Arrow Cross men came back enraged, then shot someone else instead of the brother they were after. As long as they had him there, they subjected Mário's testicles to their boot heels. Finally a gendarme officer came into the Arrow Cross building and dragged them off. A good thing.

Dr. Erdős and a group of other elderly Jews had been pulled out of 49 Pozsonyi Avenue to build a cobblestone barricade on the corner: the younger Jews had long since been taken away. Six stones high and four deep, the wall was impenetrable. The T-34 tanks that had made it all the way from Stalingrad would certainly be stopped dead here.

We children watched from the entrance as the old men, stooping against the cold, hacked at the stones with pokers and hammers, separating the blocks stuck together with pitch, then lifting them into their laps and lugging them over to the roadblock. Young men in hunting boots, black trousers, and green shirts watched over the work, prodding the old men on. One of them cracked a whip, once used by a cabby on his horses, over the old Jews' necks. They could in fact have worked with more vigor.

It was probably the fellow with the whip who outraged an older gentleman from the next building, a building inhabited by Christians. Sometimes old men stick together, even if it means crossing congregational boundaries. In any case the old gentleman pulled out his hunting rifle and wounded the young whipcracker. The Arrow Cross men thought that one of the Jews had taken the shot, and started shooting back blindly. The twenty barricade builders ran for cover and fell. Dr. Erdős himself made for the main door of the building, though taking his time so as not to draw attention to himself. I was the only one still standing in the doorway: the other children and the doorkeeper, an even older Jew, had dashed up the steps upon hearing the shots.

I opened the boarded-up entrance door. Dr. Erdős darted inside. I wanted to shut and lock it before the tall young man pursuing him could shove his way in, and the two of us, child and graybeard, pushed from the inside, but our besieger, who was twenty-five or so, took a running start and rammed us back enough to make a crack for the tip of his boot. The game was his. There he stood, pistol in hand.

He was taller than Dr. Erdős, and his lip was quivering from wounded pride: Jews slamming the door in my face just like that? A slight smile, the smile of the vanquished, flashed over Dr. Erdős' face. The young man held up the pistol and fired into the doctor's temple. Dr. Kálmán Erdős fell, his blood flowing over the muddy, pink imitation marble. Then the young man took aim at my forehead. I looked at him more in amazement than in fear. He lowered his pistol and headed out of the door.

By this time the trams were delivering ammunition crates ever more desperately to the front, that is, the immediate vicinity, yet courageous women would leave the building and still manage to forage bread. On the night of 17–18 January 1945 we moved to the inner room to sleep, since the outer one, damaged by a bomb, lacked a windowpane. Instead of going to bed, however, we crouched by the window, where we could watch the fighting. By the light of the Stalin-candles whizzing into the sky we saw a newsreel scene in all its glory, unbounded by the screen: a tank rumbling through the barricade, sweeping aside the basalt blocks, with more tanks and infantry in its wake; German soldiers, who had been on their bellies with machine guns behind the stone-piles, dashing for the park as the front moved on toward the Saint Stephen Ring.

As dawn came up on 18 January I watched the historical turning point of the war (liberation for me, defeat for others) with my own eyes. A few excited young women—teachers, fashion designers, dancers—hummed the "Internationale." Magda, a tall, strawberry-blonde dancer, taught us to sing with them. She was a communist and said we should be communists too, because they were the only party in the underground; the others were collaborating with the government. At four o'clock on that morning we gave ourselves over to the spirit of liberation.

In time Magda lost her enthusiasm. She tried to slip over the border in 1949, wearing the same ski boots she had worn during the winter of the siege. The border guards shot her dead.

At ten in the morning on 18 January 1945 I stepped out of the front door of 49 Pozsonyi Avenue. Two Russian soldiers were standing on the sidewalk in their torn coats, slightly scruffy and more indifferent than cordial. People spoke to them. They did not understand, but nodded. It was obvious they were not much interested in us. They asked whether Hitler was in the building. I had no information suggesting that Hitler was living with Budapest Jews under Swiss protection at 49 Pozsonyi Avenue. Then they asked about Szálasi, head of the Arrow Cross: no, he wasn't living there either. After a moment we caught on that "Hitler" meant Germans and "Szálasi" meant Arrow Cross. They were fairly simple boys. They went down into the shelter with a flashlight, prodding people with the barrels of their machine guns and shining their light into every nook. They found some military defectors in civilian dress, whom they let be. They did not particularly care that the building was inhabited by Jews: if you tried to explain to them you were a Jew and expected to get some kindness out of them, you didn't get very far. But they were friendly enough to us boys, and we got used to their poking around in the basement looking for Hitler. There was a man down there who spoke Slovak and could understand them a little. He immediately offered to interpret for them, and as they went through a passageway, which had been opened with a pickaxe, to the shelter next door, this Slovak-speaking Jew started barking out instructions like a commander in mufti, newly appointed from the ranks of the blanket-clad. Eventually, having conquered his last vestige of hesitation, he bade farewell to his family and ran off after the Russians.

The soldiers broke into a pharmacy and drank a bottle of Chat Noir cologne. They reached for it confidently, as if familiar with the brand. It was the closest thing to liquor there. We—soldiers in mufti, locals, Jews and Christians alike—flocked after them. The more resourceful took along knapsacks. I picked up a harmonica, which I later traded to Rebenyák for a bag of sugar cubes.

We could now leave the building at will, the building whose neutral status had protected us, though it had not been enough to keep the other half of its residents alive. A few markings in Cyrillic had begun to appear. The yellow star had come down from the front entrance and lay on a snow heap. As I stepped out as a free man for the first time, I was perhaps also stepping out of my childhood, the years when prohibitions of all sorts hemmed me in. The shooting and bombing were over, and it was safe to come out of the cellar. There were still the occasional stray shots, but now it was the Germans shooting from the Buda side.

At times an entire round of machine-gun fire showered the street, and I learned just how flat I could press myself against a wall.

Given that the apartment had been hit by gunfire and we were sharing it with thirty others, thought it best to leave for Aunt Zsófi and Uncle Gyula's apartment in Szép Street, which might be empty or at least not so crowded. We felt a sudden urge to take leave of the people in the cellar and break free of the seven-story Bauhaus ghetto into which we had been squeezed.

The hard-trampled snow had iced over the asphalt. We all wore knapsacks, clutched quilts, and pulled the rest of our meager belongings on a sled behind us. The wind was kicking up snow-dust. It was well below freezing, and as we had no gloves our fingers were purplish-red. We passed burning buildings in the darkening evening. Through black windows we saw dying flames painting the ceilings a rusty red. They were like a cross-section revealing the building's naked innards after a bomb had torn its façade off: a bathtub dangling, but the sink still in place; a heavy mahogany cupboard on the wall, but the dining table three flights down. It was the shameless, twisted humor of destruction.

Exhausted, but reviving, people were carting their belongings from place to place, going home, going in search of their loved ones, going just to go: after all, someone might be baking bread somewhere. People trudged through the streets weighed down with their goods and chattels while soldiers sat around on tanks or moved around in squads. Tongues of flame soared out of windows; people and horses lay scattered on the ground. Survivors did not carve meat from people, though they did from horses:

elderly gentlemen crouched inside horse corpses scraping frozen shreds of meat off bones with their pocketknives.

Our bundles of bedding were falling apart; we hung onto the quilts in desperation. I would have liked to earn Aunt Zsófi's praise. Once she called me her "little mainstay," but my joy at this mingled with the disappointment of being called "my little hypocrite" again for another of my attempts at pleasing her. That slightly chilly but still flirtatious irony was in Aunt Zsófi's face now too, curious to see how I would manage a bundle that was threatening to disintegrate.

The building on the corner had been razed to the ground, but 5/a Szép Street was miraculously still standing. It had taken a few cannon shots here and there, but they were patchable holes. The marble fountain in the courtyard, untouched, had icicles hanging from the stone-rumped nymph's jug.

The brass nameplate had disappeared from the front door of Dr. Gyula Zádor's apartment, and Aunt Zsófi's key would not turn the lock. The buzzer would not ring. She had to pound on the door. Out of the darkness of the long foyer a little circle of light emanated, and as the tiny grille-protected window in the door opened we saw a gray-haired woman sizing us up in a manner less than friendly.

Zsófi was wearing a light-colored fur coat, and her black hair was bound in a light-gray silk kerchief. The five of us children were standing behind her. We were curious and determined to reclaim the apartment.

"Good day, madam. I am Zsófia Vágó, the wife of Dr. Gyula Zádor, owner of this apartment and the possessions therein."

The gray-haired lady answered as follows from behind the grille: "I am Mrs. Kázmér Dravida, rightful tenant of this apartment. Your apartment, madam—inasmuch as it was in fact yours—has been officially granted to us as refugees from Transylvania."

To which Zsófi said: "Madam, the legality of your procedure is subject to several objections."

To which Mrs. Dravida replied, "I trust, Madam, that you wish to impugn neither our good faith nor our patriotic obligation to observe the spirit of our thousand-year-old state as it is embodied by the authorities in power at any given time."

Zsófia: "You might, however, let us in, Madam."

Mrs. Dravida: "My conscientious observation of recent developments leads me, Madam, to do so. I note that you have of your own initiative removed the distinguishing emblem from your overcoats, trusting that the days of discrimination are over. Well, I do not discriminate against you, Madam, and out of patriotic sympathy do hereby bestow the use of two of the apartment's five rooms to you and yours."

Zsófia: "Madam, I have no wish to deceive you into thinking that I would not have been happier to find my apartment uninhabited, but then, of course, you yourselves must find refuge of a winter's day. How else might I put it? Kindly make yourselves at home in my rooms and with my furniture to the extent that propriety allows."

We watched motionless as these two elderly people, Dr. Kázmér Dravida and his wife, deftly salvaged their vital reserves—several bags of potatoes, beans, flour, bacon and sausage on spits, sugar in a large paper bag, pork lard in a red-enameled pot, and crackling in a large pickle jar—from pantry to bedroom, lest the invading horde make short work of them.

Not until then could they bring themselves to ask, panting, whether we had brought any food with us. Well, no, we had brought nothing at all. Good will moved the Dravidas to give us enough potatoes, flour, and bacon to hold us for dinner and the next day. For the third day we got nothing, but they did not hide the news—the most useful item of all—that there was a German storehouse in the basement of the Reáltanoda Street school perpendicular to Szép Street, and though the locals had carried off most of the inventory on that day, 18 January, there might still be something left.

We boys set out with empty knapsacks to see what we could find. We heard a machine gun ratatatatting from the direction of the Danube. There would be trouble if the Germans came back: the Dravidas would have us removed from Aunt Zsófi's apartment and our feet would never again cross the copperplate but long unpolished threshold.

A well-worn path led from the front gate of the school across the snow-covered courtyard to the back staircase and down into the cellar. We saw German corpses sticking out of the snow and shone our flashlight in their faces. I had always thought the dead grimaced, but every one of the faces was peaceful, including the one lying on his back on a wooden crate in the cellar next to a depleted bag of beans, his head hanging in a rather uncomfortable position. The only possible explanation was that there had been another crate under his head. And if they didn't leave it there, it must have been worth taking.

We filled our knapsacks with beans, peas, wheat, and dried onions, which was all that remained by then, but were still interested in the crate lying under the young German. He was a tall, handsome young man with a powerful brow and a light-colored stubble on his narrow face. His deep-set large eyes were open, and he observed us with interest.

"Forgive us," we said to him as we tried rolling him off the crate.

"I will *not* forgive you," the soldier responded coolly. "I have no idea why I had to die on this crate after taking a bullet on the basement staircase and dragging myself over here. In fact, I have no idea what I am doing here. You will find this crate to contain fairly high-quality sausage, and though it has turned white on the outside with mold, after a bit of scraping you will find it perfectly edible. I have turned stiff, and you will take the crate out from under me and steal away with the goods, but I will remain here in the dark, in this cellar of death, until the corpse-removers take me to an even darker place. No, I will not forgive you."

But we persevered. "O unknown German soldier, we understand your sense of injury, since, to put it bluntly, we are not allowing your earthly remains to rest (however uncomfortably) in peace, though it might be said in our favor that by removing the crate of sausage from under you we may actually straighten you out. Still, we hasten to observe that you have come a great distance from your permanent place of residence, by command to be sure, but not by invitation. Moreover, it is probable that when the bullet hit you you were engaging in activities of which we do not approve. May we point out that it would not have occurred to us to shoot at you, but the issue of whether or not you shot at us was a function purely of the random circumstances of the commands you received. From your perspective there would have been no obstacle. You shot your innocence dead, whereas we are still innocent—though understandably cynical—young boys."

The moment we lifted the crate, we were filled with disappointment: it proved mournfully light. And what remained of the ten scrawny sausages once we had scraped off the white and chopped it into the beans on the little utility stove would not hold us for very long. Two weeks later we were resigned to the wheat, grinding it up and boiling it for hours to soften it. While it cooked, we stood around it to keep warm, dipping dried onions in mustard to trick our hunger in the meantime.

Mr. Dravida, a fur cap on his head, sat in a rocking chair wrapped in a blanket up to his waist, squeezing a tennis ball in each hand. "It works the muscles, very soothing, and helps you think." He wore a winter coat with tassels and hiking boots with gaiters. His mouth, thin but sharply delineated and outlined by an equally thin mustache, had the sour twist of scorn and pride. From Uncle Gyula's high-backed reading chair he cast an occasional glance at us noisy ghosts. "Just because you've won, you've no right to come snooping around." Next to him sat his old dog, slapping its tail back and forth. Now and then Mr. Dravida touched the tennis ball to the dog's head. "I brought Bella's food inside because you ate her baked potatoes. There are a lot of you, and you make noise, and you eat my dog's potatoes. Don't stand in the door! Either come in or get out! What's this? Garlic sausage? You've got it good. You people always have it good."

We were hungry. We ate the dog's food and stole garlic from Mr. Dravida's kitchen cabinet. Nibbling away on a clove was almost like eating. Outside, the popping of a machine gun. We exchanged glances, then looked over at Mr. Dravida, who seemed encouraged: "The game isn't over yet. If things turn around and our troops come back, you'll need my protection. You might get it, but that depends on you. If you're nice and quiet and don't eat up Bella's food, I'll put in a word or two on your behalf. Though to tell the truth you are a bother. I keep finding the bathroom door closed. Have you so much to eat that you're constantly on the toilet, you locusts?"

We boys, the four of us, lay side by side on the double couch, talking about what was to come. Once the lights were out, I imagined myself at home with my parents as if nothing had changed. I would have been ashamed to speak of this to the others, though I was curious to know what they were imagining. It was cold and dark in the large apartment, and we wore socks in bed. The fire in the utility stove died early.

Once some Russians came. They checked Aunt Zsófi's papers and eyed her and my sister like cats eyeing sour cream. My sister pulled her clothes under the covers and got dressed. Aunt Zsófi went into the bathroom. One of the soldiers followed her in, but a minute later tiptoed out, as if signaling that no youth on earth was as tactful as he. After shining his flashlight on our four deeply attentive young faces, they praised Zsófi. "Good Mama, nice Mama, many children. Good!" They growled at us not to make a racket, though we had been quiet anyway. They took a can of meat and three eggs out of their pockets and put them on the table.

"It's cold," said the Soviet soldiers, whose faces were of various shapes. They got the fire going, one of them pulled a bottle of brandy out of his pocket. They bit off pieces of bacon, red onions, and black bread to go with it and even gave us a piece or two while they regaled themselves. On their way out they offered everyone their hands. I took hold of the magazine on one of the soldiers' machine guns. "And what do *you* want?" He pressed his fur cap down on my head, then set it back on his own. They took nothing and left a smell of warmth, onions, and boots. They also left us with an uneasy feeling, since Dravida muttered something to them in the front room in Slovak.

The next day I waited in line outside the baker's, if only for the smell wafting out. The quicker ones had taken their place early in the morning, though bread didn't go on sale until ten. It was not often I managed to get there early enough to avoid coming away empty-handed. But at least I didn't have to drop down onto my belly or press against the wall as machine gun fire strafed the street. At this point the real fighting was over, even in Buda. Newsboys shouted out the name of the newspaper: *Szabadság! Freedom!* In the parks graves surged up in mounds, and in the streets people went around in search of their loved ones.

Aunt Zsófi kept expecting her husband. One day she went down to Nyugati Station in a light fur because she had dreamed he was lying in a field, his still-open eyes staring at her. She had also dreamed of a village, which she now sought. She turned to a Russian officer for help, explaining that she wanted to travel west. At first the officer didn't follow what she was saying, but when Zsófia continued in French he gave her a seat on his train and told her that no one would bother her there and she should let him know when she wanted to get off, because he would be in the next compartment. And in fact she did find the village she had seen in her dream. She inquired whether there was a mass grave within the town limits. There was. They opened it. She found her husband.

Aunt Zsófi and Uncle Gyula had last spoken on the sixth floor of 49 Pozsonyi Avenue on the balcony facing the courtyard used for carpet-beating. It was there they had kissed for the last time. In 1953 Zsófia jumped from that balcony onto the cobblestones below.

The day after our liberation I went with Aunt Zsófi to the Wesselényi Street ghetto hospital, where we found her mother, still alive, on the third floor. Her head had been shot through, the bullet entering the right side of her face and exiting the left side of her skull under the ear. She was a slight woman, still in late middle age, and even in her state could manage a bit of a smile upon seeing her daughter. A few sugar cubes were all we could take her, though we couldn't bring ourselves to put one on her lips. The ghetto hospital had once been a school and is now a school again. On that day in January 1945 I looked out onto the school courtyard and saw a hill of bodies rising to the level of the second floor. Zsófi sat next to her mother. They were holding hands. Neither asked the other what had happened since they had last seen each other. When I accompanied Zsófi there again the next day, her mother was on her way to the pile in the yard. Aunt Zsófi sent me home and tried to arrange for her mother's body to be identified and removed from the mass grave.

I didn't much feel like wandering around Budapest, as I found the city inhospitable and yearned for the familiarity of home, for our house in Újfalu. It felt miserable to come back from the baker's empty-handed and stand around stirring the wheat in the pot, the fire almost out. Even dazzling winter days can be miserable when you look out from a dark room with nothing to hope for. Nor was there anything left to steal. Those elegant gentlemen who three weeks earlier had sat in their galoshes on the ribs of a dead horse lying in the snow had now acquired the status of a comical memory: there was nothing left to hack.

By now we were just a nuisance, extra mouths to feed, and there was no immediate danger to save us from. The smartest thing would be to go where we belonged. There would certainly be something to eat there. So my sister Éva and I decided to return to Újfalu and wait for our parents. István and Pali were heading for Kolozsvár: their paternal great aunt had survived the barely survivable year and invited them there. We would go home to the village and manage somehow. Homesickness for Berettyóújfalu and our house was hard at work inside me. If my parents didn't return, then we, the inheritors, would open the business. I would invite all the old shop assistants back and behave exactly like my father, free of all Budapest arrogance and scorn. But if my parents did return, I would give my father the keys and the cash books and accept his handshake and thanks for what I had done to keep the business going.

The role of guest was not to my liking; I felt much more at home in the role of host. Once I had grown up, I would bring a woman into my father's house and make lots of babies using the method described to me by the Gypsy Buckó one day on the way to Herpály. I had once gone to visit him to see how Gypsy children of my age lived. A boy came up to me, only slightly smaller than I, wearing absolutely nothing but a cap. You need a woman in the house, with a nice-smelling wardrobe and a nice-smelling muff. And you need children for the swings and ping-pong tables.

If during abnormal times you act according to notions born in normal ones, you owe the Devil a trip. This requires a train ticket.

The news in the bakery line, which the Dravidas had also heard, was that tickets were available only at the Rákosrendező Station, a good couple of hours on foot from the center. It was a long trip, with Russian and Romanian soldiers everywhere. At times I was a bit afraid. My sister couldn't accompany me, as the city was dangerous for young girls. I had no gloves and tried to protect my hands from the cold with—heaven knows why—a hair net. The thought that I was now truly hungry and truly cold gave me a certain pride, but I also kept my eyes open, there being plenty to see.

What I saw were second-line troops, the front line having moved on from Budapest toward Vienna. These young men had collected all kinds of clothing and were not beyond wearing skirts over their trouser and women's turbans on their heads to keep warm. They were a wild bunch, making derisive remarks from their trucks. We didn't understand them, but they were always laughing. When they urinated from the trucks, they enjoyed seeing the women turn their heads, which of course made them shake their cocks with all the more gusto. I saw one of them jump down from the vehicle and offer a woman a square loaf of black bread cut in half. The woman stepped back, but the soldier sidled up to her, stuffed it into her pocket, and left the woman trembling.

I took an interest in these round-headed boys, wondering at their rag parades, their antics, their sudden impulses. As natural as it all was, it struck me as strange. Yet they did have a sense of humor. Watching the rouge-lipped Romanian officers in white gloves swinging their cameras like proper gentlemen, they hunched over and laughed up their sleeves like village girls looking at polished city ladies.

Then there were soldiers with machine guns who escorted men to do a little work, just over to the neighboring town, or country, or continent, or the other side of the Urals—"*Davai, davai!*" (Come on, come on!). Promised a *bumazhka*—an identity document—the men obediently followed them out of town to the Tisza, there to continue by rail to camps and the distant cold, and all for the illusory security of those papers. A mirage.

The number of escapees per thousand was quite small, among Jewish and Christian Hungarians alike. Many more could have escaped than did; many more could have remained alive. As for their freshly arrived solider escorts, whether ruthless, indifferent, or humane, they were always unfathomable, unsusceptible to understanding. They were not as natty, disciplined, or angular in their movements as the Germans; they were less soldierly and more relaxed. Nor were they predictable: one would give the locals gifts; another would rob them. The same man often did both. There was no particular need to fear that the Germans would rape a woman, whereas these boys couldn't wait to unbutton their flies. Yet they did not kill on principle, and even if they looked glum while spooning out their mess tins, they also were happy to smile at someone, just like that, for no reason. What they would have liked more than anything was clear: a warm room, a woman, and a meal. They would have pulled the moon from the sky for the woman who could give them that. *Davai*, moon, *davai!*

The railway station on the outskirts of town was a pile of rubble. A long line toward a temporary ticket window snaked its way under an overpass that had remained intact. Well, well, it turns out we weren't the only ones who knew this was the place to get a train ticket! Word had got out that the window would eventually be opening up. Long hours passed and darkness was falling when a railway employee announced there were no tickets—nor were tickets necessary. Whoever fit into the train would go, and whoever did not would not. A train would be heading east from Nyugati Station the following afternoon at three. All aboard who's going aboard.

We were there at noon, standing petrified, my sister and I, amidst the crowd elbowing its way up and down the train. We let ourselves be swept up by the flow. There seemed to be no way for us to get on. People were sitting on the roof, standing in the entryways, clambering onto the couplings. Some had even curled up into the luggage nets above the seats. We couldn't get our feet onto the steps; we were just not good enough at shoving. Our situation seemed hopeless.

And suddenly who did we see but Zolti Varga, the Újfalu photographer, wearing a fur-lined overcoat and pelt hat with earflaps. Varga had taken pictures of us from the time I had entered the world. I had to lie prone on a platform at three months, practically without hair and clothed with only an angry look, my ankles the rolls of fat of the well-nourished infant. Then there is the picture from perhaps three years later in which I am sitting on my father's knee in a sailor shirt, my hair long; my sister is sitting in my mother's lap, her head flirtatiously cocked.

Once Zolti Varga had stuck his head into that black, harmonica-pleated, waxed-canvas cone—the jaws of darkness, almost—we would wait (who could tell if the master's head was even in there still?) for the promised birdie to pop out. We imagined it as a canary of sorts, but then all there was was a click and no bird at all, just Zolti Varga pulling his head from out of his glass-eyed box, like a magician who, slightly flushed and perspiring, rightfully expects applause for his trick.

And now Zolti Varga stood before us. He gave us a hug and said how glad he was to see us safe and sound: How splendid. His wife and two children were with him, and he invited us to join them. I was pleased at Zolti's kindness, though I seemed to recollect he had been expecting a German victory the previous year. After fleeing Újfalu for Budapest and sitting out the siege there—they did not go further west, as they wished to avoid the war—he and his family were homesick for the old house, no matter what shape it was in. My sister and I knew we would not find our mother and father at home, but we too looked forward to seeing our house and somehow beginning our old lives again.

Our voluntary travel companion managed to squeeze my sister through a window into the baggage net of one of the passenger cars. He pressed me into a cattle car, where we were packed so tightly that an old man gave me a piece of his mind: "Stand on one leg, boy. You're a kid, you can do it. There's no room for both. Switch off."

That was my first long trip: it took a week. But it was no departure; it was a return. We were not fleeing; we were returning, returning to the scene of a questionable paradise lost. A house is always unfaithful: either it goes before you do or it survives you and offers shelter to anyone or anything. Who was living there now? Who had the key? I dared not imagine we would find things as they had been. Maybe the furniture had been rearranged; maybe the clothes would be gone; maybe it would be completely empty. There was one possibility that had not occurred to me, however: the filth. In my thoughts the house had always been so attractive it never entered my mind that my first view of it might be repulsive.

Standing there on one leg in a cattle car with eighty others, shoved in not by guards' rifle stocks but by my own free will, pressed among those bodies, I shut my eyes and conjured up images full of longing: How would I find my sister? How was Éva managing in the baggage net? How long would our beans keep or the two rolls we had bought from a young man squatting in a broken, empty shop window for an astronomical price? What would happen if the trip dragged on? Could Zolti Varga give us something to eat? Could he—and would he?

Supposedly the Russians had commandeered our locomotive, but would provide another. The train was still standing at the Nyugati Station in Budapest, but I was a little more comfortable now, because a few people had grown tired of waiting and abandoned their travel plans. From the narrow window I could see the moon shining through the station hall's now glassless ribs. The self-appointed big shots who got on and off and shoved their way through the crowd spread the word that we would leave at one in the morning, at five, at ten—yes, certainly by ten.

I slipped down and peed between the wheels. The urine froze instantly. People were still sitting on the roof, back to back, but fewer than before. The more determined cattle-car passengers were putting up with each other now, and I managed to squat down behind a fat old woman. Though we had moved not an inch closer to our destination, it felt good to have had one long night on the train now behind us.

Ultimately we set off at about two in the afternoon. It was stop and go all the way. Locomotives came and went (if we had the better locomotive, we would lose it), tracks needed repairing, military trains had right-of-way. After a while Éva and I were sitting on benches in the cattle car and getting bread and bacon from Zolti Varga to assuage our hunger. At one point we heard a round of machine-gun fire: stray soldiers frightening civilians. The usual heralds said they were going from car to car seeking women. The women got lumps of coal from somewhere and smeared their faces to make themselves look wrinkled and ugly. Even aging ladies rubbed coal under their eyes my sister and I noticed, smiling to each other. I put Éva in a corner and stood in front of her. The other women pulled their kerchiefs down to their eyes and sat hunchbacked. In came the five or six soldiers on their rounds. One of the soldiers must have been attracted to a woman even through the pitch, but when he moistened his finger and rubbed and the black came off he grew angry and spat in the woman's face. The soldiers left the train in a ruckus of dissatisfaction.

We came to a jerry-built bridge spanning the Tisza where the Allies had hit the old bridge with a bomb and what was left had been blown up by the Germans. The temporary stilts between the pylons would not have borne the train, so we crossed on foot to where another train was waiting, though without a locomotive. Eventually we were moving again, and eventually we stopped again, sitting out a February snowstorm at night in the snowed-over bins of an open coal car. The wind off the Great Plain, unimpeded in its mad rush, pounded us mercilessly. We could no longer feel our hands and had ice crystals hanging from our eyelashes. Glued shut, our eyes transported us to a happy place, and the cold came close to rapture. We stood out on the open track surrounded by darkness.

We decided to strike out on a dirt road and ask for shelter at the first house we found. The wind practically knocked us on our backs as we made our way, dragging our clumsy bags, until at last a faint light flickered on the edge of the blue-white plain. I was frozen to an anesthetic purple by the time my legs had taken me there, stumbling through clods of ice. Obediently I stretched out on the straw covering the dirt floor, and my good will was restored when a young servant girl lay down at my side and told me to snuggle up, pulling my hand onto her belly to stave off my shivering. I pressed against her from behind and buried my face in her back to fit her bottom into my lap. We were entirely one. I realized that you can love someone whose face you have never seen and respond to a stranger as you would to your closest loved one. I held onto her as if I had long since chosen her as my one and only. In the morning I thanked the residents of the house for their kindness and expressed special gratitude to my sleeping companion.

Given that the train was still standing the next day, I set out on a reconnaissance foray and came upon a flat, black, cube-shaped solid amid the tire tracks on an icy hillock not far from some horse manure. Detailed inspection revealed it to be a piece of Soviet military-issue bread, albeit hard as a rock. But as long as it was indeed bread, it could soak up the steady stream of lukewarm water from the bronze pipe of an artesian well to become soft enough to eat. My supposition was borne out, and I chewed contentedly on my find.

A woman walked past, briskly tossing lumps of goat manure from a breadbasket over the snow, as if sowing seeds, left and right, making sure to cover the entire width of the street. Watching me paw at that wet bread, she held out her basket and said, laughing hilariously, "Have some meat with it. These last few I won't sow. You'll get a nice bleating in your belly."

"Where am I?" I asked her.

"In Törökszentmiklós."

"What shall I do with the bread?"
"Leave it here for the birds."

On 28 February 1945, the seventh day of our journey, we reached the Újfalu station. It had hardly changed over the year, as there had been no serious battles in the vicinity. We fumbled our way with our bags out of the first car, which had assumed the noble rank of passenger car since Püspökladány. It would have been natural for Father to pick us up, as when we arrived with Mother and after a few words of greeting he hugged us on the yellow-brick platform and we told him our news: Just imagine, we skated on the lake in the park in Pest and fed the baboons apples in that terribly smelly monkey house and then saw a performance of *Latyi Matyi* at the Operetta (Latyi could hardly get a word in edgewise what with all the children laughing) and then touched the very rope the Regent would as he walked through the rooms of the Royal Castle and then there was an air-raid siren when we were still in the Castle district and we went down with everybody else into a deep stone cavern, a cave under the Castle, where a teacher standing next to us explained that there was a lake in the belly of the hill and, just imagine, he said you could row a boat on it. But when we alighted on the platform looking straight ahead, it was clear our father was not waiting for us. Nor was anyone else.

Where fiacres had once offered their services to travelers coming from Budapest, there were now a few ox-drawn carts. The first acquaintance we saw was my former teacher at the Jewish school, Sándor Kreisler. Everyone in our class had been killed, as had all the pupils in our school, so our teacher was naturally deeply moved to see us. There he stood, a short, plucky man with a mustache. Seeing him was almost as unbelievable as it would have been to see my father.

Sándor Kreisler had been a good teacher: reserved, but kind and fair. In addition to primary school science he gave me a few slaps with the cover of my pen-case, generally because of Baba Blau. Mr. Kreisler had been my teacher as early as the first grade, when I still had private instruction: he would come to the house and teach István and me in our living room afternoons from three till four, which was all we needed of book learning. The rest of the time was our own. Sometimes he came down into the garden with us, and once in a while he gave the ball a kick, but he never got involved in the game, being a young man and mindful of his dignity.

His father was a fine tinsmith and went in for politics. He was a friend of my father's. He came into our store every day in his work clothes, and they would stand at the oven and crack jokes. Yet I cannot recall his father ever coming to our living quarters, and where the father was not admitted the son could not feel at home. He told my father to send me to school: it would do me good to be together with other children. I got top marks but, as I have said, not a few raps on the knuckles as well. For rhythmically grabbing the bottom of the girl hopping in front of me when we squatted for the circle-dance that begins "The hare called his son out onto the green meadow." Or for the usual reason: fighting. I gave as well as I got. We were three classes in one classroom. While the teacher was busy with the first graders, the second and third graders worked on a quiet assignment. I still find it a good idea to avoid focusing constantly on one group activity: we could lose ourselves in reading, drawing, or writing.

Mr. Kreisler had returned from forced labor. His parents and siblings had been taken to Auschwitz, and all his pupils had perished there. He was as surprised to see us as we were to see him. He hugged us and kissed us, which he had never done before. He listened to Zolti Varga's story, thanked him for bringing his two pupils home, and promised to testify to Zolti's valor should he ever need it. Eight months earlier the act of taking us to Budapest had been a political scandal; now the act of bringing us back conferred political credit, which was not particularly pleasant either.

Soon thereafter we encountered a leather-jacketed young man with a holster on his belt. "Sanyi," he said, "make these kids into good communists."

"Fine," said Sándor Kreisler, and the three of us walked on.

After the war he had a distinguished career: he began as a primary school teacher in Debrecen and entered retirement as a commissioner of schools. On the day we arrived, he was primarily concerned with practical questions: where we would sleep that night and who would feed us. We were stubbornly drawn to our house. Our teacher recommended we wait until the next day. But why shouldn't we sleep in our own home, move back in and wait for our parents?

In a little main-street shop we were met by three friendly faces: Imre Székely, Márton Glück, and András Svéd. The first two were my father's cousins. They had returned together from forced labor, each having lost a wife and two children. The three of them had united forces to open a small shop where you could get everything you might need, from brown sugar to a black woolen kerchief. The merchandise—for which they traded flour, smoked sausage, and wine—was brought from Várad and Debrecen by cart. There was jubilation when we entered. Then all three of those muscular men retreated, each to a different corner, and shed tears. When they returned, they did their best to put on smiles. Then they accompanied us to our house.

There was filth everywhere, from the attic to the cellar: trampled books and photographs lay all over the floor; the bathtub, which had served as a latrine for the soldiers who had quartered there, was full of dried excrement. The only furniture left was a large, white rococo wardrobe with three doors, decorated with angels, its mirror still intact. It was probably too heavy for them to have carried off. At my feet lay a story I had written in school about a young fir tree that became the mast of a seagoing ship and engaged in conversation with the wind, an old friend from the mountaintop. There was a photo album scattered about in loose pages, the vanished faces, ourselves among them, stained and muddy. I turned to see the three men standing behind me. We were beginning to understand that what had been would never be again.

"Let's go to my place, then," said Uncle Imre. His housekeeper cut thick slices of bread from an enormous round loaf, buttered and salted them, and set them down next to cups of tea. I rubbed my eyes. Only then did we realize what had happened. The men already knew, of course, though they themselves had been in forced labor digging entrenchments near the front, not in Auschwitz or the deportation camps. Their commander, a local landowner, had led them home when the Russians passed through the village. Most of the Jews left in the town were young men. Before the war approximately one thousand of Újfalu's twelve thousand citizens had been Jews. About two hundred of them survived. They had been lucky in their commander, who had known them all from peacetime, having bought from their businesses and commissioned items from their workshops. He wanted nothing more than to return to peace, to his own house, together with his men and therefore with a clear conscience. The Soviet troops passed through after a big tank battle on the edge of the village on 20 October, and by November even the forced laborers had gone home. By the time we arrived, they knew what had become of their families and had read about the gas chambers in the Nagyvárad paper. The only question was whether their wives had been sent to the gas chamber or to work camps: they were strong young women, so their husbands could still hope that only their children had been lost. What they did not consider was that the Germans in charge wanted everything to run as smoothly as possible. Children were less likely to create noisy scenes and more likely to step naked into the showers if their mothers were at their sides. To keep the children from crying, they preferred to gas the young women along with them.

It was not easy to accept the affection of those men, those hundred-odd widowers around us who had lost their children. They were kind to us, glad to see us alive, but I could not help thinking that my survival reminded them of the death of their own. One of them said to me, "You realize, don't you, that you are living for the others, not only for yourself?"

Uncle Imre, who looked after us and was actually my father's second cousin, was a warm-hearted, frank, quiet man, with broad shoulders and a sense of humor. He waited in vain for his wife, Aunt Lenke, his daughter Panni, and his son Gyuri to return from Auschwitz, whereas I still had hope, knowing that my parents had gone to Austria, where the war was not yet over. Imre lived in just two rooms of his former house, sleeping in the old bedroom. I slept in the bed next to his—his wife's.

My sister and the housekeeper occupied the other room. Imre did not sleep much and smoked a lot. His lighter, made from a cartridge shell, would flame up now and again. From the corner of my eye I would look at his face, illuminated by the cigarette's glow. One time he cried, the way men do, the sobs welling up from his chest, through his throat, and he turned onto his stomach and pressed his face into the pillow, his shoulders shuddering, biting the pillow so I would not hear. I pretended to be asleep.

I returned to the public school to which István and I had transferred from the Jewish school the previous autumn. The teachers and pupils were the same, except that István, who had remained in Budapest, was not sitting next to me. There was no military education, from which we had been excluded the previous year, so I was a full-fledged member of the class community. Neither the teachers nor the pupils knew quite how to deal with me. The homeroom teacher asked me where I would like to sit. No one was sitting next to little Bárczi, so I asked to sit there. He was the one who little less than a year earlier had said that now we Jews would get ours, in spades. Our Hungarian-geography-gymnastics teacher had once pulled his hair while slapping his face to make the slaps more effective. We pitched buttons together and shared our larded bread.

"Where's your father?" asked my classmates, but all I knew was that my parents had been deported. There was a boy in the class whose father had fallen at the front and one whose father was a prisoner of war and still missing. Rumor had it that there, abroad, civilians and prisoners alike were starving and the weak had frozen to death. I was not alone in my orphaned state. We came to accept one another again and avoided speaking of our families.

We slid over icy paths on our boot heels and looted tanks that had been shot up. We collected cartridge shells. Once in a while we found a helmet or a belt or a cartridge bag with dum-dum bullets that explode inside your body, throwing their brass shrapnel everywhere. We would drill a hole in a plank of wood, force the brass shells in, and plant a sharp-tipped bullet in the tapered tube. Then we would hold a nail to the cap and hit it with a hammer to make it explode. A plank with a dozen or so bullets in it looked like a multi-barrel mortar. We used to say we were going out to fire the *katyusha*. There was plenty to shoot at, especially ravens, since the harvest had been bountiful in forty-four and there was plenty for them to pick at under the snow. It is a miracle we never hurt ourselves.

A year before, one of our teachers had plied us with anti-Bolshevik admonitions. He no longer did so now, though he said nothing against the Germans either. Privately he let one of his good pupils know that given their miracle weapons they might stage a comeback yet. Once the Russians had occupied Vienna, though, the teacher applied to be admitted into the Hungarian Communist Party. The previous summer the children still fantasized about those German miracle weapons, wailing like German dive bombers. One of the big kids was called Tiger, after the German tank. But by the spring of 1945 Germans had gone out of fashion, and the children's imagination was taken over by the Cossacks and their red cloth caps with fur along the sides and gold crosses on top.

The Cossacks could not sit still for a minute: they were like bad boys. They would burst in with eggs, onions, and a big hunk of bacon and ask us to fry them up. They would gobble it all up, wash it down with a tumbler-full of vodka, and munch on a whole red onion. They would get drunk and cry. We had to smuggle my sister out of the house through a side door.

Once Duci Mozsár, a pretty, buxom girl of barely fifteen, was standing in front of her gate when a motorcycle with a sidecar came screaming by. The Cossack in the sidecar reached out for her, whisked her off the ground, sat her down in front of him, and shot off. They were next seen a year later, when the motorcycle came screaming back into town, and the soldier in the side car set down Duci Mozsár with a baby and a suitcase, then shot off again as if he had never been there.

A whole squad of sharpshooters had their way with a peasant woman while two marksmen held machine guns to her husband on the porch to keep him quiet. There were times when they shot the woman and her husband if they resisted too strongly. They would drive up in trucks, bringing things, taking things. You could trade with them if you could make out what on earth they wanted. One of them just wanted us to look at a photo album he had found in the frozen mud. He had carried it with him ever since, gazing at the stranger grandparents in its pages.

I had brought back a wounded patriotism from Budapest. There were things you could not speak of. That one year had become like a bell jar of silence between me and my Christian friends, since they had been normal children even during that year.

"Why I Love My Fatherland." Such was the title of a composition we were assigned in March 1945. What was I supposed to write? Things were far from simple. I believed my fatherland wanted to kill me. There have been cases of parents wanting to kill their children. If it wasn't my fatherland that wanted to kill me, if it was only a few of its inhabitants, then what makes my fatherland different from the fatherland of those who ordained the killings and carried them out? They too spoke of their fatherland—all the time. If I am a part of my fatherland, then so is what happened to me since last year's exams. None of this could I discuss in my composition.

I was particularly attached to one image of my fatherland—our fatherland—and the place that gave me birth: the *good place*, the place where you felt safe and from which you could not be uprooted. But once you have been driven from your home and observed your fellow countrymen accepting it (indeed, rejoicing in it) then you will never again feel at home as you once had. Something has been destroyed, and your relationship to the place will never be as naively intimate as it was. My sister and I had wanted to feel at home again in the town after our weeklong return trip, but the house was empty, our parents gone, and there I stood, on the national holiday, 15 March, in the same square where I had once marched in formation to the national flag with my class.

There was a stone podium where the speakers stood and behind it a flagpole where the red, white, and green tricolor had flown at half mast before the war to indicate, as I have said, the painful fact that the country was incomplete, three-quarters of it having been truncated after the First World War. The flag would never fly at full mast until the lost territories had been reannexed. We wore dark blue trousers and white shirts. I can even remember some bright spring mornings when shorts and short-sleeved shirts were warm enough. The Catholic, Protestant, and Jewish schools stood side by side.

In my boyhood I was as unhappy as anyone that the flag was at half mast. I considered it unacceptable that the train should stop so long at the border, after Biharkeresztes, whenever we went to Nagyvárad to visit my grandfather and the tangled network of our relatives there, that one uniform should replace another, that we should have to go through passport control and customs. Once we crossed the border, we saw cement fortifications, as if war were imminent. From Berettyóújfalu to Nagyvárad is only thirty kilometers; from Berettyóújfalu to Bucharest is seven hundred. So Nagyvárad was more mine than the Romanian king's.

The family's oral tradition embraced a number of cities. In addition to Berettyóújfalu, there was Brassó, Kolozsvár, Debrecen, Miskolc, Budapest, Pressburg, Vienna, Karlsbad, Fiume, Heidelberg, Trier, Manchester, and New York. Rabbi relations may have lived in those great distant cities, but Nagyvárad was the true center of things, Nagyvárad with its cafés and theater, with its riverbank where, from the balcony of one of my great aunts, I would watch events unfold on the surface of the Körös through an opera glass.

If Nagyvárad was the sun, then the moon was unquestionably Berettyóújfalu, seat of Csonka-Bihar County. We had our county hall, our county prison, and our county satrap; we had balls and literary evenings at the Military Youth Center, sponsored by either the gentlemen's club or the Jewish women's organization. In elementary school we studied the geography of Berettyóújfalu and then of Bihar County, reciting in wonder how everything was to be found there: plains and snowy mountains, rivers, forests, mines, and—in the very center of it all—the modern city of Nagyvárad with eight hundred years of history behind it. I was a patriot of my region as well as of my fatherland and would jealously defend Berettyóújfalu against Derecske, its neighbor in the district.

Noticeable changes cropped up in the speeches given on the national holiday in 1945. Recalling 15 March 1848, a speaker called it more than a war of independence; he called it a "revolution." My position at school was that of polite outsider, and it continued to be so. The community that sang "Be unshakably faithful to your fatherland, O Magyar, for it is your cradle and some day your grave, nourishing you and covering you," a community that loved pathos, could not expect my Jewish classmates, present only as ghosts, to join them, because the fatherland in question had no interest in their graves: they had been turned to ashes in a small town in Poland, those two hundred children whose lives I was living, if I was to accept the mourning father's words.

The townspeople had generally made no comment about the Jews' being carted off. Some had even laughed at the sight of the old people struggling with their bags, and indeed they were laughable, thinking they would have need of their things, their familiar pillows and blankets, when what was awaiting them was the crematorium. The fact that they were loaded onto trains was met with the same indifference as news from the front or draft notices or the appearance of bombers over the town on a sunny morning: they were all so many historical events over which one had no control. It was the indifference that comes of an acceptance of fate mingled with fear and perhaps relief. "The town has become Jew-free," the local newspaper proclaimed. Hungarian had found its equivalent for the German adjective *judenfrei*. Most people probably felt that with husbands and sons at the front they had enough trouble as it was: news of the fallen kept coming, the harvest had to be brought in, the shops they had always frequented were closed. Then there were those who thought that it was their turn to own the shops, that their little girl should play this piano, their little boy sleep in that brass bed,

viving mirror and nodded at the little fellow who had found his way home after all.

A woman captured my gaze: a naked woman's body, a display-window mannequin. She was obviously a woman: she had breasts and inked-in pubic hair. Her eyes had been stabbed out with a dagger, her body riddled with bullet holes. Why did they shoot at her seeing she was a woman? I heard a rustle behind my back: Gypsy children were looking to see what I was after or had found, because there might be something in it for them too.

Walking along the main street on those late-winter mornings. I would be invited into one shop or another. It was a nasty March: muddy, gray, inflexible. We were apprehensive, between destinations, yet found it natural enough to be there and have someone provide for us. This was the place we had longed to be. We had looked forward to taking over as adults, but we were just children after all. The wind blew through the family letters in my old room and the prayer-book pages in the synagogue.

Our weakness was palpable: we could no more begin a new life than remove all the rubble; it was cold in our rooms and noisy in the kitchen, and the town had no library. I dawdled in the thinly stocked shops of the men back from forced labor as I once had in my father's. Two or three of them would team up, one buying, the other selling. Friends from the camp. Having lost their families, they had nothing else to do. For a while money could buy processed sugar or flannel or hoes, but soon the only valid currency was eggs or flour. Still, the door would open and customers come in. The young widowed men began looking at women again, the Jewish women trickling back from the deportation camps and the Christian women of the area, former typists, nannies, and housekeepers. If a wife had been killed, her younger sister might still be alive. A woman would enter house and bed, and children be born by the year's end. The loss of the original family was no longer a nightmare, rather a painful reality. If things worked out, you could mourn the dead in the company of a new wife and new children, though more in silence than in words.

But in 1950, just as returnees were getting on their feet again—gathering goods to sell, furnishing houses, filling them with families—the People's Government took over all businesses, all workshops, all houses, everything. You could see it coming. This was the second blow, the final blow to the Jewish community in Berettyóújfalu. The first had occurred in 1949, when a number of the men hung "Back Soon" signs on their doors, went out to the edge of town, and climbed into a truck, destination Israel. Jankó Kertész the shoemaker continued telling his juicy stories on a three-legged stool in Naharia in Hungarian: he had no lack of Hungarian-speaking clients. Jankó had lost his wife and two children.

In November 1944, after the Soviet troops had passed through Berettyóújfalu and set up their headquarters in the district courthouse, Balogh the blacksmith, the strongest man in the village, was elected president of the National Committee. During the few weeks of the Hungarian Soviet Republic in 1919, he had been the president of the Directorate. He was a man people trusted in extreme situations, though there was nothing particularly pleasant about him: he was a terrible grumbler, a malcontent. Nor with the black scarred pits in his face where sparks had landed could he have been called handsome. Loose oilcloth trousers, black boots, and shovel-like paws tipped with dark nails completed the picture. He would lug things here and there in anarchic bundles, meting out justice by giving a poor farmer a rich farmer's porker, though not doing himself any damage in the process.

Anyway, one day this Balogh went to headquarters (the former county courthouse) to lodge a complaint with the potbellied colonel against a Soviet soldier who had gone to the woman next door with a goose he wanted cooked, and taken her eiderdown cover to trade for bad moonshine. The commander stood the guilty party in front of the smithy's coal-cellar door. Then taking a running start, he gave the soldier such a kick in the rear that he tumbled down the stairs. There were no witnesses to what followed, but I heard that the soldier got nothing but water for three days, and when he was good and hungry, the colonel sent for him.

"Do you regret your offense?"

And *how*!

He would get something to eat then.

The colonel got on fine with the blacksmith, but the powers that be did not. Back in 1919 the gendarmes who took over after the fall of the Hungarian Soviet Republic had beaten Balogh the blacksmith black and blue, but he was still the strongest man in the village. In 1945 he again proved stubborn, and because he could not get along with the authorities he returned to his smithy. It was he in 1956 who led the demonstrations, carrying the national flag and becoming the president of the local Revolutionary Committee. When the old guard Communists came back to power, they, depraved weapon-happy drunkards that they were, dragged him out to the edge of the village and took care of him. He died soon thereafter.

My sister and I remained in Berettyóújfalu for another month. I don't remember how we got word that we would be going to Nagyvárad in a Russian truck, but László Kún, a cousin of mine who lived in Bucharest (the son of Aunt Sarolta, my father's favorite sister) went there to pick us up. No one asked us if we wanted to go, but my father's friends took it for granted that we needed to go where people would take us in for the long term. My cousin, a textile manufacturer and businessman, arranged for our lodgings in advance. The gray-green truck had a tarpaulin roof and benches in the back for passengers and was carrying so many packages of black-market goods that we had no place to put our legs. Behind the driver sat a sergeant who had learned the language of every country that the Soviets had moved through, and instantly found his place in each of their local economies. He sold me a Cossack hat and traded me a dagger for an alarm clock. (Today I still think warmly of that grinning sergeant. More of him later.) That autumn Nagyvárad and Berettyóújfalu had been in the same country, even the same county; by then, early April, they were in different countries. But by then it wasn't Bucharest or Budapest giving the orders; it was the Russians, along with the local authorities that always seem to pop up.

My sister Éva and I were taken to an address in Nagyvárad where some plump women were engaged in looking after a baby. My sister was happy to join them, while I gave myself up to pleasant solitude. I lived in an apartment one floor up, home to a forced-labor returnee who had lost his family. He was a prosecutor who traveled a lot on business and did not sleep at home, so the spacious apartment was virtually all mine. I would sit on the balcony sampling the liquors I found in the cabinet. It was perfect springtime weather, and I watched the fast-flowing Körös sweep everything away like paper boats. Lounging on the balcony with a book in my hand, I wanted things to stand still; I wanted to hold them as they were and protect them.

There are times during childhood, times of inspiration, when we know what we do not know even though we do not particularly need to know it, because merely existing, walking along the river or a row of shop windows or a peristyle is joy enough.

I make my way by smell in my grandfather's house, seeking a cupboard, an oak tree, a dining cabinet covered by a lace cloth, the porcelain figurines in a glass case easily penetrated by a bayonet. The inner turns of the garden remind me of dinners under the arbor. To live well you need more than means; you need a certain lightness, but most important, you need to stay alive. You need to give the beef broth and the coffee and the cigar each its proper due. There used to be a life in which everything had its time and place, with tasks to be done that stacked up neatly like ironed shirts in the wardrobe: a time to read and write letters, a time for the *Neue Zürcher Zeitung* and the *Pester Lloyd* and the government and opposition papers of the capital and provincial cities, a time to nap, a time for the café, for a walk, for the theater. There used to be a life in which there was no reason for grandfathers to hang their jackets on any but the same coat rack before changing into a tobacco-colored camel-hair housecoat.

In those earlier days of the late thirties there was plenty to talk about at table—once I was old enough to weigh the adults' words, that is. The rebellious sons of the bourgeoisie traveled to Paris and London, not Vienna or Abbazia. They did not go to Moscow. They were leaving Berlin. They would make impatient declarations at supper, eating with silver cutlery whatever the housemaid (or, in more modest households, the cook) served them when the kitchen buzzer rang, its button built into the table (or, in more modest households, hanging above it) to send the message that she could clear and bring the next course.

A serene permanence seemed to abide in the weekly menu and starched caps worn by the house staff. Even if faces changed from Juliska to Piroska, from Erzsi to Irma, from Regina to Vilma, there was little change in the preparation and serving of food. The younger members of the family were at a loss to explain what intolerable problem lay behind a change in staff, as they were satisfied with all of them, from Juliska to Vilma. They all married properly, with a proper dowry. Nor could the younger generation understand the odd new relationships being forced not only on themselves, but on everyone around them. More than one of the well-provided for heirs made the case for cohabitation.

Now those days were gone too. I stood on the balcony in an overcoat, watching the spits of foam jostling on the rocks: the Körös was a sweeping mass of water even when low. I went to see *Six Hours After the War* with its images of camp prisoners and the unforgettable inside-left soccer star: every day an armed policeman in one uniform or another would take them to clear rubble. Once I had spent the requisite amount of time with the baby and the plump women in the warmth of the second floor, I would go up to my room and read or close my eyes and concentrate on the river's thrum, gripping the armrests of my chair and waving my head back and forth until I was dizzy and could no longer think.

My month there passed quickly, even though I visited the bureau for returned deportees every morning. Camps began to be liberated at the end of April and the beginning of May. The men and women would arrive in their striped uniforms or various combinations of striped and civilian garments. They were gaunt, and their voices seemed to emerge from the bottom of a well. Their eyes were on constant alert, anticipating the next blow. The clients—the deportees—gathered in a large hall. Behind the windows at the counter, clerks would refer to a list that might shed light on who was alive and who dead. They also distributed civilian clothes. Many departed carrying the striped garments; others left the camp uniform there, better forgotten.

I asked the none-too-friendly woman behind the window whether she could tell me anything about my parents, which she could not. Leaving her our present address, I sat down on a chair in the hall and waited for them to come, because here they would receive not only civilian clothing but also a bit of money and information about where we were. And where would they go if not here? My mother, who was from Nagyvárad, would naturally come here: everyone went to the city of their birth. And it was from Nagyvárad that her older sisters and their children and grandchildren had left for the gas chambers. Someone might come back, though not the children. They would most certainly not be coming.

I tried to imagine my parents entering the hall, stepping up to the window, and asking after us, imagine myself dashing over to them and touching them. I wondered whether they had changed much, whether we would spot one another easily. Returnees showed us photographs of faces looking out at the camera with candor. The intervening year had carved the knowledge of death and mourning on one and all, even the most ordinary. One told me my parents' chances of survival would be better if they happened to have ended up in Austria rather than Auschwitz, though nothing was yet certain. So I found myself hoping that my parents were in what was still German-controlled territory—in other words, in constant mortal danger—because it would have been worse to imagine them in liberated Auschwitz.

I had heard about what had happened there. Since no other Jewish children from Nagyvárad and the surrounding region had survived, I was the only child waiting for parents at the bureau. The women sitting on the bench next to me explained that the Polish–Jewish inmates would take the children from their hands and pass them to a grandmother or other old woman: they wanted to save the younger women from having to accompany their children to the gas chambers if so directed by Dr. Mengele. The doctor must have particularly hated children if he sent young women and others still capable of working to be gassed just for holding the hand of a child: the children had to die, immediately, unconditionally. Children and those in physical contact with them were motioned by the doctor to the right the way you snap your hand over a mosquito buzzing around you in summer on the terrace. He saw my coevals as pests, not children. He saw the children's faces, yet did not see them, his eyes cataracted over with words, an officer, intelligent and imperious, carrying out his command to the letter. And since the command was to exterminate every last trace of them, there was no place for individual consideration: each Jewish child was a mere speck in the mass. It did not matter what sort of children they were; all that mattered was that they were Jewish. People said the doctor was no more than a vain young man with a handsome face, more interested in twins—that is, his scientific career—than in his anthropomorphic guinea pigs. What a nice gift for the Führer if medicine could help Germanic—or preferably just German—mothers to give birth to twins and limit the propagation of others. In a short time Europe would be teeming with fertile Germans.

At any rate, I was a real curiosity at the bureau. Some parents would not look at me; others looked at me and cried. One wanted to give me something I didn't accept; another shook me, then cried like the others. It was too much in the end. They had my address; they could find me. I stopped going.

I recently had a visit from a Berettyóúfalu acquaintance, the writer Tibor Tardos, who is now seventy-eight. For me he will always be the legend, the big boy. His father, the lawyer Henrik Tardos, was a friend of my father's who died of diabetes at the age I am now. I remember his bald pate as if it were yesterday. A clear-sighted man, he sent Tibor to Paris, where he preferred chasing women and tennis balls to studying: he wanted to be a writer. Bored with politics, he would not have thought of leaving on his own, but in 1938, after Munich, his father realized that the Allies would not protect Eastern Europe from Hitler —in other words, that our fate was sealed. He was a tall, affable man. He dressed well and thought straight. Not one to fall for rhetoric, he sensed the interests behind the words. He presented the county health officer with a gold cigarette case, and Tibor was released from military service and allowed to return to Paris. There he wrote surrealist books that his father would proudly show me, though he understood not a word. When he sent his son a telegram, he would ask my mother to translate it, since she was the only one in his circle of acquaintances who more or less knew French. After the war I stood before their bookcase as his father took down Tibor's books like relics. And relics they were.

"It was a good village," said the aged Tibor to me. "People lived side by side in peace until those German insanities started happening." Life had an order to it. In the movie theater owned by the father of our friend Karcsi Makk, the boxes on the left were for Jews, the boxes on the right for Christians. They would tip their hats to one another and nod their ambiguous nods. They were separate, yet together. Young peasants sat in the cheaper seats in front of them, Gypsy children in the first row. On Sunday afternoons the Apollo Theater offered a cross-section of village society.

The generation of our fathers needed no incentive to work. Diligence was in their blood, though there were those who aped aristocratic ways: hunting, playing cards, and taking drink with the gentry. Jews had their own tennis court, right next to the Christians', and the Jewish bourgeoisie engaged German governesses for their children and had them taught French or English if they could afford it. Friendships were separate from professional interests. Henrik Tardos in his capacity as lawyer for the Berettyóújfalu Jewish community demanded that my father remove one meter from a newly built multistory house. The community held that the house infringed upon the three-meter-wide service road running from the back of our garden to the synagogue behind it, the road I looked down on from the balcony every Friday evening. That is when the men in black hats would walk three abreast, their tallises rolled up under their arms and their prayer books in their hands, deep in conversation and not the least cramped for space. But the community leaders, friends and former classmates of my father, proved unmovable. They may have been annoyed at the idea of a multistory house on the main road, the only one at the time besides the community center, because on the Great Plain towns tended to expand horizontally into the distance. Imagination moved horizontally, and my father's vertical vision needed curbing. The proceedings went all the way to the Supreme Court, and although my father won the suit his friendship with Tardos remained intact. Nor was the subject broached at their Sunday-afternoon gatherings over coffee, cake, and liqueur.

I was surprised that Tibor did not know what had happened to his father. He was aware that he had been deported to Austria, but not that the Gestapo had arrested him with my father and one of the Kepes brothers. The other Kepes brother was taken to Auschwitz but came back with a number on his arm. They were robust men, not particularly well-educated but quick to take the initiative, worthy of respect, and full of good will. One was a lumber merchant; the other dealt in wines. They saw to it that their children went to university, but like Tibor's father they never left Berettyóújfalu. Their wives died in Auschwitz with one of their daughters. They were beautiful, educated girls, like Dr. Spernáth's daughter. Dr. Spernáth's son was a strapping young man. He is alive to this day, having survived the war, thanks to false papers, as a Wehrmacht officer. His parents were killed in Auschwitz.

There was reason enough for the Jews of Berettyóújfalu to be politically active and save their children by sending them away, even if they themselves remained. They were fine where they were: they had built houses, made lives, and earned reputations in plain view of everyone. Be it honor or shame, they had brought it upon themselves. They were known for the quality of the firewood, the wine, the cart-axles they sold. My son Miklós used to make fun of me when I asked him about the shoes he bought. "Are they nice and comfortable?" He may have realized I was quoting my father, but I approved of my father's concern wholeheartedly.

My mother and father came back from their Austrian internment camp at the end of May 1945. They cleaned out the house and started up the business again. They did not give the issue a second thought, as it would never have occurred to my father not to pick up where he had left off. At first there were just four shelves of goods, then six, then twelve. The shelves filled fast, as there were five children to support.

As a survivor, I owe my greatest gratitude to Providence, yet much as I would like to regard it as something other than coincidence, I am uneasy with every case of providential mercy. For if the Lord of the Fates willed my survival, then why not the survival of the other children? They were no more guilty than I, after all. I cannot be so generous as to hand over Vera, Gyuri, Kati, Jutka, Baba, Jancsi, Gabi, or Ica, to say nothing of Aunt Sarolta, Uncle Dolfi, Aunt Giza, Uncle Náci, Aunt Ilonka, Uncle Pista, Aunt Margit, Uncle Béla, Uncle Gyula and the rest to complete oblivion.

In place of a childhood there is an absence, a story that has not been and perhaps cannot be fully told. Two generations after the fact, I feel prompted to preserve the memory of the Jews of Berettyóújfalu. The synagogue is now an iron-goods warehouse. There was some talk of turning it into a concert hall, but nothing came of it. The Jews who return to visit generally go to see Annus Lisztes, a sharp woman in her eighties, one of the original inhabitants, who lives in the house of the former rabbi. "Come more often. It's your home town, isn't it?" she said to me last summer.

In August 1945 we got a phone call from the border crossing at Biharkeresztes informing us that István and Pali, two orphans traveling from their aunt's in Kolozsvár (which had once again become part of Romania) to their uncle's in Berettyóújfalu, were waiting there to be picked up. My parents happened to be taking a summer break in Hajdúszoboszló, and my father had left the business in my hands. I went to a carter who said he was too tired to go anywhere, but his horse and cart would go if I drove them. This was a staggering offer on his part; it was tantamount to entrusting a boy of thirteen with an automobile. Until then I had been allowed to hold the reins only if the coachman sat next to me on the box. Anyway, the carter hitched up the horses, and I climbed onto the box and gave the reins a tug. I could have taken the old road, but chose the new one, so I could drive the length of the town.

The sun had abandoned the stubbled field, leaving the landscape to cool. It was dark by the time I reached Biharkeresztes. I would have liked to hug István, but he just held out his hand. I babbled something about the horses. He had come from a real city where the cream of the Transylvanian Hungarian intellectuals were regular visitors at his uncle's villa. Whatever I told him was a mere village anecdote.

"How is stabilization going?" asked István, to raise the level of conversation. He was referring to the monetary reform. I was proud to give him some kind of answer and disappointed he had no interest in my cart, whose progress he called slow and bumpy. This was undoubtedly so. He barely watched while I watered the horses at the sweep. When I mentioned that horses had been stabled at the Újfalu synagogue by the Germans, then the Hungarians, then the Soviets, all he said was "Hm." He was through with Jews now that they had been swept away by history. I mentioned Uncle Béla, but this too irritated him. I still had my parents, whereas he was orphaned and had no reason to love his parents' bourgeois reality. He said that he had become a communist and that his father, had he survived, would be his enemy.

István had read Stalin's *The Questions of Leninism* several times and had even taken a crack at *Das Kapital*; I had read nothing of the sort. István had put up communist posters; I had put up nothing of the sort. I had attended various election rallies, drawn by the fact that there were several parties: what I liked about the communists was that they were communists; I liked the smallholders because they were smallholders. István had joined the Hungarian Communist Party at the age of thirteen. By fifteen he was an official Party activist, earning a salary by teaching *Das Kapital* to adults. At twenty he was expelled from the Party and the university for something he had written, and at twenty-three he played a significant role in the Revolution in Győr, so significant that when the Soviet tanks rolled in, his boss and friend, the elderly Attila Szigethy, told him to leave the country. Szigethy himself waited calmly to be arrested, and a short time later was to fall from the fourth-floor window of political police headquarters onto the cement courtyard below. I never joined the Party and never thought I should leave the country, not even after 1956.

István was more theoretical than I and had a more sensitive and radical morality than my own. He was a revolutionary, while I am conservative by nature: I prefer to let things be. My worldview was eclectic, and I did not adhere to any doctrine. Flitting about and refraining from headlong commitment, I could always correct my excesses the next day. Everything István said had an intelligent beginning, middle, and end. If I took a stab at something and he liked it, he would make an approving click with his tongue. He formulated every problem as if speaking to himself.

"This Revolution," he said to me at the end of October 1956, as we stood holding machine guns on the student national guard truck, "is not only against Stalin; it has no use for Lenin either." I was not the least shaken by this statement. By that point István had run through every conceivable issue based on an analysis of data he had smuggled from the State Planning Office and on his experience in the countryside.

"The only benefit of emigration is that I've got hold of a copy of Kierkegaard," he wrote to me from Oxford. What came after the defeat of the Revolution, a slightly less-communistic, more bourgeois communism, was something István did not find particularly tasteful. No one could be homesick for *that*! Had he not emigrated, he might well have hanged. If that kind of thing was to my liking, I was welcome to it.

István pretty much knew all three volumes of *Das Kapital* by heart, but capital itself left him cold. He was found dead in his bed in March 1960, a doctoral student at Trinity College. Gas poisoning, signs of suicide, no note. The previous night he had returned to his rented flat from his brother Pali's birthday party. He had moved out of College lodgings, which he regarded as a rubber-walled sanatorium and where he had had a servant. The housemaid called the police. He was buried in Oxford. The Budapest *Esti Hírlap* printed a small obituary on the last page. Not long ago someone said he had it on reliable authority that István had had "suicide committed on him." He was the best mind of the young post-1956 Hungarian diaspora, which may have given rise to the statement. Pali looked into the matter, but the source had gone silent.

Some time in the seventies I traveled to Berettyóújfalu with my children and our American cousin Tony, Pali's son. We cut a path through the man-tall weeds to the family plot, where Tony cried out, "Jesus Christ! I'm standing on my grandmother!" It was Aunt Mariska's marble grave. My daughter Dorka, tired of the graves, wanted to swim, so we sent her down to the Berettyó. The water smelled like pig manure. One of the cooperative stables was emptying its wastewater into it.

We walked the length of the town. The single-story middle-class houses on the main street, the homes of vanished Jews, stood gray and peeling. I drank *pálinka* in the railway bar. Everything was as it had been forty years earlier except that the hansoms were gone and the restaurant had become a bar. On the train an elderly Gypsy had given his son a slap for suspecting his father of stealing his money. The boy put up no defense, only cried and vowed to kill him. "I cannot strike my father, but I can shove a knife into his throat." A policeman with a German shepherd and a truncheon appeared on the scene. "Jesus fucking Christ! Why don't you respect your father? Put down that knife, and don't you be stabbing anyone on me here in the train. You'll get it back in Budapest."

"It's so *real*!" enthused Tony.

"Father feels most at home on trains like this," my son Miklós noted somewhat acridly.

Until 1948, when I was fifteen, I would regularly visit my parents' house in Berettyóújfalu. After that my father's hardware business and house were taken over by the state and my parents moved to Budapest to be with my sister Éva and me. From then on only letters came. They came from the local Party secretary to my university, saying that my father was a bourgeois and not merely a petit-bourgeois, meaning he was a class enemy, meaning I was unworthy of a diploma granted by the authority of the people.

Later, in the seventies, I went to the village of my childhood on several occasions to visit my friend Tóni Baranyi in the psychiatric ward of the hospital, which was run by a superb doctor, István Samu. Many of us had had great respect for Tóni's sharp mind and sardonic sense for the heart of any matter. He had his own room in the hospital, where he could smoke and read as he wished, and he sometimes put on a white robe. He could leave the hospital at will, but still required Dr. Samu's fatherly support and the friendship of a doctor couple. He helped work up patients' case histories through thorough questioning, thus playing the role he had filled in other mental institutions, the inmate prince who in intellect and learning towered over patients and doctors alike. His talent as a writer was evident primarily in the musculature of his formulations: his words hit their mark the moment he opened his mouth. At home in Pesterzsébet he would mostly just sit in his armchair and stare out of the window into the street at the similar working-class house opposite or read the only book in the room. He gave away all books once he'd read them. Having no desire for possessions, he was finicky only about his trousers. Otherwise he was no dandy. He would go down to the garden gate several times an hour to see if anyone had rung. He was ready to deal with any intruders, by force if necessary.

Tóni Baranyi always felt better after seeing his doctor friends in Berettyóújfalu, where he would go to the beach and have a swim in the Berettyó. The time I visited him, we had an animated conversation in the former Lisztes Restaurant. I was the only guest in the upstairs hotel, where I found the Gypsy boy who played piano at the restaurant in the evening playing chess with himself. Tóni and I sat in high-backed chairs in the restaurant's large main room, digging into wild boar sausage and garlic cabbage, drinking a heavy red wine, and watching a row concentrating fully on the process to the exclusion of each other and lifting the marrow on toast to their excited mouths.

The long-limbed, slightly tipsy waiter gave the waitress a kiss on the neck. She recoiled. The hostess behind the old-fashioned cash machine drummed her fingers while studying the varicose veins in her legs. A row of cars decked in flowers pulled up, and guests poured in, half-happy, half-drunk, taking their seats around the long tables. The waiter started bringing out the brandy; the music was not far behind. Men in thick furs, leather jackets, and boots breathed in the aroma of the hot stew and cautiously bit into the pickled peppers. The guests discussed the trend to smaller portions. "They're looking out for our figures," said one. An enormous young butcher in a bloody apron danced into the kitchen with half a pig over his shoulder and flirted with the cook, while her apprentice, in a carefully ironed and folded white cap, extricated herself from the strident din.

A squat gentleman on our left, his ring digging deep into the flesh of his finger, was courting one of his lady colleagues. They had left headquarters for a fact-finding investigation, and now that the meetings were over there was time for a little celebration. Young workers on sick leave arm-wrestled. A crumb quivered on the mustache of a thick-armed Gypsy fellow, his broad fist hanging motionless. The walls were adorned with woodcuts of distant wars of independence. The waiter said the best thing to drink with wild-boar sausage was genuine Bikavér, Bull's Blood, which he poured from a special bottle. A salesman pulled a little bag of bicarbonate out of his pocket, removed a pinch with the tip of his pocketknife, and mixed it into his soda water.

A bearded young man who had gone through his cutlet and buttered peas was looking disgruntled, though there was nothing for it. He was telling a blond schoolteacher with a narrow face that knowledge is not the basis of love, because the more you know someone the more relative that person becomes.

"You mean the better you know me the less you'll like me?" asked the teacher.

This is not what the bearded young fellow meant: he was thinking metaphysically.

"I see," said the teacher, relieved. "Only metaphysically." (Why couldn't the fellow relax and stop pulling her leg?)

"The road to familiarity leads to exalted regions, the realm of icy peaks. Only a greengrocer would suppose that we find warmth among great minds. Chill breezes blow about us, perchance the indifference of sanguinity."

"You mean from your icy peaks I look common to you?"

This is not at all what the bearded young fellow meant. "We do not love the one who deserves our love, but the one that we in fact love."

Now what was the teacher to make of that?

The young man raised the ante: "God must needs be a believer, but the God He believes in cannot be He himself. If God knows of God, then he cannot be one with himself, but must then be as divided as I myself. In short, God must have another God. And so on, ad infinitum. Better not to think of it."

Tóni took a pill that, he claimed, sliced off the cerebral cortex. He washed it down with beer. In a short time he felt a bombing raid approaching and asked to go down to the bomb shelter. He spotted an emergency exit along one wall, but as it was blocked by a table of four corpulent guests he went over to them and said, "Please follow me through the emergency exit to the bomb shelter!"

The four large guests looked at him quizzically. "Where is it?" Tóni pointed to the blank wall.

"Leave us in peace, will you, Comrade?"

Tóni gave up his evacuation plans. They can bomb us if they want. A few years later he blew up his heart with drugs and vodka.

The next day I continued my solitary walks. My legs knew automatically where to turn. A schoolboy waited in a window.

"Who are you waiting for?"

"My parents."

This is where the domestic would lean on her elbows, waiting for the lady of the house to ring, while over in the next window the daughter leaned on a pillow, taking refuge from her French lesson. As a child, I knew who lived in all these houses, but by now the names were unfamiliar. The only familiar names I found were in the cemetery. A row of children's hats and women's legs in boots filed by, and faces stared through the fence waiting for what was to come.

In 2000 I accepted an invitation to Berettyóújfalu from City Hall (it was a city now, not a town). I was to give a reading to an audience of local citizens in the building that had once housed Horthy's Military Youth Organization. The reading and the discussion that followed were a bit on the somber side, whereas my hosts would have preferred that I be more emotional in my nostalgia: nurture warm memories, express my love for the old Berettyóújfalu. They wanted my heart to beat faster whenever I saw it rise on the horizon, this town that all three of my wives unanimously dubbed a dusty hole, but that made my heart quicken, that I found beautiful, the town of towns with the most intelligent arrangement of space. Approaching the former community building and national flag on the former Erzsébet Street, with the Calvinist church and school on the right and our house, somewhat higher than the rest, on the left, I had the sense of being at home. How many times had I experienced this sight on sunny afternoons, heading home on my bicycle from the river. I was sad to see the artesian well gone and the cinema disfigured, but at least the post office was its old self. I had a framed picture of the past inside me that overlay what I was now seeing, but even with the best of intentions I was unable to portray it with anything like the sweet reverie my audience expected.

I could not veil the deportation of the Jews or the plunder of the survivors by state appropriation with sentimentality. The town had deported its Jewish citizens and viewed all their possessions as its own, moving strangers into their houses. At the time my father called it highway robbery, and I agreed. Today the town is coming to see that my father and the others did it honor and were model citizens in their way. The vanished Jewish citizens are becoming a venerable tradition.

I found my grandmother's and grandfather's tombstones in the abandoned Jewish cemetery. My great-grandfather's tombstone had probably had another inscription carved on it. The hospital director, an intelligent man, told me the cemetery serves more than a hundred villages in Bihar County. Sometimes elderly visitors come from Israel and walk out to it. These children of émigrés are sober, naive, and cordial and take a hand in preserving the monuments, as does the town itself. The black-haired women with prominent cheekbones look familiar. The woman who is deputy mayor, a local and very kind, told me how much the town had looked forward to my coming and mentioned that her parents had known mine and me as a child. I felt my Bihar County roots that day. When something during my visual inventory caught my fancy, I felt the pleasure of one who belongs. True, they have filled in Kálló Creek, and the garden where we played soccer among the cherry trees is gone, as is the walnut tree by my window; indeed, the window itself is gone, filled in. And the synagogue is still an iron-goods warehouse.

II

Up on the Hill During a Solar Eclipse

ON A DAZZLING SUMMER DAY IN the last year of the twentieth century I had the opportunity to watch the world change colors and sink into gray darkness from the porch stairs of a crumbling wine-press house on Saint George Hill.

The noontime bells are pealing. I arrived yesterday. The countryside was beautiful, my family even more so. My account of the trip elicited laughter from my most critical audience, and I was pleased by the quantity and variety of the gifts I received: Áron had painted me a rich landscape with a wonderstruck deer that bore a striking resemblance to his father; Józsi had carved me a walking stick with the inscription *To Papa*, a nice long stick that will soon take me up the hill.

I had spent the entire day in travel—first by plane, then by train—but by evening I had reached this place of repose. Now, my back propped against the uneven masonry, I sit on the acacia-wood bench in the garden between lilacs and the walnut tree listening to the rush of the wind and swallows' chirping. I can feel waves beating between my forehead and the hill, which in primeval times seethed with volcanic magma, though for thousands of years now it has exuded nothing but fruit, water, and fragrance.

Most of the houses are inhabited by widows now. They have a better rapport with life than their menfolk had: men tend to pace and fidget, get in the way, wondering what in the world to do with themselves and ending up messing with varieties of afterlife; women potter around in the one we have.

When I sit at my desk with the window open, I can see the village world of Hegymagas: my sons eddying up amidst a horde of friends, the elderly neighbor women, the tractor man, the bulldozer driver, the housepainter, the groom, the vintners, the Gypsy family that always marches in a group, the young mothers pushing their infants up and down in carriages or leading them by the hand, the old ladies bent over their little purses, out for a wholesome stroll, the old men stepping gingerly, leaning on canes.

The locals parading by my window exchange greetings with me. The poorest old man in the village sometimes topples into the flowerbed in front of our house on the way home from the pub or nods off on the bench there under the linden tree, propped on his cane. If he had more money, he would just drink more. The old fellows are on their own now. For a while they can go on without the people who made their lives, and then comes the day when they cannot.

The days grow shorter now that summer's back is broken, though the sun is still well up in the sky. The noontime bells are pealing. A veil of fog covers the ridge of Long Mountain. Wheel marks escort me across the meadow, my legs practically whisking me over the springy ground. Untroubled by ragweed, I take a good whiff of the undergrowth. I run into a shepherd who complains about his right leg; I'm having trouble with my left. The shepherd feels better if he lies on his left side, but since it's bad for you to lie on your heart he spends the night twisting and turning. Clean spring water gurgles from the mouth of a century-old lion carved of wood into a mossy basin where tamarisks are budding. The smartest thing to do is to keep going up the hill.

Zsuzsi kneels beside me on the bench. "I'm going to draw something beautiful, so beautiful you won't believe it, and I'm drawing it for *you*." She draws a kind of latticework in red pencil.

It is soon done, and she asks for another pencil. "It's so beautiful: droplets falling from branches," she whispers.

I will be eighty when she is twenty, if I live that long. The fun was short-lived, like a holiday. Over before you know it.

Every afternoon we go down to the lakeshore, where Jutka rents a kayak for Józsi, who was paddling away at the age of seven, climbing walls, scampering up ropes, speeding along on his bike in every possible position. Jutka got a new bicycle for her birthday and rode through the neighboring villages in white slacks. She came back flushed and enthusiastic. The other day she said she was despondent at feeling stupid. I attempted with great conviction to argue the contrary, but to no avail.

"So what if you *are* stupid? You're smarter than I am."

Jutka laughed.

"How long is there a point in living, Son?" my mother once asked me.

"Until we die, Mother," said I. "Till then for sure."

The mood at the breakfast table is bright for the moment. Not even Jutka has a headache. True, Áron was attacked in his sleep by a venomous snake and upon waking noticed a red spot on his leg right where he had been bitten, but he complains of no pain. Józsi asks about the plan for the day. Has the Bureau of Parental Services arranged for the proper abundance of entertainments for the People, the Little Ones? A full day's worth?

I give my assurance that we will arrange a trip to the circus in the afternoon. I call to ask whether there will be a show. Yes, they tell me, elephants included. I sit beside my wife in the car, passing her crackers to munch and water to swig. She never takes her eyes off the road.

Meanwhile there is no break in the process of enchanting the children and hushing them and taming Zsuzsi and coming up with ideas and encouraging them to shut their eyes and try to catch a few winks. I just stare ahead lazily, passing her the water. If Jutka is dissatisfied or (*horribile dictu!*) starts grumbling, I put up no resistance, because this is the best of all possible worlds. Even the physical decline that awaits me, the series of defeats that is old age, is more interesting than the hereafter. As for resurrection, well, of course I believe in it. It happens every morning until the show gets canceled for technical reasons.

Jutka will be forty-five the day after tomorrow; I will be sixty-six tomorrow. Both of us are Aries. We have been getting to know each other for twenty-some odd years. I sense what she is thinking even when she says nothing. Three children and a husband on her back, and all the practical issues of their daily lives. It takes no small effort to stay on top of it all, to pass out praise, find refuge in a corner, come up with incredible stories, talk through the day that has passed, and preside over the evening's ceremonies from the English lesson to the brushing of teeth to the climbing into bed. Once she emerges from the children's room after nine o'clock (often closer to ten), she too will go to bed soon. She has done her most elemental job.

Everything is so perfect at this moment that I fear something will come along to upset our lives, in which bitter tears and hysterical cries and nightmares and self-enforced exiles and escapes cast their shadows only up to a point. Each member of the family will remember only the happy moments when they think back on the old days.

I feel I have simply turned up here where I am now. The world has fallen into my lap or I into its lap. And some day I will simply be turned out. In a cool room on a hot afternoon I begin a story. I do not yet know where it will go.

In the middle of April 1945 I got a message saying my cousin László Kun would be arriving at four-thirty. He was thirty-seven at the time; I was twelve. I knew his first stop would be to say hello to the women of various ages in the downstairs apartment, including my sister Éva and the little baby (I no longer remember whose). Then he would come upstairs to the floor that at the time was mine alone, with its balcony overlooking the Körös, its library and liquor cabinet. Nothing was forbidden me. I could spend the entire day reading and wandering with no one expecting an account of my time (though I would not have minded being questioned and chided if I proved ignorant). This older presence was a soothing influence, Laci Kun representing the next generation in the family tree, and it had been decided—perhaps by Laci himself—that he would be our guardian, our bread-giving surrogate father until our parents, carried off in May of 1944, came back from the camps once the war managed to end. *If* they came. So I expected some direction from him.

Seated at a large round table, I fixed my eyes on the front door of the Nagyvárad apartment belonging to György Pogány. Then city prosecutor, he had started out as a lawyer, but soon had to serve in the forced-labor service units for Jewish men. His entire family had disappeared. When my cousin László Kun from Bucharest made his entrance, it seemed as if my father had walked in, but a head taller, broader in the shoulders, larger in every dimension, and ten years younger. He was a self-assured and elegant man in a flawless suit. You could see he had made it his own.

The new arrival was more urbane than the locals and had been spared the humiliation of being sent to a camp. Former prisoners, happy to be alive, could not afford his generosity: all they had was what fit in their knapsacks. "The Swedish Lord" was what I called Laci to my sister, though fully aware no such thing existed. Laci sneered at lack of generosity in others and could sometimes be haughtily, curtly dismissive of people. His parents had been of modest means, and he had no wish to follow suit. It is hard to be small-time when you are over six foot three.

He asked few questions, wishing only to know whether I was satisfied with my circumstances, and he assured me that we would not be long in that apartment: he would return in under a month to take us to his family, a wife and two children, in Bucharest. Then we too would be his children whether our parents returned or not. That was the last time we discussed such intimate subjects. When I asked him what I should do until he came, he took a wad of paper money out of his back pocket and set it down before me, saying it was mine and my only task was to spend it. He assigned my sister Éva the same task.

After that I ate a lot of cream-filled pastries and went to see the Soviet film *Six Hours After the War* several times. I understood neither the Russian narration nor the Romanian subtitles, but after several viewings I could follow the action. A young woman once flashed me a kind smile from a window. I went back several times, but she was gone. I could deal with loss.

I was growing a little wild: I would unbutton my shirt, reach under my arm, and scratch. This did not escape the notice of Aunt Zsófi.

"Oh, Gyuri, what has become of you? How you've let yourself go! It's only six weeks since we separated, and you've taken up such crude ways!" True, she smiled and may have been joking, but her words could be taken seriously.

A pair of brothers in transit sat at the dinner table, spilling the black humor they had picked up in the labor camp, where violent death was as common as seeds in a watermelon. They vied to win a smile from Aunt Zsófi, a smile whose unmovable reserve filled me with bliss.

Aunt Zsófi went her way early the next morning, while I walked up and down the Körös watching labor servicemen marching off to clean up rubble under the escort of an armed but shabbily dressed policeman. It would have been easy for them to escape, but apparently no one did. I looked for the house where my grandfather had lived three years before, and found strangers living there. They were not interested in my grandfather. They said they too had been bombed out of house and home. They offered me some rolls and jam, but didn't mind when I declined the offer with thanks. There was a little girl drawing in a corner of the kitchen. During the few minutes I was there she raised her head no more than twice, but even so we had a good look at each other. After that I walked past the house a couple of times hoping to run into her on her way back from school, but those meanderings did not bring the hoped-for encounter, which I had even fleshed out with a bit of dialogue. In my head we had some very serious conversations.

Later I stopped walking down that street or even in that general direction, because I happened to run into my Aunt Gizu there. She gave me a kiss, but I extricated myself from her arms, unable to forgive her for having abandoned us in Budapest without notice at the beginning of the Arrow Cross regime. I made no promises to visit her. She had found her way here to Nagyvárad to take over the house and possessions of her relatives. I left her with a remonstrative smile, without telling her our address.

Our upcoming trip to Bucharest filled me with a powerful curiosity, heightened by a yearning to travel and the excitement of anticipation. I had heard there were more Hungarians living there than in the outlying cities of Hungary itself. We had a long road ahead of us in the big, black Chrysler Imperial that Laci had purchased from the Queen of Romania, chauffeur included. Now that he was allowed to work again, he was doing business everywhere between Bucharest and Transylvania, including Kolozsvár and Brassó, and we had family to stay with all along the route.

Looking back, I see that I climbed a few rungs on the cultural ladder that year, moving from rural petit-bourgeois to urban intellectual circles, the latter calling for an ironical style as opposed to the naive nostalgia of my family background in Berettyóújfalu. People smiled at me when I expressed a desire to return there. I said I belonged in the village and considered everything else a mere way station.

Both our guardians—Aunt Zsófi, a fashion designer and historian of fashion, and Laci, a textile engineer and wholesaler as well as Romania's breaststroke champion and the assistant concertmaster of a distinguished amateur orchestra—would gladly have left their parents' origins in obscurity. This I could not accept, since I loved Laci's mother, the tall and robust Aunt

Sarolta, who knew just how to make me happy. Whenever we visited them in Nagyvárad, she would sit me out on the terrace overlooking the Körös and, if a wind was blowing off the river, wrap me in a silky blanket. Then she would set down a chocolate pastry with strawberry jelly and an opera glass so I could watch the water gurgling over the rocks and the fish jumping clear out of it. I could spend hours on end there. Now and then Aunt Sarolta would replenish my supplies from the adults' table and at my request give a brief summary of their conversation, which dealt mostly with the family and Laci's marriage to the tall, blonde, elegant, and noble-spirited Iboly, who always knew best and may have exceeded even Laci's ideal of perfection.

Iboly was from a good family in Kolozsvár, had attended university, played tennis, did gymnastics, spoke German, French, and a little English, and came with quite a nice dowry. She was unsurpassed in the theory and practice of manners. A movement at the corner of her mouth would register the faults in others' upbringing. She never said a word, and she was forgiving, but she noticed all the same.

Her father-in-law, Uncle Dolfi, had like my father been in the hardware business, but both his shop and his stature were smaller than my father's. I did not understand why Laci avoided mention of his parents killed at Auschwitz. Out of shame perhaps? Did he not want to look the horror in the face? Or perhaps he saw it all too well and found it unseemly to mention. Should all talk of humiliation and murder be taboo? My father had only the greatest love and respect for his older sister Sarolta, who had treated him with the utmost tenderness from earliest childhood: she always had something to give him—an apple, a spool of thread—and if there was uneasiness at home, if my grandmother got worked up over something (what with five children and a house full of people there could always be reason for pique), Sarolta would go into action and make so amusing a remark that my grandmother would turn red from cackling and her annoyance vanish—together with its perfectly valid basis. What is more, Sarolta had a perfect sense of judgment and proportionality. Witness her choice of the diminutive Uncle Dolfi out of all her suitors: he was the most human of the bunch. Uncle Dolfi looked upon his monumental wife in wonder. It probably never entered his mind to betray her, and Aunt Sarolta was the very embodiment of tranquil satisfaction, her only concern being for the children.

Sarolta's daughter, Laci's sister Magda, was the most beautiful girl I knew as a child. Once she summered with us in Hajdúszoboszló, where my passions included nuzzling up to her in the early morning to trade purrs and inhale her scent. For the most part I was the one to wake her, though she was not always in the mood, sometimes whimpering for me to wait and stop squirming under the blanket. But once her eyes were open, she had strange things to say.

She would say, for example, that only bad people amused her and that she would like to meet a pirate some day or at least an adventurer. She wanted to have a look at an honest-to-God decadent seducer, because the only people she encountered at the Nagyvárad theater or the pastry shop or the women's club ball or in the synagogue garden on Jewish high holidays were well-intentioned young men. The ones who looked interesting to Magda all left town for the big cities. Her own brother Laci had outgrown Nagyvárad and felt at home only in Vienna or Bucharest. He had so many girlfriends he couldn't count them on his fingers and toes combined.

Laci's visits were red-letter days for Magda. Together they would go down to the public bathing area on the Körös and show off their backstroke, breaststroke, and crawl, sinking their arms deep into the water and gliding gracefully forward. In Nagyvárad Laci generally appeared in the company of Magda, who was not beyond the occasional acerbic remark should any of her friends show conspicuous interest in her brother. Though I did not lay eyes on him until I was twelve, I had heard a lot about Magda's fabulous brother and seen him looking dashing—decked out in a riding jacket or tennis shorts—in photographs. I had also heard that Laci once gave such a slap to a young man for an undignified remark directed at Magda that the fellow tumbled backwards over a bench in a park square.

Magda let me in on her suspicion that her brother was not truly in love with his wife but she would at least give the children an excellent upbringing. I found it odd that Laci would use the familiar pronoun *te* with Iboly while she would address him with the impersonal *maga*, but they made a fine couple at evening events. In 1942 Magda made the acquaintance of a man twenty years her senior, broad in the shoulders and tanned to a copper hue. He was balding somewhat and working on a paunch. Now here was someone whose state of decay had a certain mystery about it. The interesting thing about bad people, she said, was that they were good anyway, in spite of themselves.

His surname was Flóra, and he ran rackets, or at least that is what my governess Livia informed my mother. This Mr. Flóra came for Magda at the Gambrinus Hotel in a Steyr Puch sports coupe and took her for long drives. This made both my mother and my governess uneasy. After lunch Magda would disappear, not to return until after dinner. He fancied unusual dishes like breaded chicken shaped into sticks; I was less drawn to such innovations. Once I saved one of the chicken sticks for Magda, but she didn't seem interested. She said she had eaten marrow custard at the Golden Bull Hotel in Debrecen. That turned my stomach.

Once an incandescent Magda and I were sitting on the terrace at the Gambrinus Hotel when Mr. Flóra took a seat with us.

"How old are you, sir?" I asked.

I saw that he did not appreciate the question. Magda tried to skewer me with her gaze, but gave up. We sat in silence, letting Ákos Holéczy's Jazz Band and his singer Stefi Ákos move us, probably with a song of farewell. I despised that old coot with the woman's name—Flóra—and tried to trip him up.

How did he like the Alföld region? If he was less than enchanted, his goose was cooked. And so it was. He came up with the dullest of criticisms: it was flat and empty, there was too much distance between the one-horse towns, the cobblestone roads connecting them were hard on his roadster. I grew more pleased with his every word. If this fellow is so stupid, Magda won't be long in turning him out. But this was not to be. To my silent horror Magda happily concurred, even raising the ante: she understood him completely, this Flóra, this ape who lived on Budapest's fashionable Gellért Hill and skied in the Tyrol. She was of mountain stock herself—in spirit anyway—living, as she did, close to the Bihar Range. So it was the two of them against me, the Alföld yahoo. (Can you really be conspiring with *him*—you and he a *we*, and I just a *you* to you now?) This little roly-poly of a Flóra will come to regret his little fling, and you'll see what a slug he is! He'll make you retch! That very year proved me right: Magda, pregnant and abandoned, failed to cough up the sleeping pills she swallowed, and closed her eyes forever. Lying on the bedside table next to her, tied with a silk ribbon, were the letters she had written to Flóra. He had returned them.

Laci's arrival was a real event. He would rise up tall out of the back seat to greet everyone scurrying to meet him, then get a full report from each member of the family and its employees, dispensing praise and a few witticisms to point up our intellectual debility. You could never be sure on what grounds he would disapprove of what he heard. I sensed there was a sensitive instrument, quivering to every stimulus, working inside him, consigning everything clumsy, excessive, or petty to the black zone. I suspected he used his pipe to keep him from answering too quickly, and although the remark would have had more bite had he come right out with it, the contemplative pause carved veritable epigrams out of the smoke. There was no reason to take his words to heart, but if he trained all the power that was in his eyes on you, you were done for.

Laci was nothing if not talented, particularly when it came to starting good-sized businesses. When Austria aligned with Hitler in 1938, he had to make a quick exit from Vienna, where as successful executive and exquisite equestrian he had gained entrée into high circles. His quips and sparkling, intelligent smile, his flawless decorum would have sufficed to keep him there, but he also had a dignity, a power that drew others to flock to him: he was the kind of man upon whom people danced attendance, for whom they put their best foot forward. It was not easy to win the boss's approval, but they kept trying.

By the time Laci returned to Nagyvárad just under a month later, we had set our hearts on his becoming our guardian. Perhaps the reason I trusted him was that he so strongly resembled my father.

He was a good man even if Mimi, one of his girlfriends, was more often unhappy without him than happy with him.

One day a well-dressed young woman called to me on the street, asking my name with a lilt, suspecting who I was, based on Laci's description and our physical resemblance. I nodded. "Yes, I'm the one." I was amazed at having such a sweetly scented beauty in furs recognize me or even find it worth her while to do so. She removed her hat in the Japort Pastry Shop, let her dark golden hair tumble down her back, and ordered a tea. She placed her elbows on the marble table, rested her chin on her fists, and had a close look at me. Then she smiled as if to say, Let's get to it then!

I had been there several times and religiously ordered the cream pastries (scented vanilla, which had been my favorite at Petrik's in Berettyóújfalu as well), but this time, to make my new acquaintance happy, I responded enthusiastically when she pointed to the pastry case and said, "It's all yours!" This led me to conclude that the lady was inclined to excess. Mimi inquired about Laci and the family, wanting to know everything because, according to her, he was so taciturn and irritated by anyone's curiosity. "I will listen to what anyone tells me, but I won't ask anyone a thing," he once told me after I had barraged him with questions.

Mimi had a quick mind and a quick tongue and claimed to have read *Les Thibault*, a thick, two-volume *roman fleuve*, in two days. I had had a rather uncomfortable relationship with the book during the Budapest siege in the domineering presence of Aunt Zsófi: she made me hold a volume under each arm to keep my elbows at my sides and prevent me from leaning on the table "like a cow." Though properly trained thanks to the efforts of my mother and governesses, I was nonetheless inclined to recidivism when it came to elbows on the table. "You're not in a bar, you know!" was something I heard a lot. ("More's the pity," I would say to myself.)

In any case, my relationship with this ample novel, so filling and always ready to provide further nourishment, continued in Bucharest, because Iboly too had noted my pernicious propensity to rely on my elbows, to say nothing of fingering tumblers, as I had seen men do in the bars in Újfalu whenever I peeked inside. No sooner did I tell her about my grotesque connection to the Thibault family than she reached for the bookshelf and pulled down the very same edition. It had lost none of its heft in Bucharest. She tried to civilize me further by requiring me to lift buttered steamed peas to my mouth on the convex bottom of the fork rather than the top. (A decade or so later I wrote a long paper on Roger Martin du Gard out of chivalry perhaps or as a tip of the hat to that reliable master as I sampled proper bourgeois virtues after the intervening turbulence.)

The day I mentioned Aunt Zsófi's pedagogical procedure to Mimi, provocatively placing my elbows on the table, she said, "Your family is a bunch of scoundrels!" and tousled my hair. Her nails were long and, of course, painted red, which one month before the end of the Second World War was, I would venture to say, an uncommon spectacle even in the Japort Pastry Shop. She asked after our family. Her own was largely gone and had not been all that extensive to begin with. Mimi was the product of a less than regular marriage and had decided as a girl to grow up rich and famous. She later amended this with another wish: to stay alive. She thought she looked like Magda, or vice versa. The two of them had been the prettiest girls at school and were often compared. They got over this by praising each other's beauty. They never became close.

With her too, Laci refrained from speaking of his parents, victims of Auschwitz, but neither did he bring up the beautiful Magda, who never got there. "Thank God for that," Mimi would have added. Even so, she had not had an easy time of it: she had fled to Southern Transylvania in Romania, where Jews were not being deported to Poland, only shot by the tens of thousands in their own land. Like many others Mimi was taken to an island from which there was no escape: all those who tried were shot, and by spring only their remains were left.

Still, you could slip through the cracks by means of a paper marriage or bribery or indifference on the part of the authorities: Mimi arrived in Nagyvárad not long after the Russians and watched over her mother's apartment there, filling it with furniture of her well-to-do deported aunt, lighting the candles in silver candlesticks. She came to know Laci's tastes and cooked his favorite meals, taking the edge off some and improving on others, getting hold of the ingredients through mysterious, semi-obscure supply chains. "That finicky cousin of yours is quite a gourmand. It's begun to show on him. Have you noticed?" Mimi divulged that she had let Laci's trousers out herself. A seamstress by training, she hoped to open a fashion salon in the center of Pest, Szervita Square, perhaps—yes, she had picked out a spot next to the Rózsavölgyi Music Shop. Laci would find her there after the war, assuming neither of them got shot. Mimi had reckoned with the possibility that Bucharest would not be enough for Laci, that he needed Budapest, Budapest and Vienna, where he had spent some good years. He had even divulged to Mimi what the name of his company would be: Technicomp.

"Like the sound of it?"

"Hmm."

Laci would not have a partner because he liked making all the decisions himself. Maybe he would use her in the clothing factory as a fashion designer, Mimi said, though nowadays it was work clothes that were in demand. Well, they could be attractive too. Laci was supposedly stunned by her productivity: each time she came to Nagyvárad she showed up in a different outfit, designed and executed by her at astonishing speed.

"Your despot of a cousin does love novelty," said Mimi, "but don't worry, he won't trade you in! He's just a bit difficult and won't let himself be loved. He doesn't spoil me either, but you'll be fine," she added with a touch of envy, "because you'll be able to have lunch and dinner with him every day, while he's my eternal fiancé." She talked with a dreamy sadness and fretted about having let her hair down, but she had divined that Laci enjoyed talking to me.

And so he did. Laci and I even talked politics. He asked me to pick him up a copy of *Scînteia*, the Romanian Communist Party newspaper. When I asked why he wanted that paper in particular, he told me the same thing I had heard in Budapest from my beautiful dancer friend Magda, a few years before she was shot in the back while trying to escape over the border. She had reasoned then that the Communists were the most determined enemies of the Nazis, the Arrow Cross, and the Iron Guard, so they were the ones she trusted most. I replied that this was only partly true, since I had heard stories in Újfalu about Arrow Cross people turning Communist —once a bigmouth, always a bigmouth. But Laci chose to believe that industry was about to pick up and finally usher in the age of enterprise. I told him stories about the Russians and their drunken shooting sprees, about how I'd pulled one of them back to save him from falling into the well in Uncle Imre's courtyard while he was emptying his bladder.

Oh, of course, he said, he had stories of his own like that, but I should keep in mind that they were the liberators and I owed them my life. I acknowledged this, though I was a debtor on so many fronts simply for making it to twelve that I was growing lazy in matters of gratitude and felt that Laci's optimistic generosity towards the Communists was overly hasty.

As did Bibi, his assistant manager in Bucharest, who said, "*Les idées sont belles, mais le pratique, bon dieu, c'est tristement douteux.*" He would phone early in the morning and announce in his piercing, somewhat impatient voice, "Bibi here!" He was amazed I could not pass on his messages in French to Laci. When I offered to do it in German, he thanked me and said he'd rather not, German being a language he was steering clear of for the time being. Bibi was not at all impressed that the Russians had commandeered ten thousand automobiles in Bucharest in a single day, and made his feelings known at the table where he often took dinner with Laci and his family and they conversed over cigars and cognac like proper capitalists.

But to return to the despondent Mimi: it became clear during our conversation in the pastry shop that she was not only waiting in vain for her eternal fiancé but would go on waiting even if she married another. "And if some day that cousin of yours leaves his clever stick of a wife, and says, 'Come to me, Mimi,' then crazy little Mimi will run as fast as her feet will carry her. She'll dump her husband and family just to feel your precious cousin's heavy hand on her head."

A few lovely teardrops trickled down her nose, and she wiped them away with her scented handkerchief. I never met Mimi again despite her promise to visit me. I did see her once, however, though she did not notice me, or pretended not to. She had just come out of a building when a large, black Morris driven by a man in a crew cut, black glasses, and leather gloves pulled up. Mimi climbed in next to him and ran her hand through his hair. In light of what I had seen I considered Laci's passion for Mimi a reckless investment of his energy, yet despite my moral ruminations I concluded that Laci's putative infidelities did not make him unreliable as far as we were concerned.

Thus my sister and I decided to let Laci in on our secret: the buried gold. There were two kilos of it in a stainless steel box, about half in bracelets and other jewelry, the rest in different forms. The day after we arrived in Berettyóújfalu we made an energetic inspection of our house's grounds, which were nothing but rubble. We also peered into the warehouse that opened onto the courtyard and determined that the crumbly ground in one corner indicated some digging, but that there were no traces of it on the hard-tamped earth floor starting a meter from the doorpost.

We gave each other a nod: any nitwit would have thought to dig in a corner, but a meter out from the doorpost and the wall was an unlikely hiding place. While one box was gone, the other might still be in place, underground. But if we dug it up, it would not be safe with us. So we told Laci our secret and left it to him to work out where the goods could be stored. On the evening of the third day Laci said we would start digging at nine the next morning.

We took three cars and were escorted by five or six young Jewish men with holsters under their short coats, former labor servicemen who had lost their families and thought they were helping the sole surviving pair of Jewish children in the county. They had brought shovels and guarded the gate as they dug. It was a good while before the tip of a shovel struck metal. They lifted the box and placed it in a sack. We headed back immediately so as to meet the same border guards and Russian soldiers who had let us into Hungary that morning at the new crossing, approving our passports with a compassionate glance. They said something I could not understand, and off we went.

If our parents ever returned, they could not accuse us of being careless. We had no intention of letting Uncle Andor in on the secret, though he was very curious about our parents' hidden valuables. We said we had no idea about anything of the sort. We were very good at playing dumb.

We soon left Nagyvárad. I still remember the long goodbyes to the older women who had managed to stay alive. I had been accustomed to such staircase sentimentalities from earliest childhood. I recall the loud, almost paroxysmal greetings of my mother's sisters (Margit and Ilonka, destined for the gas chamber and crematorium) when I would recoil so as to be spared all but the final slightly mustachioed kisses that accompanied those yelps of joy. My mother, now ninety-five, still mentions her long-dead sisters and talks of having visited them recently or of their imminent visit to her. She asks whether I have seen one or the other recently. My attempt to awaken her to the truth feels fatuous and uncalled for even as I say it: "She's been gone for sixty years, Mother. You know that. They killed her at Auschwitz."

"Did they now?" asks my mother in amazement. "Killed her?" She might have been hearing it for the first time. She knows the truth; she just doesn't want to acknowledge it in her mental slumber. She would rather think of the childhood games they shared. She no longer recalls my father. What brings her the greatest happiness is a visit from her grandchildren and great-grandchildren or a certain gray tomcat when it springs into her lap on the balcony. Zsuzsa, the sensitive economist from Munkács who works as my mother's nurse, calls the cat Bandi; she feeds him and elaborates humorously on his character. My mother will sometimes do a little drawing or reading or walk through the garden on my arm. She eats what is served her, then falls silent, then asks a question, then falls silent again, then starts laughing.

When I visit, she holds her cane in her right hand and takes my arm with her left, and we take a few turns around the garden. Her forgetfulness may help her along the one-way course of years: she is letting go of her burdens, and the tapestries of memory slip from her consciousness layer by layer, leaving a smooth, unfurrowed optimism that asks only to be caressed. I stroke the soft gray hair on the back of her head and praise her, tell her how beautiful I find her latest drawing though a two-year-old might do better, and often feel the same dizzy optimism in myself, a tolerance and aloofness from the world, a mask that says, Any way at all is just fine. I feel my mother's face against my own and my father's smile coming to my mouth. Sometimes I come out with one of the silly things he used to say, the few that I recall. When I do, my sons give an ambiguous smile, not knowing what to make of me and my verbal oddities.

But let me return to my original story. There was silver in one of the boxes we dug up: trays, cutlery, sugar bowls, and candlesticks. My parents meant to sell it if we lost everything else. In fact, some of the rest ended up with relatives, and what little remained was still there a few years ago, at the end of the twentieth century (of glorious memory), in my mother's glass cabinet. Then one day, when she happened to be alone in her ground-floor flat, two stout old hags rang the bell. "You remember us, don't you, dearie? We shared a room at the hospital." They told her all kinds of stories about herself and their close friendship there, none of which my mother denied, though she had never actually been in a hospital. Why hurt their feelings if they were nice enough to pay her a visit? While one of them talked a blue streak, the other removed my mother's savings book from the drawer and her silver trays from the cabinet. They packed the goods into a bundle and took their leave, expressing their sadness at the prospect of not being able to return for a while. In response to their kind words my mother saw them off with a kind farewell of her own.

Before we approach the eight-hundred kilometer trip from Nagyvárad to Bucharest during the last month of the Second World War, this time under the patronage of my cousin Laci and in his elegant, once-royal, still chauffeured car, stopping on the way to visit my second cousin Ferenc Dobó at his house and garden near the Greek Orthodox Church in Kolozsvár and my uncle Ernő Klein, director of the Hotel Korona in Brassó, a bit of perspective is in order.

In the fifties, after the communist takeover, Laci became a department head at the Romanian Ministry of Industry (then the Ministry of Foreign Trade). Although he had been chief engineer at several factories, a respected expert who oversaw international negotiations, he remained under suspicion because of his bourgeois background: technically speaking, he was a class enemy. To determine whether he was a class enemy in spirit as well—or to use the parlance of the time, whether was also *subjectively* so inclined, the appropriate entities were mobilized.

One night, lying in bed next to his wife, he awoke to the glare of artificial light: four shapes in trench coats stood over him, each with a flashlight, grilling him about the whereabouts of a missing document. They took him to the Ministry, where he found the document in question, which was in the wrong folder. The whole thing turned out to be a farce, and they let him go, though from then on he no longer slept soundly. Thus the next visit by flashlight did not wake him from a deep slumber; indeed, he had been all but expecting it. He left the Ministry and sought a simple job: all he wanted was to keep his family in modest circumstances and be left alone. But this was not to be. Laci could not shrink into a small enough package to escape their harassment and interrogations. Iboly bought a knitting machine and started making sweaters for a cooperative.

In 1956 they filed a request to emigrate to Israel: it was the only way to leave. The entire family was released in 1958. We met briefly in Budapest, whence he was off to Vienna. There a friend asked Laci whether he had officially informed the municipal authorities that he was moving away for good when he left in 1938. Laci did not recall having done so. He looked into the matter and found that this was in fact the case. So after twenty years he was still a registered resident of Vienna and could apply for Austrian citizenship. Which he did, successfully. Thereafter he opened an elegant office in the center of town under the name of Technicomp. He particularly enjoyed traveling to Budapest as the representative of German, Dutch, English, and Swedish companies, arranging the purchase of chemical, oil, and food industry equipment for Hungarian enterprises. He sent his daughter Kati and son Stefan to the best schools in Vienna, but Stefan, the light of his life, died suddenly of meningitis.

Once Laci had more or less emerged from mourning, he and Iboly went to the Konzerthalle every week. He read all the major German-language newspapers and lunched in Mr. Kardos' restaurant not far from Technicomp. Every morning he crossed the City Park on the way to the office until one day he collapsed on a bench, having lost all desire to reach the leather armchair behind his enormous desk. Frau Reisner, his aged secretary, did not understand what had put Herr Kun into such a catatonic state, though according to Frau Kun it had happened once before: he had been interned in one of the better mental institutions in Bucharest, where he would stare at the puddles in the courtyard and give the tersest of answers to her questions. Here in Vienna it was the brick wall of a stolid public building from the previous century that he saw across the street, though he was not inclined to look out of the window.

In time he managed to pull himself together and make another go of it. The work intoxicated him again. He took up with a woman named Edit, a good match: elegant, intelligent, svelte, tanned at the pool by early spring, now a citizen of South America, originally a Nagyvárad Jewess. He enjoyed her witty, malicious pinpricks like a good massage. With ever-increasing momentum he traveled the world—America, Japan—putting together complicated deals for his clients. He often came to see his cousin Gyuri Gera and me in Budapest, paying amicable court to our young wives, until the secret service called him in and tried to get him to report on his domestic and foreign business associates and his burgeoning circle of friends. If he refused, there was not much chance of his doing business, as they could revoke his multiple-entry visa. "What can these people be thinking?" he asked us, as if his own experiences back in Bucharest had not made it perfectly clear to him what these people were thinking. They were thinking that if he did what his character dictated (and what I respected so much) we would not be seeing him in Budapest in the foreseeable future.

We were sad to see the end of our cousin, though thereafter it would have been more disturbing had he been allowed to visit. He wasn't, and our meetings were suspended for a long time. Laci lost his taste for Vienna as well. After seeing to his wife's funeral, he remarried in America and lived near his daughter Kati. Later he moved to Florida and from there to the world of shades.

I have presented these developments to give the reader a sense of the future trajectory of the man who sat to my right in the front seat of the car. In the back sat my sister and two women we knew, whom Laci had taken along as a favor. Behind their heads was the sack containing the heavy strongbox. Coming into Ploieşti, the driver swerved off the road and hit a milestone. The box flew into the air and hit the head of the woman who talked the most and loudest. The Chrysler ended up in the ditch below with the milestone on its roof. A Soviet military truck had veered towards us out of the opposite lane—its young driver may have fallen asleep—and the queen's chauffeur had skillfully yanked the wheel to the left. As a result there were no serious injuries—except for a bump on the head of the talkative lady.

We were picked up by a truck in the pouring rain. Laci sat in the open back, wrapped in a waterproof tarpaulin; we sat in the cab, where it was dry, with our lady guests. The entry into Bucharest was less triumphant than the departure from Nagyvárad.

Crossing rainy boulevards, we arrived at a fin-de-siècle boyar villa. Deep in the garden stood a three-story Bauhaus building completely overrun with woodbine. The garden also boasted a sandbox, a swing, and a small pool. Standing perfectly straight in the doorway of the third-floor apartment, wearing a soft camel-hair robe and exuding a faint scent of lemon, was the broad-shouldered Iboly. We found in her a good surrogate mother, mindful of her obligations, from meals to bathing to clean pajamas. Everything fell into place more or less as at home, before 1944: I had a bed and a desk, we had lunch at lunchtime and dinner at dinnertime, we were to be civilized at table, and we were to toss our underwear daily into the hamper, because a clean change was waiting in the wardrobe. After the morning bath I was allowed to go to the garden or shops with my two-and-a-half-year-old cousin Kati, who served as my interpreter: What I said in Hungarian, she repeated in Romanian. Invigorated by our team spirit and well-matched roles, we dutifully accomplished our appointed tasks, garnering praise from Iboly and Viorica the cook, a loud, amusing, passionate woman who called me a Dacian savage when she was dissatisfied with me. Laci's baby son Stefan, tossing and turning in his little bed, was the only other male in the apartment, because Laci left home early and returned late and was often away on long business trips.

While the Queen's Chrysler was being repaired, Laci drove around in a red Škoda sports coupe that was requisitioned out from under him somewhere between Torda and Kolozsvár by the Soviet soldiers who were always standing around in groups by the side of the road. Laci expressed his outrage, insisting on speaking to the commander and having the case officially recorded. The sound of the word *protokol* got the soldiers' dander up. They gave Laci a shove in the chest and jumped in the car. Laci, always one to do things by the book, found this an unorthodox procedure, but was still capable of laughing at finding himself once more in the back of a truck in the pouring rain.

Born under the sign of Aries like myself, he saw adversity as adventure and was unable to stay angry for long. He merely moved on to the next item on his to-do list, earning the money for a new car and accepting from the outset that it would turn out a losing proposition like the last. In those days luck was an ephemeral guest if it came at all, glittering in one spot for a spell, then evaporating just as quickly. He had two good years after the war, then four more after emigrating, but the last time I saw him—we were walking along Fifth Avenue looking for a certain tobacconist's where he had seen a cherrywood pipe in the window that had caught his fancy—I realized he had resigned himself to the pensioner's view of the world: he spoke highly of walks by the sea and had stopped making plans.

My father was unsuited to prosecutorial statements. Instead he would reflect, "What is this fellow trying to pull out of himself?" as if everyone had a few extra characters lurking inside, like suits in a closet. I imagined him saying to me, "And you, my boy, what do you want to pull out of yourself?" "Nothing, Father. I'm just waiting for the bell to ring in the front hall. Maybe I'll go down to the garden with Kati, but I'll always be where I can see you in case you come home."

One day Laci phoned from Nagyvárad to say that our parents were alive. They were at home in Berettyóújfalu, and we would be seeing them soon. How soon? *Soon.* He refused to go beyond the essentials. Our parents were probably as thin and sickly as other returnees. I didn't relish imagining what their fate had been given what I had heard of concentration camps.

In the meantime I hunkered down in that apartment so little like home. Everything exuded normalcy, yet things could have worked out much less favorably. In the last year of the war two English pilots had hidden out in the room where I was staying. Their plane had been shot down, and the resistance network brought them here. One evening during dinner the concierge rang the bell and asked who was living there besides the immediate family. "No one," said Laci. The concierge wanted proof, but Laci would not let him in. When the concierge tried to push his way in, Laci gave him a punch in the face that sent him tumbling down the stairs. "You won't regret keeping quiet about this," said Laci, helping him to his feet.

Even as we spooned our soup from Rosenthal porcelain bowls, the image of our parents taken from Nagyvárad and Kolozsvár to the gas chambers had floated in the air above the chrome-plated silverware and the covered soup tureen. Whenever they were mentioned, a silence would fall over the room and Iboly and Laci's faces strained to hold back the spasms tightening their throats.

With a nod from Hitler and Mussolini Hungarian troops re-occupied Northern Transylvania—and hence Nagyvárad and Kolozsvár—from Romania in 1940. In 1944 the Jews in Northern Transylvania were deported to Auschwitz, while the Jews in Southern Transylvania remained under Romanian rule. Thus my uncle from Brassó and cousin from Bucharest survived that critical year, while my relatives from Nagyvárad, Kolozsvár, and Berettyóújfalu, except those few young men drafted into forced-labor service units alongside the army, perished. Some of the men in the labor units were eventually shot into mass graves anyway, but others were left to live—the decision being determined at their commander's whim—and made their way back home. In other words, the fate of the Jews sent to forced labor depended on whether their company commander happened to feel like killing or rescuing them at the time. If he was a hardened fascist who stuck to his guns or if such a one replaced the softer and more feeling reservist, the Jewish men's days were numbered. Although I avoided imagining where my parents might have ended up, I had heard enough at the Office of Deportee Aid in Nagyvárad about what happened to those who managed to pull themselves off the train on the platform at Birkenau, where prisoners were divided into groups depending on their usefulness. If they had gone to work in the fields, they would occasionally find something edible.

We had no idea when Laci would arrive with our parents. Each day could be the day. The excitement of anticipation was great.

Suddenly I was no longer able to give my full attention to little Kati's meanderings in the garden. Yes, even Kati, to whom I owed a new fairy tale, could wait. The tailor in the ground-floor shop—he was supposed to measure me for a new suit, though I was perfectly content with the old one—could wait too. Indeed, I was glad I wouldn't have to hear him ask on which side, right or left, I put my "tool." I needed time for the most important thing of all: retiring to an elevated spot in the garden that let me keep track of all who arrived.

Finally the rumble of the familiar car, the slam of its doors, and the voices of several people, most prominently Laci's. Then a woman's voice: my mother's. I ran out to take my mother's bag from her hand. Éva too appeared, eager to take my father's rucksack. Bickering about who would take what was a restraining influence on the excitement of falling into one another's embrace. It would give the kisses time to dry. Walking into the garden, my father squinted in the bright June sunshine and dropped behind; my mother held out her arms. I had to gulp back my tears. Yes, these were my parents.

They were smaller, thinner, and older than the image I had been carrying in my mind. The eyes of both held the same probing question: Who are you, you who have been in my thoughts for so long? Laci left us to ourselves. There was a long silence during which we held one another's hands. I looked at them and nodded, then said the words *Mother, Father*. Then we did all sorts of things: we walked to a park my sister and I now knew inside out; we treated my parents at the Italian ice-cream vendor's. Gazing at a girl with black curls drinking from her palm at the fountain, then sprinkling the water over her hair, I felt a bittersweet peacefulness settle over me: how nice that the people around us had no desire to stake us out, turn us in, have us dragged off and exterminated. You can relax when no one around you wants you dead.

After dinner, in our pajamas, we squatted on our parents' bed and listened to one another's adventure novels. My mother told their story, my father commenting with an occasional grimace. On the forced march from Vienna to Mauthausen a dozen of them had dashed into the woods at a bend in the road at my mother's instigation. They were so quick that the guards failed to notice. It was early spring and survival in the woods was difficult. They encountered an SS unit and passed themselves off as Hungarian refugees. The soldiers were glad the group spoke German and was willing to cook the hares and deer they had found in the forest, so they all sat around the roast in a friendly mood. A pretty young girl among the escapees rather caught the fancy of the young and handsome unit commander, who engaged in some coy flirtatiousness in the interest of good relations.

This sylvan idyll, which lasted two weeks, turned out to have saved their lives, since none of those who reached Mauthausen—those who had not dared to escape at the time—remained alive.

My father's role in the adventure was to keep his mouth shut, as his acting would not have got him far: he was incapable of cheating or lying and had always kept his books assiduously, always paid his taxes, and never bought on credit (though he also enjoyed the minute discount he received from paying in cash). He would repeat ad nauseam the German saying *Ein Mann, ein Wort*—a man is as good as his word—but such simple-minded piety was dangerous. He would never have survived the war had he not yielded to Mother, who in the face of authority and laws was stronger-willed, more tenacious, impulsive. The commander, ever more frustrated by the forcefulness with which the young woman rebuffed him, eventually reported a band of escaped Jews hiding in the forest.

So in April 1945 they were packed into a wagon by Austrian gendarmes and traveled for days to reach a multipurpose camp located amidst cherry trees in bloom and housing people of every origin, a great many prisoners of war included. It was not an extermination camp, though, and it was there, in Krems, that my parents were liberated.

Mother's quiet yet determined resistance predated their ordeal. Take, for example, the case of the broiled sausage. The market square in Berettyóújfalu had an open kitchen stand from which the aroma of pork sausage wafted far and wide, enticing not so much mother as son, who had fallen into temptation. From whatever angle I sniffed, the sausage would win out.

Not that it had no competition: I was particularly partial to the smell of sunflower rolls—leftover sunflower seeds pressed into a disc and used as fodder—that filtered through that olfactory cavalcade. I was also drawn by the gentle whiteness of the tables where old ladies sold sour cream, butter, farmer's cheese, and ewe-cheeses big as a child's head. Ultimately my mother ceded to the pressure and bought a twist of sausage. Daringly we sneaked bites before lunch, sitting on the pinewood chairs in the kitchen and using my pocketknife. We ate quickly, like conspirators, hoping to conceal our assault on Jewish dietary proscriptions from my father, ever the good son, who though resigned to the fact that my mother bought rump of beef along with the shoulder, would have found the appearance of pork in the house unconscionable. In any case, our attempts at concealment failed: my father happened to come upstairs in search of my mother and got an eyeful of the sausage champers. And yet he pretended to have seen nothing.

My mother was willing to lie, to break the law if necessary. She had led the eager Gestapo officers and Hungarian gendarmes around the house and denied what needed to be denied. Women are better at that sort of thing. When my mother was arrested with my father in May 1944, they were first held for two days at the fire station in Berettyóújfalu. I thank my stars that my mother had the nerve to get herself locked up, leaving us children on our own. One of the gendarmes accepted a bribe to let my father into the room where my mother was being held and she told him in no uncertain terms to demand an audience with Chief Constable György Fényes at the local police headquarters, which was well disposed towards them. She thereby saved both Father and herself, since the train they were packed into went by mistake to Austria instead of Auschwitz, and in Austria chances of survival were sixty percent. She also saved us, because had she been at our side the gas chamber would have been our lot—mine for certain, and most likely Éva's as well. I never held her leaving us against her: a woman's place is at her husband's side.

At noon on the third day we took them lunch. Even food was now a political statement, an expression of solidarity and protest.

But there was no longer anyone to deliver the food to. At first we were glad to see that the doors to the holding area were open, but it turned out to be empty. One of the gendarmes told us they had been taken to a place near Debrecen, and next day we learned from the Chief Constable that they were on a farm that had been converted into an internment camp. He advised us not to go there, however, as we would not be allowed in. We took the roast home and nibbled at it, then put the rest away for dinner and played ping-pong all afternoon. At the camp the gendarmes questioned my father about the location of our valuables. He said that he had none, that all his capital was in the business. I don't know what they did to him, but by sticking to his story he saved our chances for starting over, at least in part. That gold, which he would trade for nails, wire, and pots when peace came, was for him what a last manuscript is to a novelist. They did manage to get information out of Uncle Béla, however, so they came to the garden and pulled the steel box out of the well. I remember hearing the water they pumped out gurgling into the street.

They were packed eighty at a time into cattle cars. My mother got hold of some Ultraseptil for my father, who was weakened by a fever, and whenever the train stopped she would help him off. They did the work they were required to do on the property of the Dreher brewing family in Schwechat under guards who were strict but not particularly cruel. They were lodged in a long barn. Nearly all the local day-laborers had been conscripted, so the group hoed the fields for potatoes, sugar beets, onions, and beans, occasionally slipping some under their shirts or into their pockets. They worked until winter, huddling together in the cold and keeping each other's spirits up.

In December they were taken to Vienna to clear rubble. They lived in a school building in Floridsdorf on the left bank of the

Danube, but worked in the center of the city, climbing over mounds of bombed-out houses to set the rubble into piles. Most of the Viennese pretended not to notice them, though a music publisher gave them buttered bread wrapped in paper and invited them in the evening for hot tea amidst carved mahogany music stands.

Laci encouraged my parents to stay in Bucharest for a while and rest. My father could eventually join his firm, Laci said, but first they had to shore themselves up physically and mentally. He probably made a few disparaging remarks about Berettyóújfalu: Why would my father want to go back after all that had happened? What was left for him there? As long as he was starting over, why not go into a more serious line of business? My father nodded, though to himself he must have been saying something along the lines of "Just keep talking, cabbage head." To his mind Laci was a megalomaniac.

So my father would return to his hardware business, for this was his trade and there was no one better at it in all Bihar. All he wanted was to be the person he had always been and greet the first customer who came into the store that summer. Things would have to be put in order. He would start with a few goods on a shelf or two over in the right-hand corner. Then he would expand gradually until ultimately the entire store, basement included, was stocked. The authorities would leave him alone. He still had a few friends in the village.

As for Mother, she had her heart set on Budapest, where the children had managed to stay alive. She rejected the notion that Berettyóújfalu was the place to start over. Everything had been split into separate nationalities. What had been was no more, nor would ever be again. Better to forget what cannot be restored.

But her Józsika was too stubborn to be dissuaded. He went on about his father and his grandfather and the fact that he knew virtually everyone in town by name. The madness had passed, and it was time to get to work. He took possession of his house, had it cleaned out, had new locks put on the doors. All he wanted was to be at home in his own house, to live where he had made his reputation. The fact that everything had been taken from him, that he himself had been taken off, was a passing insanity and could not happen again. No question about it. He would be stocking the finest English merchandise.

My mother kissed him on the forehead. “Oh, Józsika!”

I put my hand on his. He squeezed it and said, “That’s how it will be, won’t it, son?”

“Of course, Father, if that’s what you’ve decided.” Újfalu, naturally, yes.

But Újfalu proved a less than feasible option. First of all because only four years later my father ended up having everything taken from him again, this time in the name of the proletarian dictatorship, but also because retreating into the familiar little nest and longing for days of peace in the village—days that had never existed or existed only in Father’s imagination—was little more than an obstinate, sentimental dream. Yet I have no trouble understanding my father’s naive attachment to the village where he was born, the home of his parents and grandparents.

Laci was a bit annoyed at us for not accepting his offer. He had come to like us and regard us as his own; he had prepared for the day when we would become his children, and knew that to give us back to our parents was to lose us. Why shouldn't we all stay in the same city? In those days it was still possible to imagine Romania turning into a good country, and it was no fault of his that it did not. Neither did Hungary for that matter.

As a department head in the Ministry of Foreign Trade he negotiated with German and English clients who came to Bucharest, but since his colleagues did not understand the conversations they were in no position to write the requisite reports to their superiors. They suspected Laci of making secret deals with his visitors. The moment he received the slightest gift or sign of attention from them, they had him hauled before the political police for interrogation. He was trailed on the street; his house was searched. When he took sick leave, they moved a woman into the apartment as a cotenant, a woman who irritated Iboly no end with her transparently insincere coquettishness. Later, when Laci escaped from it all into a sanatorium, they moved an informer into the room's other bed. Posing as a patient, he would go through Laci's pockets as soon as he left for the toilet. Once Laci scribbled something on a slip of paper, then tore it up and tossed the shreds into the wastepaper basket. He came in from the corridor to find his roommate bent over the trash, retrieving the bits of paper to fit them together. They *wanted* him to know that he was surrounded, that the authorities needed more than a loyal expert who remained a political outsider. They needed all of him.

He became a truck driver instead: he had the physical strength to carry huge baskets of bread on his back. One day while he was making a delivery, a shopkeeper happened to hear him whistling "Yankee Doodle." Before the scandal got out of hand, Laci moved back to the sanatorium, grew a beard, and spent his days standing around the garden in pajamas or dishabille watching the leaves falling, silent for long stretches of time. Thanks to the intervention of a kind doctor he had access to recordings of classical music. Once they allowed him and his family to emigrate, he left everything behind. He would have done anything to remove his loved ones from that insane country.

Everyone could see that my father with his humble smile was the mainstay of the family. Though the fifth of the six siblings, he was the only son. The financial situation of his sisters was more precarious, and the younger generation disparaged his bourgeois decency, sense of proportion, and self-knowledge. I could sense my cousins' arrogance, the arrogance the intelligentsia feels in the face of middle-class stability.

My father was not at all receptive to communist slogans, always returning to the principle of free elections and rejecting the revolutions taking place all over the globe. "In an election you have many choices, son. That is all I know." He listened to the BBC during the war and after. He would also spend hours with Radio Free Europe, delicately turning the knob to minimize the jamming.

The trip back from Bucharest was a long one and mostly in trucks. Anyone with any kind of vehicle set up benches on it and became a chauffeur. There were about twenty of us seated in a very old contraption. Speed was out of the question, but limping along in a group made the trip easy to bear. I was interested to know who was sitting next to me and across from me. Who were these people with whom I got off occasionally to stretch? Opposite me was a Romanian girl about my age who ran down from the embankment at the edge of a wood and gave a shout of joy: *Vai, ce frumos!* (Oh, how beautiful!), though there was still plenty to worry about and many dead to mourn.

In Brassó we again visited Uncle Ernő, the hotel manager, stocky, polite, relaxed, though sometimes reticent. Before the war I had spent long summers with him in the woods belonging to my grandfather's family. He lived then in a large, wooden house in the snowcapped mountains of Máramaros, where he had been delegated by his family to plant trees and produce lumber. The company had a sawmill and a train of its own chuffing merrily up and down the mountainside. I felt on top of the world at five or six riding that little train hauling stripped tree trunks over the wide mountain tracks. My grandfather traveled all the way to and from the mill in his own upholstered passenger car.

I can see them now—sturdily built men, broad-shouldered, tight-bellied, and mustachioed: Uncle Ernő, my mother's older brother, and one of her brothers-in-law Pista, a misanthrope who, once the passion for cursing Jews had seized him, could be calmed only by the application of leeches to his back. Whenever I was a guest at their house, he heckled me after lunch, mocked me by saying I attended a *cheder*, a Talmudic school, which I did not—we simply lived near it—but old Pista was not one for fine distinctions. He was angry because his attempt at settling in Palestine had failed, and he was tired of constantly being a Jew. He loved the woods and fishing for trout in icy creeks. He loved feeding the pigs growing fat in their sties, and giving them a friendly kick in the rump, sprinkling groats for the chickens and decapitating them with a swing of the axe. Once he took me up to a part of the mountain where they burned wood for charcoal. He bought wild strawberries in glazed pots from the Gypsies. That rascally girl was there, the one who would frighten me by laughing and rolling her eyeballs so only the whites showed. I wanted to touch her, but lacked the courage. No one could top Pista at lighting campfires or roasting meat, and no one knew the crevasses and waterfalls better than he. It was a joy to help him skewer the bacon, chicken legs, onions, and peppers. And we had a good laugh wolfing down all traces of bacon as soon as we heard the chuff-chuff of the locomotive, which at this hour of the evening could only be carrying grandfather in his personal car.

The old gentleman liked to sit out on the porch of the wooden forest house, where his papers would be delivered to him, always a bit late. He would leave it only to accompany us to a small town in the Carpathians, where next to a lovely square stood the local prison. On Sunday afternoons the inmates would reach through the bars to sell their handiwork: wooden whistles and pipes, clacking roosters, birdcages. Their cells were their workshops. We would stroll along the tree-lined gravel path, watching them whittle. One of them had killed a man, we were told. He made slippers.

Grandfather, a cousin of the head rabbis of Trier and Manchester, read the masters of modern Jewish scholarship. He had been president of the Nagyvárad congregation at one time. He did not much bother himself with the details of the lumber industry.

When imaginary bats fluttered too thickly around Uncle Pista in the dining room, his head would grow so red that my great aunt Ilona had no choice but to bring out the pickle jars holding the thin, balled-up, wriggling leeches. Aunt Ilona would have her husband straddle the chair backwards and take off his shirt. Then she would set the leeches on the vast expanse of Uncle Pista's back—it was almost as wide as the dining table—one by one, in rows. They would set to work—pumping assiduously, growing thick and fat—and suck the red right out of Uncle Pista's head. Within a quarter of an hour Uncle Pista would reach the point where he lost all interest in the Jewish question: it was nonsense either way.

If I was in the mood, the two of us would cross the creek on a narrow plank, then proceed stone by stone across its other branch and arrive at a clearing where we could watch the deer walking along the path. When they caught sight of Uncle Pista, they would flinch and give a start, but he would just blink his eyes innocently and they would go back to their grazing or have a drink from the stream and move on along the path in a group. I very much enjoyed having Uncle Pista take me along on these excursions. He even forgave me for wetting the bed after a big lunch. Since I was already five, my mother would have punished me for such slovenly behavior by canceling all afternoon entertainments, but Pista would sneak me out of the house to the ice-cold creek, where, standing still as a statue he would reach into the water and in a flash grab a silver trout. Then we would settle down on a mossy outcrop, where Pista checked the brandy flask to see whether there was still some marc left, for what else can one do at dusk if one's feet are cold but have another pull from the flask.

In May 1944 Pista tied three trunks to his landau, took his seat on the driver's box in front of his wife and son, and like the other patriotic Jews in the region drove to the Nagyvárad ghetto. A freight train took them northward. Uncle Pista and Aunt Ilonka, my mother's favorite sister, were soon turned to ashes. Their son Gyuri Frank, my most kind cousin, died of typhus a year later in Mauthausen. He had taught me how to make world-champion soccer players out of overcoat buttons using a file and some pitch.

My uncles did not do a good job of analyzing future prospects when they conferred in the Golden Eagle Café in Nagyvárad. My mother's oldest brother Imre had held various jobs: he had been a croupier and a maître d', going from table to table with a friendly word to everyone. He always kept a table for his current girlfriend, a strawberry blonde, like all the previous ones. Imre had broad shoulders, a dark-brown tan, and a pin-stripe mustache, but he was bald and short. Sometimes he mounted the orchestra platform and took the leader's violin from him. Grandfather was less than enthusiastic about all this and steered clear of the café where his son Imre wasted his time with such madness.

Uncle Pista and my two Uncle Ernős would go there to see Uncle Imre, and the four of them would put their heads together and take counsel about how to survive the war. The most successful solution was the one Uncle Ernő Schwartz came up with: a coronary. No more did he hop into his smooth-riding Citroën and have his chauffeur take him on one of those sometimes mysterious trips of his. Whenever he was ferried to the kind of woman who made demands on him—the kind that gossiped to her girlfriends about who gave her the new ring or fur—Uncle Ernő had no choice but to stand in the doorway of Aunt Margit's room, rest his brow against the doorjamb, and complain to her about how low the human race had sunk: "Just imagine, my dear, they're going on about me again! This time about X and me!"

"Poor dear. Don't they have anything better to do? Maybe it's because you're such a big, handsome, strapping man and they're jealous of me and the children."

The children—Uncle Ernő took good care of them. He gave Éva's hand in marriage to a highly reputed pharmacist and arranged for Bandi to study in England and become an architectural engineer. His son Pál, though, whose triumphs at Exeter were more on the tennis courts than in the medical labs, he brought home and installed in his company: he, at least, would not organize a strike against his father as son Bandi had done after marrying a robust, red-haired woman active in the left wing of the Workers' Party, an lifelong advocate for the poor in Parliament.

Uncle Imre was killed in Budapest by the leader of an Arrow Cross patrol who refused to recognize his exceptional status. Detecting an inappropriate tone of voice in the officer, Uncle Imre informed him that he was speaking with a reserve lieutenant, whereupon the officer unceremoniously shot Uncle Imre in the head. My cousin, the architect Bandi Schwartz (later Andy Short) survived the war as an English doughboy. The beautiful wife and daughter of his easygoing younger brother Pál were sent together to the gas chamber because the mother would not let go of the girl's hand. Pali escaped from his forced-labor unit and organized a group of partisans of various nationalities and religions in the mountains of Máramaros. They lacked the weapons to conduct major operations but did manage to disperse the smaller units sent to pursue them.

Éva, the youngest of the three siblings, ended up at Birkenau, but a Polish prisoner pulled her daughter Kati's hand from Éva's and put it in the hand of Aunt Margit, the girl's grandmother, and although the two of them went to the gas chamber Éva remained alive. She worked in a factory, growing weaker and weaker and moving from camp to camp, until finally she received word in a hospital barracks that her husband Pál Farkas, a pharmacist and perfumer, was alive. Word of her got back to him as well, and taking heart at the prospect of meeting again they recovered and returned home.

In our family the older generations were generally bourgeois liberals and, if forced to choose a party affiliation, identified with the Social Democrats. As for the younger generations, they were radicals, Communists for the most part. Perhaps that is why I felt uncomfortable when my father, returning from the deportation camps, thought of nothing but reopening the hardware business in Berettyóújfalu and taking up the life he had once had. They might have known that nothing could be as before. But even though the young felt that radical change would affect everything in life and I might well have taken my place at my cousin István's side in that sneering communist chorus, I identified with my parents. When I asked István who could better manage our fathers' businesses in Berettyóújfalu (Ferenc Dobó's books, Béla Zádor's textiles, József Konrád's hardware) than they themselves, who had done it over a lifetime, he dismissed the question as insubstantial. "One of the assistants will take over," he said.

My father still believed in the return to what he thought of as normalcy: he would reopen his business in the ransacked house with a fraction of what he had once had and the customers would come and greet him and hold profound discussions on questions both timely and eternal, sitting in upholstered armchairs and eating food they had brought from home in their wagons—garlic sausage or paprika bacon or plain old salted bacon with bread and red onions—and drinking the fresh artesian water he provided. The staff, my father, and his regular customers, all on familiar terms, had so much to talk about in winter as they warmed themselves around the enormous iron stove or in summer as they enjoyed the cool, spacious room.

The younger family members, who had professional or humanities degrees and whose parents had been killed, wanted a radical break with the old order. "Why do you want things to be as they were?" they asked, seeing us move home—or at least to what we imagined to be home—with all our chattels. We should be happy to be alive, the sole surviving Jewish family in Berettyóújfalu, parents and children reunited. When our friends and relatives brought up their gassed wives and children, my parents maintained a somber silence.

People did not stop telling me I was living for the others as well as for myself. That frightened me. If it had been a mere bombastic phrase, I would not have minded the rebuke implicit in it, but I knew there was more involved: now I had to act as they would have acted had they still been alive or at least act in a way calculated to win the approval of my murdered childhood friends. Even with relatives I felt a mixture of tribute and antipathy in their response to my having survived and being able to return to the nest and live happily ever after.

Another issue soon insinuated its way into our talk: Were we bourgeois or communist? "Had my father lived, he might well be my enemy," István had told me. I was no enemy of my father, nor did he harbor ill will against us. It was only natural for him to take István and Pál Zádor, the sons of his late sister Mariska and cousin Béla, into his house. He did the same for my cousin Zsófi Klein. István and Pali spent a year in school in Kolozsvár, skiing down to the main square in winter, but by the summer of 1946 it was clear that Transylvania would revert to Romania and they came home to Berettyóújfalu.

The new age began for me in the summer of 1945. The family was together and out of mortal danger. Our old life had resumed its course, after a fashion, in the house at Berettyóújfalu, the hardware business having reopened on the ground floor. My sister was soon attending the *gimnázium* in Debrecen, taking room and board with the family of a retired officer. As for me, it was the dawn of freedom: I was now being privately tutored—meaning that every once in a while I went to see a teacher—and working in my father's shop, where three shelves were now filled with goods brought in from Budapest, Salgótarján, and Bonyhád. (They came in Studebaker trucks, now in Russian hands, which were used in civilian commerce and sometimes escorted by the Soviet military on roads not yet free of danger. Everything of course had its price.)

In December a second cousin of mine arrived on the scene. His name was Ernő Steiner, and he was a good-looking, active young man who refused to acknowledge the border separating Berettyóújfalu from Nagyvárad. He and his friends would race their jalopy of a truck across it through frozen fields carrying goods. "I always take two or three shots in the air to get the border guards to look back." Ernő had been liberated by the French in May. He could converse with them and had developed a taste for Calvados and Gauloises. Arriving home in the summer, he learned that his parents and younger sister had not survived, and although other families were living in their former house Ernő reoccupied his old room, telling the new residents to behave themselves and showing them the pistol he carried under his jacket. Ernő did not want to stay long and soon began carrying people, not just goods, westward. Many young Jews of his ilk had been sailing from Marseille to Haifa after returning from labor service to learn they were without families.

"I'm ready," said Ernő one day.

I gave him a questioning look.

"Ready for anything," he said dryly. His knapsack held everything he owned.

"Why not take over your father's business?" I asked.

Ernő gave my arm a stroke. "That chapter is over." But to acknowledge that I too had a point, he added, "Your father's still alive. You're helping him."

From the wheel of the truck he reached down to shake my hand one last time. I stood in front of our house and waved as he pulled away, en route to the Holy Land. Holy, he said, because they had given their blood for it. The next year in Haifa he would be active in disabling or sinking English patrol boats so the passengers on immigrant ships could maneuver their rowboats to the shoreline.

I wanted my own space and took over my old room so as to escape the wheezing and snoring of others and have the freedom to turn on the light whenever I pleased. I needed a room where guests could sit and talk, but where no one could just come traipsing in. My craving for privacy came from a desire to know the terrain: if the dogs reacted to late-night passersby, I wanted to know what courtyard they were barking from.

Although the churchyard adjacent to the garden had once provided many playmates, I currently had only my cousins István and Pali and Zsófi Klein. Zsófi had returned from Bergen-Belsen thin but tenacious and with no other place to go. There were now five children in the house. It was never quiet. We cooked in enormous pots. Leftovers were unknown.

My father took it for granted that he should support us all. He enjoyed being back in the saddle, watching the stock gradually spread from one wall to the next and rehiring his shop assistants. Some of the old customers hugged him and squeezed his hand seeing him there again by the door. "My Józsika," they called him, a form of address dating back to his childhood. He well recalled that there had been no hugs the previous year, but never mentioned it.

By the tile stove, which was still beechwood-burning in the winter of 1945–46, I listened to the conversations of the people who came to visit. A girl named Kati and I would cut holes in apples to remove the core and fill them cinnamon and molasses, sugar not yet having returned to the market. I was particularly interested in the opinions of Laci Nyúl, Kati's broad-shouldered and obstinate cousin. He had returned from labor service a tough customer and later barely escaped imprisonment by the Soviets. He wore a short leather jacket and high laced boots. His family had owned the local slaughterhouse, and he helped out at the butcher shop, where kosher and non-kosher products now coexisted. Immersed in blood to the elbows, he sliced pork legs and chops all day long. On the way to our house he would rub cologne into his chin. He had dreams of sties housing hundreds of pigs and a thoroughly modern meat-packing plant, a dream he would punctuate with endless views of the great figures of Hungarian literature. He held Mihály Babits in the highest esteem, knew the poems of Attila József, and brought a number of living authors—Milán Füst, Lajos Nagy, Lajos Kassák, Tibor Déry—to my attention. My sister would see him to the door; I humbly retired. Their parting words seemed to take longer than absolutely necessary.

On other evenings I would listen to the admonitions of the blacksmith's son, who provided me with sexological advice—for example, which notorious women in the village were best avoided. He had plans of becoming a mechanical engineer in Budapest. Laci Nyúl wanted to stay in the village and made us swear to vote for the Smallholders' Party, because if the Communists won he'd have to, as he put it, kiss his meat-packing plant goodbye, and my father his house and business. The Russians, not the Americans, would be giving the orders then. On dark winter afternoons he brought along a book of poetry. We had managed to trade up from a petroleum lamp to a gasoline one with a pump of its own, the white mantle growing taut and burning with a crackle when the flame caught it.

I would cut tobacco and stuff it into cigarette papers (I no longer remember who paid for it, though I'm afraid it was my father); I had fashioned a spinning wheel out of a bicycle wheel and would spin the long, white fur of angora rabbits for my mother to knit sweaters with; or I would move off somewhere to read. My time was my own. I spent summers on my bike, riding with my cousins to the swimming area or down to the Berettyó, where we would climb the pylon of the railroad bridge.

One day I found myself next to Marika on its sun-drenched concrete surface. Because she was four years older than I, it was an honor for me to lie next to her. Soon thereafter the activity repeated itself on the sofa of a cool room whose blinds had been lowered. Leaning on my elbows as she lay there on her back, I tried to reach under her skirt and stroke her thigh. Her resistance was mild, and as I touched her skin I had the impression she was not entirely lacking in interest. We both held our breath. Marika's aunt would leave us alone together for long stretches.

On days like these I should have been reeling off Latin declensions and conjugations for my blonde yet dull private tutor. When she phoned my father, he took me aside and asked whether I was going to my Latin lessons. "Of course I am," I said. "Most of the time." My father's gaze darkened, and he walked away. I wanted to spare my tutor, but I can't deny that I always took pleasure in skipping classes.

Inflation brought chaos. My father was not good at riding such waves or, rather, he could not do it at all. After the billions came the unfathomable trillions and then the period of barter, when customers brought wheat and bacon in exchange for his merchandise. My father having no use for wheat and bacon, they went moldy in the cellar. It was beginning to look as if commerce were utter nonsense, but my father kept at it, and once reliable money was minted in 1946 it began to accumulate. Whether he could keep his business, however, was unclear. The reassuring announcements being made could be interpreted in many ways. But then the Communist Party in its passion for state appropriation was moving from large companies to small businesses, with the result that after five years of a second flowering my father's hardware business was taken over by the state, which then turned him out of house and home with no reparations. Such was the law. The Smallholders' victory meant nothing: the Communists took over anyway. But he had reckoned with losing everything again. At least now they did not want to kill him.

Laci Nyúl's dreams remained just that. He enrolled at the Technical University in Budapest and went to work at a slaughterhouse to earn his keep. One day he fell asleep in the bathtub and the gas flame in the water heater went out. The gas poured noiselessly over him, and the exhausted Laci Nyúl slept on, forever.

In August 1947, when the last parliamentary elections were being held, I would ride my bicycle to the town hall in Berettyóújfalu, where they posted the results on a large board the moment they were phoned in. During the preceding weeks I had attended the campaign assemblies of every party and found something stimulating about each. I was fourteen and had completed a year at the Debrecen Calvinist Gimnázium with highest honors.

The previous September my parents had taken my cousin Pál and me to the four-hundred-year-old institution in a cart, together with our fees in the form of a chest full of food—because over and above the fees for room and board payment was required in staple goods: flour, sugar, bacon, smoked meat, beans, eggs, and preserves.

Debrecen was a big city in my eyes, unfamiliar and inscrutable. After lurching along the wide Market Street, the cart arrived at the entrance to the student dormitory, where bronze heads commanding respect stared out at us. An inscription on the interior facade admonished all that this was a place for prayer and study.

On the third floor a bleak, pave-stoned hallway led to sleeping quarters packed with iron beds. This room also served as the study area. The daily schedule specified that *silentium* was to be observed from three until five in the afternoon, during which time we were all to sit studying at the common table. The wake-up bell rang at six in the morning, when we ran laps around the courtyard. At the filthy sinks we could wash only down to the waist. A cowbell would summon us down to the cellar dining room, where a roux-thickened soup with cumin awaited us every morning.

We stood behind our chairs in silence while the others mumbled grace: "Dear Jesus, be our guest today, and bless what Thou hast granted us . . . He who food and drink hath given, let His name be blessed in heaven." I could have said the Jewish blessing "Blessed art Thou, Eternal God, King of the Universe, who bringeth forth bread from the earth," but I was not the praying type in those days.

The serving spoon would make the rounds from room monitor (whom we were bound to obey) down, according to age. The prayer did little to dampen the abuse of rank. The serving order went by class, the oldest class going first, the youngest last. If there was a big steaming bowl of goulash in a big porcelain tureen, it was only natural that the highest class should spoon out the most meat for themselves and all that was left for the "little buggers," those of us under fourteen, were the potatoes at the bottom. As a member of the fourth class I was in the lower school and therefore subject to commands like, "Bugger, bring me a glass of water!" A raw sense of fun made the vulgarity of it all seem natural. Endless jokes about farts filled the dormitory.

Pali was in the first class, at the bottom of the pecking order, while I, in the fourth, belonged at the top of the lower school and was thus ripe for rebellion. I put up with the hazing as long as I could. I even put up with the prank they called the star-kick, which consisted of sneaking up to a new boy at night and sticking strips of twisted paper between his toes, then lighting them. When the flame reached the skin, the victim would make huge kicks in the air and bolt up in alarm to see the flaming paper wafting through the room. Something to snicker at. (Even the little buggers had their established order, whereby one might end up sniggering at one's best buddies' misfortunes—or one's own.) I put up with the fact that packages coming to me from home were opened with the room monitor's approval and devoured without consulting me. (I was familiar with his type—a "cackler"—and as I will relate I eventually put my foot down.) Otherwise we got on well enough. I was good at my studies and let them play with my four-grooved Cossack dagger, which they would throw at the doorpost. My classmates, sons of village schoolteachers, priests, choirmasters, artisans, and farmers, wavered

from the Golden Bull Hotel in Debrecen with my mother aboard after three days in Debrecen, time mostly wasted in a group shopping tour to buy shoes for my sister Éva and cousin Zsófi. They would try on pair after pair, first in shops that seemed to hold promise, then in ever-more disappointing establishments. My mother was patiently respectful of the process, but I was bored and did not pass up the opportunity to express my scorn when the girls ended up with the shoes they had tried on in the first shop. My remarks were received with cool disparagement and labeled barbarian. My original inclination, to go into the first shop and buy the first thing that more or less appealed to me, remained unshaken.

This philosophy of random choice guided me in other areas as well: "God is good, and what he gives is good." My life has been shaped by chance meetings and telephone calls: the best dinner is always at the nearest restaurant; my first woman—I was fifteen at the time—was the nearest one in the raft of women lining up before me in the salon of the old-fashioned house of assignation. The approach probably had something to do with hunger: I barely grew at all that year. You had to take what there was.

Like Debrecen, for example. It was the closest of cities (with good schools) to my parents' house. The dormitory destroyed a few illusions perhaps, but I had excellent teachers.

My favorite place was the library. Whenever school got me down, I would go straight there. No one would ask me whether I had permission to be there or was just skipping class. Good as the classes were, I enjoyed reading more, so I often found myself at its entrance, a flight of wide, sloping wooden stairs worn down by many thousands of feet. I had to stretch to reach the handle on the door and was immediately captivated by the smell of floor wax and old books.

One day, while reading a light novel whose spine I had seen earlier on my mother's bedside table, I felt a tactful hand land on my shoulder. I turned to see our class advisor, Dr. József Salánky, who taught Latin and History and inspired both respect and fear.

"If my suspicions are correct, you, young man, should be in class right now. Is that not so?"

"Yes, it is."

We were face to face. I could deny nothing.

"I hope you are reading something worthy at least."

He had a look at the book by lamplight in the November darkness.

"This one is hardly worth missing class for," he said disparagingly.

I felt reduced to near nothingness but had to respond somehow.

"And what *would* be worth missing class for, sir?"

It was a cheeky question, but by saying "this one" he had given me a lead-in. He looked at me and said, "Wait!" He had access to the library's inner sanctum, forbidden territory to students. While he was on his mission there, I found it hard to return to my novel. He reappeared with a stack of books, set them down on the librarian's desk, and said to him, "If this boy comes back, give him these to read in the building." He winked at me and left. The librarian called me over with a glance and set the top book before me. It was *Crime and Punishment*. Later, in the school corridor, Dr. Salánky remarked to me that it didn't matter if I understood only a little of what was in those books. Whatever I did understand would be worth more than all of a bad book that was easy for me.

Eventually I had to leave the dormitory. What led to my expulsion was the practice of our being allowed out into the city after lunch (though we had to be back by three, which was the beginning of *silentium*, when we were expected to do our lessons, not play with jigsaw puzzles or tops or that wooden figure whose little red peanut would pop out when you pulled on a string). On one sunny November day I was on duty, which meant I was responsible for taking the key to the common room when we left for lunch and being there to open it for those who preferred the dormitory to town, perhaps because they felt insecure and needed to stick to their nests or because they wanted to study or simply because they were lazy. After a less than glorious lunch I forayed into town. I may have bought a jam roll from one of the glassed-in stands or a cluster of the grapes sold on corners. At any rate, I completely forgot about the damned key. In thrall to the pleasures of sights and tastes I got to the door of our common room to find ten pairs of eyes glowering at me. I arrived in a lighthearted mood, giving the boys a warm hello and making a casual apology. No one said a word, but I got a good slap in the face from the room monitor. Taking a step back, I charged into his belly with my head, which landed him on his behind. When they pulled us apart, he said I would regret what I had done.

The regulated life was no longer for me. I asked my cousin Zsófi whether Pali and I could move into her rented room, and she said yes. The next day the three of us were living in Zsófi's room in the Bishop's Palace. It had a fine view of the Great Church together with Market Street and the Golden Bull Hotel, where the Municipal Philharmonic Orchestra played Mozart and Liszt in the Blue Salon under the inspired direction of Dr. Béla Pukánsky, director of the Academy of Music.

In the fall of 1947 I moved from the ponderous Debrecen Calvinist Gimnázium to the lively Madách Gimnázium in Budapest. I rented a room in the flat of an elderly couple. I was a village boy, unsophisticated and starry-eyed, but Budapest was much to my liking. And this time I could wander the city as I chose, with no yellow star on my coat and no worries about danger lurking everywhere.

The school was nearly as interesting as the city. It had its own parliament and government, two newspapers, and a court with a judge and jury, prosecutors and defense counsels, and all sorts of cases, serious and otherwise, awaiting adjudication. There was a student representative at all grading sessions, and if he disagreed with the mark the faculty wanted to give to one or another of his classmates he had the right to veto it.

Politics was in the air, and there were Communists among the student body, although the boys generally preferred to play historical roles: Danton would observe that Robespierre, sitting at one of the desks in the back of the classroom, had a glowering countenance. Chénier was a kind, light-haired Jewish boy. We used to walk together on Margaret Island, reading Dante in the Babits translation. He would soon escape over the border, which in 1949 was no longer easy, and emigrate to the newly founded state of Israel to become general of a tank division. There was a good deal of role-playing in our class and a tremendous number of debates. I defended Mallarmé against the great Romantic Victor Hugo and the aforementioned Danton, who later became director of the Opera. (His fondness for spectacular effects was already in evidence.) We read a lot in those days: the second or third time I admitted to my friends that I hadn't read this or I hadn't ever heard that name, one of my friends called me an ignorant country bumpkin.

Yes, this was an age of politics, even at school. When was it permissible to kill? That was a burning question. Or should boys like us, fifteen or sixteen years old, go to a brothel (and if so, which one?) or *go out* with a girl? A girl? From a girls' school? What would you talk about? Your homework? One opinion was that you were better off talking to your Latin master. Ours was a wise man, though anarchy held sway in his classroom. (A translator of Plato does not get bogged down in discipline.) Mr. Kövendy would sit in the last row, and whoever gathered round him could drink in what he had to say while the rest went on with their racket.

The couple I boarded with was Arnold Konta—a former wine wholesaler and rowing and walking champion, then past eighty—and his wife. They could not afford to heat their large apartment, which was crammed with carved mahogany furniture, Shakespeare in English, Goethe and Schiller in German, Flaubert in French, plaques in black glass cases, ponderous paintings all over the walls, and bronze statuettes in every spot not taken up by something else. I found it all very depressing. At fifteen I detested the fin-de-siècle style and its eclecticism, and even the Jugendstil (or Secession, as we called it); I loved the cubism of modern architecture.

Mr. Konta was a short man; his wife Elza was quite tall. Every Sunday morning the natty old gentleman reached up and took his wife's arm (her shoulders were higher than his head), and they walked to the Museum of Fine Arts in Heroes' Square. He used to say you could look at a good painting a hundred times. He read some *Faust* every evening. Before sitting down to his desk, he murmured a short Hebrew prayer. His face was pink and jowly and fragrant from shaving. He took his meals in a housecoat redolent of tobacco and tied with a rope.

I would be walking along the Ring, and who would step out of one of the noble old buildings, each forming a quarter-circle, but Zoltán Kodály, white beard and all. (Whenever he appeared on the balcony in the hall at the Academy of Music, the house would give him a standing ovation.) I would bow my head as we passed, and the old man would nod. The garden and red sign of the Stück Pastry Shop filled me with melancholy. This is where I had sat with my father before accompanying him to the Nyugati Station whenever he visited me at the end of one of his buying trips. Much as I enjoyed sitting with him, I smiled to myself more than once at his naive but well-intentioned notions.

Every morning I would feel compelled to step off the sidewalk as I walked along Andrássy Boulevard two blocks down from the Ring: the building at number sixty, with its *gravitas*—and the heavy chains that bound its concrete pillars—would order me down into the roadway. In the last year of the war it had been called the House of Loyalty, the headquarters and torture chamber of the Arrow Cross. Anyone taken there had little chance of coming out alive. There had been concrete-walled torture rooms in place in the cellar by then, but the setup was not modern enough: the new regime dug deeper. Buildings outlive regimes, and this formerly upper-middle-class apartment building was home to the political police of the new system. The reconstruction was the idea of Gábor Péter, once a tailor, then a librarian for a fashion magazine, then head—general—of that police force. A major sat on either side of the padded door to his office, effective advisors no doubt. After 1956 they became official humorists, writing hilarious Christmas radio and TV programs.

With Gábor Péter at the helm of the State Security Agency, the Andrássy Boulevard facilities embarked on a visually dazzling expansion, gobbling up the large and lordly buildings around it one by one. No sooner were the inhabitants expelled than industrious stonemasons set about making it fit for the uses of the Agency. Red geraniums bloomed in a flowerbox outside every window, but guards carrying machine guns stood in every doorway and on every corner, and no one would have dreamed of playing games with them.

Soviet Pobedas, light brown and gray, and large, black American cars with curtains in the windows rolled out of the driveways. The next block was also part of the picture. The windows of the Lukács Pastry Shop on the corner—once a showcase of cakes and liqueurs, of glass chandeliers, velvet draperies, and marble tables—had been replaced by glass bricks impenetrable to the eye: it had become a club for State Security officers.

I later learned that prisoners who had signed confessions were assembled there among the Art Deco decorations to learn their show-trial roles. Since the baker and his masterpieces had been kept on, the prisoners got pastries for reciting their canned self-accusations by heart. By then they had gone through the preliminary phases of confession and torture. Most people proved capable of slandering themselves, even condemning themselves to death. All bets were off once the prisoner found himself alone in the cellar, crawling into his cell on all fours like an injured animal. As soon as you signed the papers and redeemed yourself, you got a hot bath. Now all you had to do was play your part. And this was theater at its most imaginative. You were spirited up from the cellar to the vanilla-scented paradise of golden angels and chandeliers and garlands and whipped cream, where a clean change of clothes and a dignified stroll along the slightly sloping marble floor could put you in the mood for any role. Down below, all relationship between the ego's visible and invisible aspects had been severed, the visible (and thrashable) part doing what it must, the invisible part looking on, astonished.

In 1949 I did not know much about what was going on in the cellar, but from the BBC I learned that the accused in show trials would say all sorts of things to incriminate themselves, that they were mere puppets, their will having been broken with beatings and chemicals. This seemed plausible, as they spoke like automatons, reciting more than repenting, as if meaning no longer mattered.

The cameraman father of a boy I knew told his son that the proceedings were filmed without the knowledge of the accused. Moreover, the trial was staged more than once, and the accused never knew which the "real" one was. The final film version was spliced together from several takes. Could the whole procedure have been just for the sake of the film? The director supposedly had friends among the accused.

A bit further up Andrássy (soon to be Stalin) Boulevard there was a private lending library that was taken over by the state in 1949. It was intoxicating for me, at fifteen, to take out novels by Steinbeck, Hemingway, Martin du Gard, and Malraux. The same neighborhood also boasted a respectable private house of assignation run by Madame Clarisse on the second floor of a neoclassical apartment building. By the end of the year it was all over: the private library, the private *maison de rendezvous*, and everything else private, including the private individual. Nor were we left in peace at school: we had to sing hymns of praise to the working class after each ten-minute break. Sometimes we slipped in a dirty rhyme or two.

When in the early sixties the State Security Agency moved out and the space reopened as Specialty Pastries, I would drop in after long afternoons spent investigating the living conditions of people on file at the Public Welfare Authority. I would sit with friends in velvet-upholstered chairs beneath the chandeliers' gold curlicues and Venetian glass and surrounded by blue-silk walls and gold-leaf friezes as trolley buses, the pride of Soviet technology, rumbled by. I was always on good terms with the old ladies in the cloakroom. I had many dates there, dates with beautiful women and odd women, with clever women and madwomen: I had just divorced my first wife. Those women are dead by now, or elderly.

Late in November 1983, when I was on a fellowship at the New York Institute for the Humanities, my wife Jutka and I rented an apartment on the corner of Fourth Street and Avenue A, four blocks from St. Mark's Place. One morning while walking along the latter we came upon a street fair. There were bands playing and a woman prancing around on stilts, enticing children to dance. We bought a table lamp for two dollars, and the seller wanted to prove to us it worked. We walked into a precinct house to look for an outlet. "Your honor is at stake," the policemen told him, smiling as they pointed to an outlet. The lamp did not light. They had a good laugh, black and white, men and women alike—then took pity on the salesman and pointed him to a working outlet. The lamp was fine. Filled with a sense of dignity, the salesman then told us that his mother was Hungarian and that he was happy to have us here in this part of town, properly called the East Village, not the Lower East Side.

I am standing at a Tarot reader's shop front surrounded by iron pipes, iron plates, and iron gratings. The mustachioed old fortune-teller likes to snooze in a rickety armchair in the window. The next two shops are bookshops. My novel *The Loser* is available in both. Back home it had to be published in the utmost secrecy, which bestowed an aura of heroic transgression on the publisher, Gábor Demszky. Here in America I ran into a samizdat plain-white-cover edition. It is so tightly spaced that the whole novel fits into two hundred pages instead of four.

Iván Szelényi and I also single-spaced our typescript of *The Intellectuals on the Road to Class Power*. The fewer the pages, the easier it was to smuggle it outside the country. That accomplished, I could turn back to my novel. But one day Biki (Tibor Hajas—poet, essayist, photographer, body-artist, film director, watchman, and warehouse worker) told us there had been a house search at Tamás's (Tamás Szentjóby—poet, painter, film actor, and Fluxus artist). They had been looking for pornography, but discovered our manuscript instead. They suddenly lost all interest in pornography. No, they had a 132-page typescript dealing with ideological issues and containing all sorts of seditious ideas. "Looks like 127/b is your genre: incitement against the state," said the good-humored, portly lieutenant colonel entrusted with my arrest and interrogation.

Now here we were, nearly ten years later, our consternation having shriveled to a series of comical anecdotes, standing in St. Mark's Place, looking over the offerings on the sidewalk. People put out anything with the slightest chance of selling, trusting to the market gods to make the proper match. Nor did the market gods let them down. For among the pulp novels and one or two good books were two familiar-looking soft-cover volumes—red on top, yellow underneath—with a Hungarian title: *Társadalmi*

Szemle (Review of Society), the theoretical journal of the Hungarian Communist Party, November and December, 1949. Stalin, then celebrating his seventieth birthday, was on the cover.

I picked up one of the yellowed volumes. Now the young black man proffering it was certain you could find a paying customer for anything under the sun. Supine on a New York sidewalk the *generalissimus* was none too imposing, but in the autumn of 1949 the whole world was sending him gifts, including a trainload assembled by the grateful Hungarian People with enough material—a sea of miniature locomotives, machine tools, and children's drawings—for an exhibition. What is more, there was a statue of him in every shopwindow. In butcher shops, for example, the wisest leader in the history of mankind was rendered in frozen lard, the artist's honorarium being paid in kind: fatback.

Suddenly there was a vacant flat on the first floor of the Andrássy Boulevard building. Its former inhabitant was the son-in-law of the President of the Republic, a self-assured squat little man with an equally self-assured and squat spouse. In the autumn of 1949 the shutters were rolled down. The son-in-law of the President of the Republic had been appointed ambassador to Cairo and moved there with his family. Then he was ordered home, denounced as a spy, condemned to death, and executed. It didn't take long. The large American car stopped coming for his wife. The movers came and took all their possessions heaven only knows where.

The year 1949 was the year of the Great Change, the great new rigor, as peace-loving, progressive mankind prepared for the seventieth birthday of the Lighthouse of the Peoples. The brass band of the Hungarian State Security Agency, as part of peace-loving and progressive mankind, had recently moved into the spacious apartment of the freshly executed Hungarian ambassador to Cairo, and there they rehearsed the *Stalin Cantata*. I was forced to listen: I lived on the opposite side of the courtyard. They rehearsed it bar by bar, playing each one hundreds of times, boring it into my head. "Stalin is our battle, Stalin is our peace, and the name of *Sta-a-a-lin* will make the world a better place." (The last line had slight meter and rhyme problems, but was ideologically pure.) Sometimes a booming chorus would sing along. It was all very festive.

In 1949 Stalin thought there would be a war with the West, so the eastern half of Europe needed to be unified according to the Soviet model. The Soviet model meant trials. They started by sentencing Archbishop József Mindszenty to life. Then came the tall, handsome, and popular Foreign Minister (previously Minister of the Interior) László Rajk, who was selected for the role of arch criminal and duly tortured until he testified against himself. The BBC called him a victim of the very methods he had introduced.

People were no longer as they had been. A kind of rigid intoxication seemed to have infused their faces. The fear radiating from the walls of 60 Andrássy Boulevard seemed to grow stronger as the geraniums in the windows grew redder. Every afternoon a million sparrows perched on the lindens and plane trees, turning the street into one great vibrating river of chirping. Might there be some ruse lurking deep in the innocence of sparrows? Like the newly refashioned puppet theaters waiting to receive jackbooted kindergartners with machine guns?

The brief period of normal civil life that followed the Germans' collapse was over now, I realized. Gone were the days of burning class records, of back-talk, of speechifying about Hugo and Apollinaire, Ady and Babits. My *gimnázium* days enabled me to experience the whole city, its swimming pools as well as its libraries, or visit my sister, or sit in a café with a boy who could really play the saxophone, or admire the classmate sitting behind me, who could belch the whole of *Rhapsody in Blue*, or hire his neighbor to drive off every teacher from my vicinity with his farts and thereby let me read in peace (though of course I had to smell as well as pay).

My Hungarian literature teacher encouraged my readings, inviting me to his apartment and lending me books. When he opened his glassed-in bookcase to me, it was as if a beautiful woman had undone her robe. Those were the days when I discovered manifold meaning in every line and found profound wisdom in clichés.

I was sixteen and entering my next-to-the-last year at the *gimnázium*. I walked into the room on the first day to find two students standing by the window. The others were sitting at their desks, looking stern and singing songs of the workers' movement with great enthusiasm. They scrutinized the latecomer with lowering anticipation to see what he would do. Would he take a seat and sing with us? One class, one community, one heart, one soul. If not, he could go and stand by the window with the other two and pretend not to know that standing there made him conspicuously suspicious, dead to the ideological and political unity that flexed its muscle in common song! There they stood—Pali Holländer and Laci Endrényi, the most sensitive boys in the class. Tall and thin, learned, dripping with irony, inveterate concertgoers, readers of Hemingway's *Fiesta* and Huxley's *Antic Hay*, and, as Junior Tacituses, fully equipped to enjoy the historical transformation in all its vulgarity.

But the brightest student in the group was sitting in the back row near the window, bragging that he had traveled to the border in a State Security car as a volunteer to denounce his Zionist schoolmates' escape. He had always been malicious, but his sarcasm was grounded in power now: he was a high official in the student association. Though he still had to attend class, he would seek out other student officials in the corridor, where they would discuss important, confidential issues of the Movement under their breath. No outsider could come near. And he was the one who gave the speech on the occasion of Stalin's birthday in 1949. He spoke of a Golden Eagle, of an unshakable will that pursued its goal ruthlessly, without mercy. On the first day of classes he read aloud a passage from *The Road to Volokolamsk* about how cancerous meat had to be hacked out of a body or the body would rot. He then spun a pretty little speech on the topic, repeating the word "rotten" several times while glancing my way.

When József Révai, a member of the Politburo, condemned the harmful delusions of the philosopher György Lukács in a page-long analysis, I was the only one in the class who stood up for Lukács. It was intolerable that a *gimnázium* student should disagree with the Party leadership. I was summoned to a disciplinary committee chaired by a student my age. His name was Ferenc Fehér and we later became friends. He despised Lukács at the time, but later saw the light. In a required paper on the Three-Year Plan I wrote that for me it meant the state takeover of my father's business and house, for the tired worker I used to see on the stairs it means long hours of work for low wages. My literature teacher could not bring himself to grade the paper ("There is nothing I can do for you, son; I have no jurisdiction in such matters") and passed it on to the headmaster. It wasn't long before I was expelled from the student association.

What I really wanted was to be expelled from the school. "You have outgrown this place," the literature teacher told me. "You are intellectually over-age." Which was flattering enough, though I couldn't tell whether he just wanted to avoid the unpleasantness that came from having me around.

My friend Pali and I once invited him to come rowing with us on the Danube. Sitting in a bathing suit on the coxswain's thwart, he displayed a fairly large belly, but also the broad shoulders to match. Now that we were *à trois* and on the water, he confided that he could not make his peace with Marxism and expected difficult years to come. "Terror," I said ambiguously, "is history's sacrificial festival." My teacher did not completely understand. Perhaps I did not either.

That summer, the summer of 1949, Budapest played host to the World Youth Assembly, and young Communists flooded in from the Soviet Union, China, and the countries of Eastern Europe. After the trial that condemned László Rajk and his associates and led to their execution the city was brimming with a vibrant energy. It might have been said that the only people not yet arrested were the ones whose trials the authorities had lacked the time to arrange. They were scheduled for the following year.

"This ice cream represents the penitence of the alienated mind," I said one day on the way home at an Italian gelato stand that had not yet been appropriated by the state. Pali gave a good laugh. His violin teacher had called Kant the only respectable thinker, so he was primed to appreciate my Hegelian quips.

Soon the *Weltgeist* gravitated to the brothel. We set our elbows on a piano covered with a large embroidered cloth and peered down from the balcony at the Ring sinking into shadow. We set out on a hunting expedition. We stepped through the door of that neoclassical apartment house with its spacious courtyard, its pale pink marble staircase, its slightly dirty red carpet. The bell gave out a restrained buzz behind the heavy brown second-floor door. First a servant girl, then Madame: "Do you want Éva again?" Yes. Éva was thin with small, pointed breasts and an indecipherable, lovely scent. Her hair was red—everywhere—and she had an identification number from Auschwitz tattooed on her left arm. She was nineteen, I sixteen. "Explain the Rajk affair to me," she ordered, because I had always been able to make things clear. Her breasts got goose pimples. "I don't want to be tortured!" She had a fur, and on occasion there was a car waiting for her. Sometimes she took my money, sometimes she didn't. When she did, I paid with the proceeds from books I had sold from my library.

Pleasant as it was to sit in the brothel kitchen, all those thighs together tended to dispel illusions. Later, when they closed the public houses and socialism retrained the girls as taxi drivers, the only one left leaning on her elbows in the second-story window was Madame. She underwent a second flowering, because the drunk and disenchanted men whose feet mechanically took them her way were happy with her for want of anything better. Her neck was wrinkled, but the skin lower down on her body was smooth. She would bend over the lace bedspread dramatically and spread her legs passionately. The lips of her sex were large and swollen. She kept it shaven and screamed in the soprano register.

Be it by cart, bike, or train I would go home to Berettyóújfalu for holidays whenever I could, but once I began my studies in Budapest I became a city boy. The story of my village boyhood was over—if a story can ever be truly over.

This was my last summer in Berettyóújfalu. On the hot weekday mornings the daughters of the town's proper families would lie out by the railroad bridge. When I was fifteen, I had sat with Marika by one of the hot pylons, a veritable box seat for viewing the daughters of the pharmacist and chief physician, district court judge, and Calvinist priest rubbing oil into their thighs down on the sandy riverbank. Whenever the train rumbled past, I would put a protective arm around my girlfriend.

Once a group of sweaty, dusty Cossack soldiers galloped down to the water from the embankment. They rubbed their horses down stark naked and, once the hides were shiny, splashed and tumbled and pushed one another under the water until, suddenly cold, they emerged, their bodies stark white atop the dark brown, wet beasts. The young ladies averted their eyes. Then the soldiers slapped on their red felt hats and rode in ever tighter circles around the tanned young ladies, whose hair peeked out from under swimsuits barely reaching their thighs. The sun shone fiercely. Then from nowhere came a whistle followed by a command. The soldiers snatched up their uniforms and boots and galloped off as quickly as they had come.

In the summer of forty-nine I often lay on a sofa under a crimson Persian rug in the Berettyóújfalu dining room reading *Remembrance of Things Past* and *Doctor Faustus*. I would lift Marika onto my bicycle and take her to the Berettyó for a swim. Those were the days of first love. Marika was a couple of years older than I was and sat in front of me in neatly ironed white clothes. I was honored. I rode down from the dam to the riverbank and came to a stop with a nice tight turn, which I always executed just so, with a hard brake and a tail skid. Once, though, under the weight of the two of us, we rolled into the water, still on the bike. This little accident did not do our love any good. Soon thereafter a guest of ours, a saxophone player, asked me whether I had serious intentions about Marika. When I pointed out I was a bit young to be thinking about marriage, he told me that *his* intentions were serious indeed. With an eye to Marika's domestic happiness I generously let her go. The saxophonist had tricked me: his intentions had nothing to do with marriage.

When I was fifteen and entering the sixth year at the *gimnázium*, I moved with my sister and cousin into a narrow street in the middle of the city, Vármegye. I lived in the servants quarters in flat number five on the sixth floor. Entrance to the booth of a room—it was barely big enough to house a table, a bed, a wardrobe, an armchair, and a bookstand—was from the vestibule. I was free from adult supervision, but received a monthly allowance from my parents, which I husbanded as I could. Once in a while my friend Pali Holländer and I took lunch at the Astoria Hotel. We would discuss the offerings on the menu in detail and even order a Napoleon brandy after dessert. The waiter did not ask young gentlemen their age. Certain practices had remained alive.

By the end of the month, however, I would be eating at the Astoria's stand-up restaurant on the corner of Lajos Kossuth Street and the Museum Ring. If I had enough cash, I would get layered cabbage for 3.50, if not, then bean soup with beans for 1.10; and if even that was too expensive, then the 70-fillér bean soup without beans, which, cheap as it was, came with bread. But then there were the terrifying moochers who came and stood in front of me, mumbling, hacking, whining, showing their toothless gums, fixing their eyes first on my plate, then on me. Sometimes I could make a deal with them: "I'll leave you half. Just don't stand right in front of me, please. Move over there!" But they never went far; they just watched, anxiously, to see whether I would keep my part of the bargain.

I knew the Astoria inside and out and had even stayed there in earlier days on one of my father's trips to Budapest. It had the smell of that special cleanser I had enjoyed sniffing at the Hungária. My father's lifeline had been cut, while mine was just beginning. With everything still before me it seemed natural to be starting from zero. That I lived in a cubicle of six square meters and needed electric light to read even in the afternoon, that all I had—and needed—were a bed, table, wardrobe, and bookcase, none of this was humiliating; it was uplifting. I liked having my own room, a bell jar where I could hide away, where another world was constantly in the making inside my head. I could easily step from one world to another, for a book was as much another world too as the strip of sky I could see from my window.

On the other side of narrow Vármegye Street stretched the yellow county hall, a large, ancient structure with an irregular roof that made me nervous, because workers nonchalantly clambered up and down it gnawing on snacks of bacon. "Parisian style," said people who had never been to Paris. No one lived directly opposite, so I could gaze out over the roof to the antennas, towers, cupolas, siren horns, and clouds.

Below us lived the wife of Baron Villy Kohner, and on the next floor down Baron Tivadar Natorp. I took a liking to the baroness, a lithe, tanned woman who went around in sporting clothes, and to the baron, stooped over, examining the ground before him with a cane. Both were forcibly relocated in 1951, as was a beautiful woman with a deep voice, a smoker who wore plaid skirts and let her thick and (naturally, I believe) red hair tumble carelessly down. She worked at the Turkish Embassy, where she was arrested. Yet another neighbor, a banker, was resettled outside of Budapest. A

Council chairman, a former *gimnázium* teacher, moved in below us. The young son of a military officer on the fourth floor came upon his father's pistol one day and shot the daughter of the postman on the seventh floor while playing with it.

I can still picture the friends who turned up in my apartment, sitting in the unupholstered armchair across from the bed or stretching out on the bed. István would speak of his comrades in the Movement and those dull, official rooms where they discussed how to make everyone just like them, the "new men." Actually István himself was somewhat "new" for me in this phase of his, different from what he had been (and would later be, when curiosity would drive him to chase the elusive tail of a truth that was just beginning to take shape). Now his words were more judgmental and at times directed against friends in the name of Party justice. The Party's logic was enough for him. For a year or two.

But he could also speak respectfully of a girl's hair or artistic talents or mock his colleagues for their human weaknesses, to remark of a great thinker that "It wouldn't hurt for him to bathe more often." He said the most intelligent things about the crisis of the planned economy, making his points with hard statistics. As part of his professional training, he was permitted to work in the State Planning Bureau and would smuggle out data on scraps of cardboard, holding them in his hand like Aladdin's lamp or a kind of theoretical miracle weapon to condemn the system in revolutionary language as retrograde. At twenty he realized that the market exists and can be done away with only at the cost of lunacy. My eyes grew wide as I meditated on how Uncle Béla's business acumen had resettled into his son, though István was interested in the market merely as a theoretical construct and had no intention of taking part in it.

I was a boy from the provinces in one of Budapest's best schools, the Madách Gimnázium. I was a cautious young man whose accent and dress betrayed his country origins. Mr. Tóth, the tailor from Berettyóújfalu, made my suits with golf trousers, which none of my classmates would be caught dead in. But what I yearned most for was a pair of what were then called "ski boots," shoes with a double leather sole, a strap on the side, and a buckle. I believed they would give me a more forbidding, masculine air. Ski boots were for making an exit, giving the slip, taking a powder, the kind of footwear that wouldn't tear up your feet or fall apart on you if you were being pursued.

I loved films with chases and never identified with the pursuers. I used to flesh out stories of friends' escapes over the border in my imagination, taking them through creeks and mined bogs. Pali and I had plans to row down to the southern border and suss out the possibilities for crossing, but the motorboat border guards never let us get close. We still fanaticized about swimming out underwater using a reed as a breathing straw or strapping a motor-powered propeller onto our bellies, even to the point of wondering whether the propeller would harm our private parts.

Yet when emigration became a realistic topic of conversation, when Hungarian Jews, too, could move to the newly founded state of Israel, even take all their possessions with them in large chests, when our parents asked us whether we would be willing to emigrate, my sister and I said no. Everyone we had feelings for, everything we enjoyed was here. I had by then a good few years invested in Budapest and had learned to take the bad with the good. I held fast to the places where both had befallen me.

"We'll stay," I said.

"What for?" said my father, and with reason, since he had been forcibly removed from everything he had created for himself. Although he never could understand the point of it, he acknowledged its reality and went on to earn a pittance by managing a hardware store in one of Budapest's side streets. As ashamed as he was to tell his customers day after day that he was out of this or that, he rejected with disgust the under-the-table deals made by his subordinates. He took a dim view of state-directed commerce. "Tell me, son. What's the point of all this?"

Since he was nothing if not insecure in the conceptual universe of scientific socialism, there was no use in my telling him what he should say the next day if it was his turn to discuss the Party organ's daily, *Szabad Nép* (Free People), at the half-hour ritual morning meeting, when basing their comments on the previous day's issue, the store's employees would condemn the web of deceit spun by the imperialists to destroy the cause of the working class. Neither my father nor the imperialists were up to the task.

"I'm no good at speaking," he would say, though in fact he had the gift of gab. Once retired, he would go shopping at the Great Hall and spend the entire morning chatting up both sellers and buyers, then stop on the way home to hear out his concierge.

I never spoke to my family about wanting to be a writer. All anyone saw was that I read a lot, pounded the typewriter, and published a few book reviews during my university years. My diploma qualified me to be a teacher of Hungarian literature.

Mother would have been happier to see me in medical school, but I would never have been accepted, given my bourgeois background. I had an "X" by my name, which meant, in communist terms, that I was more than a class outsider: I was a class enemy.

I had applied for a concentration in French and Hungarian, but was rejected. I could count myself lucky to gain entry into the Russian Department, which was soon renamed the Lenin Institute, its purpose being the education of reliable cadres with a strong Marxist-Leninist background. But we "X's" never lasted long anywhere, and during my second year, two weeks after Stalin's death, I was barred from the university during the general mourning period. Once Imre Nagy came to power, the Ministry of Education allowed me to continue my studies in the Department of Hungarian Literature, but I was expelled again after Nagy's fall in March 1955. It was only through the intervention of my professors that I was permitted to re-enroll and complete my studies.

After receiving a degree in Hungarian Literature in the summer of 1956, I did indeed become a teacher, but also a member of the editorial board of a newly founded (though not yet circulating) journal *Életképek* (Pictures from Life). I did not have much time to enjoy those positions: my fellow students were fomenting a revolution. We got hold of some machine guns and formed a university national guard regiment that tried to defend the university against what proved an overpowering force. In the end, we surrendered.

I have mixed feelings looking back on those five years of study. I feel the same ambiguity I feel whenever I visit a university anywhere in the world to lecture on literature, give a sociology seminar, or simply talk to faculty members and their enthusiastic students. Gaining an overview of an entire field of study, having the chance to study all day (a chance that may never return later in life), agonizing in preparation for examinations, recognizing personal capacities and limits, worshiping some professors and disparaging others, thinking through the strategies for turning knowledge to use, living the excitement of first love, conversing with friends deep into the night, entering ignorant and exiting relatively well educated—no, we didn't waste our time. But even these memories are tinged with irony: I see the faces trying on various masks; I see an army of fresh self-images marching along a road of careers. Looked at one way, it is an arrogant new elite, but from another angle it is a nest of newly hatched eggs. Yes, it is a diploma factory, but then there is the master–student relationship, dramatic and elegiac for both.

Clearly politics deeply permeated my years at university, permeated them so deeply that it was a permanent backdrop for both professors and students. Being locked in and locked out, dealing with weapons inside and out (machines guns within, tanks without) is anything but normal. Any normal student role soon went by the boards. But even at the height of the Revolution I had no desire to shoot anyone: in the face of the armored units' overwhelming advantage I deemed speech to be the opposing force that would prove decisive in the long run, a conclusion I arrived at through concerted contemplation with all those who did not stream across the temporarily opened border to the West.

Half my classmates left, most of them becoming professors, mainly at American universities. We, the more recalcitrant ones, went underground, thinking that if we couldn't have it our way now we would provide the spirit of freedom with a mantle of disguise while we consolidated and reinvigorated the culture. As long as we were locked in, we might as well get to know our city, our country. Compulsion breeds intensity. The plan was to learn from people of experience, to spend part of our days in the library and part in tenements and back courtyards trying to save the lives of neglected children.

As for our evenings, we spent them in the literary cafés. Our post-university lives were thus a continuation of our university lives: the same circles of friends and lovers, a few professors, and the literary crowd. Word got out who was who. Everybody knew everybody else. It was a world with the intimacy of confinement about it, with the air of a guild. The university was merely a relatively brief interval in a lifelong course of study, though arguably it was the most stimulating, because everything was new: first exams, first serious writing, first apartment (or room at least), first lovers' cohabitation, first public role. These win out ultimately in the contest of memories, as their smells and colors are stronger than those that follow, perhaps because of the great hunger that precedes them. Who can possibly digest all that food, those books, those bodies, those experiences. Once the student years have passed, the marvelous hunger dissipates. My university career, deformed as it was by political vicissitudes, nourished my hunger for reality. I envy today's students their freedom, because politics does not stand between them and knowledge and they are spared the many senseless obstacles that affected our lives so harshly. At the same time, given that we can learn from the provocations and shocks of fate, no matter how unwelcome, I have no regrets that such was my lot.

Many years ago my mother tried to give me my deceased father's wedding ring; it did not fit onto my finger. Even during my first marriage, the moment I walked out of the door I slipped the new ring into my pocket. One day I forgot, and an entire class at the girls' *gimnázium* gave out quite a buzz.

From that day on they thought Daisy and I were married. During her last year at the university she demonstrated her outstanding pedagogical gifts in the same school where I was a teacher in training. I used to observe her from the back row and unsettle her with mocking glances. They could have seen us in the golden spring of 1956 after the earthquake and flood or before the Revolution, strolling arm in arm through the neighboring streets.

Later, they could see me with Vera, my wife, as we walked the length of the Parliamentary Library (an afternoon home for many) along the thickly bound issues of parliamentary minutes of earlier days, then turned off into the last of the so-called research rooms, which were glass-walled and lined with colorful panels. From there, a heavy door opened into a corner room: the *sanctum sanctorum*, a room reserved for us, the chosen ones permitted to keep a typewriter, György Szekeres and me. He was forty, I twenty-three. Through the thick, heavy window behind my enormous desk I had a stunning view of the Danube, the chestnut trees lining the promenade on the Buda side, and behind them the six-story palazzi in various states of disrepair, towering with lordly dignity, with the placidity of the beautiful who know they are beautiful, even if the man in the street kicks up a fuss, even if bombs start falling, even if people are lined up along the embankment and get shot into the breaking ice floes, even if excursion boats thrum about on the green-gray water. But there is nothing thrumming about now, only the sound of a piano and drums from the boat by the Hotel Dunapart, whose nightclub stays open until four in the morning. Couples coming together in the bar can rent little furnished cabins.

I usually took the number two tram to get to the Library of Parliament, whose entrance, tall and fitted with brass doorknobs, faced the Danube. You had to pass by the guards. I would nod to them with respect. After all, they were guarding the gate that led to the very summit of our country. Going up and down the steps, students would report to one another on the subjects discussed in the colloquia that went on there. Girls from humanities departments would be sitting side by side beneath bronze-stemmed lamps, future scholars with double fields (French and Hungarian, History and English, Psychology and Folklore) gazing at the current scholars, the higher caste, the chosen ones permitted to do their work in the four-man "research rooms," which were separated from the large reading room by wooden-scrolled doors with panes of colored glass, their large windows looking out over the Danube and the Castle.

Girls in the humanities were generally in love, or wanted to be, and could be quite dramatic in their breakups. They would tell their girlfriends they had just poisoned themselves in their grief, that cruel animal having told them it was all over. In a quiet little Buda bar, while everyone was dancing, that . . . that *cad* had said it would be better to put an end to it now rather than later. But the truth is, it's no good putting an end to it ever, sooner or later. So now, when her head fell to the table, he would quake at the humiliation of it all. But her true-blue girlfriend would abandon her own private students and drag her off to the hospital as her mother had done before, and later that scoundrel would sit on the blonde angel's hospital bed, and she would open her eyes and fix her gaze on him, and they would rejoice in each other, shedding tears of gratitude, both of them forgetting all that stupidity: the boy that their love was over, the girl that her life was over as a result. Now nothing was over, and the library would be open again the next day from nine to nine.

Libraries were places of refuge, asylums furnished with things of lasting value. In the library of the Institut Français I found books that spoke openly and open-mindedly of things taboo here at home. I had access to journals in sociology and psychology. There were art books as well, and novels by the latest authors. At the Parliamentary Library I was granted a pass to the research rooms—white instead of pink—which gave me access to even the classified publications of the Telegraph Office. I shared space with some odd birds involved in mysterious research and horribly boring types who used their white passes to take notes on textbooks of Marxist literature, that is, to extract meaninglessness out of meaninglessness. They looked at me suspiciously, since everything I read inspired alienation in them. Still, I was tolerated and felt at home there; in fact, we were a large caste, the merely tolerated yet still comfortable.

I glance out of the window at the Danube: Vera is coming to pick me up. We loaf a bit, our arms around one another's waists under the arcade, or sit on the embankment steps if the weather is nice. This is an appropriately humble spot: compared with the contents of the library, my knowledge was zeropoint-zerozerozero and remained so for a long time to come. I stare longingly at the tugboats on the Danube. They had a cabin at the stern where the captain lived with his family, and in the morning his wife would hang his freshly washed shirts out to dry. Watching the lazy tugboat pull those white patches along with six barges attached to its stern, I would fantasize about learning the captain's craft and, after seeing to my daily tasks, sitting in a reclining chair and reading or indulging in free-flowing ruminations.

I had a typewriter at home and one in the library, old, black portables. Gyuri Szekeres at the next desk and I would out-clack each other by turns. I wrote without restraint on my Triumph, whose handle had come off, though I rigged up another from an old belt. My machine clattered like a cannon, though no more loudly than my colleague's, who had been sitting at the next table since his release from prison. In front of me, on a table covered with crimson felt and standing on lion-legs, lay books by Albert Camus, Raymond Aron, Emil Cioran, István Bibó, László Németh, and Miklós Szentkuthy that I was entitled to borrow for in-house use with my white researcher's card, obtained through recommendations from the Writers' Association and the monthly *Új Hang* (New Voice). Without the card the librarians would have spent a long time debating whether to lend me a book of suspicious orientation; with it they gave me most of what I asked for. The rare refusal, with the explanation that a special permit was required for the work in question (for which I would have to pound the pavement and work out some clever tactics), came not from some repressed, balding employee with a puffy mustache in a white smock but from a stunning (though white-smocked) blonde wonder, her every movement—like her voice and gaze—wispy and smooth. She had a large, vulturelike nose, and the corners of her mouth were sensuous and arch though she never smiled. She seemed enveloped by a silvery bell jar, and much as I toyed with the idea I made no particular effort to break through it: by gaining her, I would lose the library, because I would eventually leave her. This made librarians holy and untouchable.

Szekeres would tell us stories about university life in Paris, stories of right- and left-wing radicals alike. He told us about the time when during the German occupation he had been caught in a raid and patted down. He happened to have had a revolver on him, a revolver wrapped in a newspaper, so he held the newspaper over his head while they searched his pockets and found nothing. Hearing about this brilliant stroke of heroism, all we twenty-three-year-olds could do was blink. We had a good laugh when he told us about the time in prison when the inmates suddenly took heart because despite the horrendous political situation the food situation had improved substantially, then lost heart when the political situation started looking up but the old slops returned. It turned out that a highly reputed cook had been arrested when times were bad and released when they got better. So the bad food didn't mean the regime was cracking down; it meant the old cooks had come back. He didn't go into detail about the interrogations. All he said was that realism lacked the means to depict them. He told us to read Kafka, because only his overarching metaphors could approach our reality and he did not consider himself up to the task. We used to compete to be the first to read the latest issue of the *Nouvelle Revue Française*. I knew that the French secret police had delivered Gyuri to the Russian secret police on Glynecke Bridge, the Bridge of Melancholy, near Potsdam, because he had refused to return home or tell the French Secret Service about his role as a Hungarian operative in Rome, their price for a residency permit. As a result, he had to choose between becoming a traitor and spy or being handed over to the Communists, who had ordered him home from the embassy in Rome (he had protested against the Rajk trial in a letter) and eventually sent him to prison.

He was a learned man and handsome, with snow-white hair, a slight limp, and a deep, powerful voice—a true gentleman, *un homme de qualité*. He was a major in the French Army, a hero of the Resistance, a master of conversation, an editor of Proust translations, and a fine translator in his own right. Later he worked as a proofreader at the prestigious Európa publishing house, where he was eventually promoted to head of the literature division.

Sometimes my wife Vera Varsa dropped in, and the three of us would sit in the heavy armchairs under a portrait of Kossuth and talk. I noticed that Gyuri's warm and civilized way of addressing his words to her, looking into her face while deep in thought, was not a matter of indifference to her. She was also taken with his masculine modesty, his self-isolation, his kindness. She had a deep voice and would give serious thought to our conversation, lifting her upturned nose, wrinkling her brow, playing in her excitement with her thick, unruly bronze locks, opening her mouth as she followed the train of thought, then making an occasional comment expressing anger or enthusiasm. And there, in the typewriter room of the Parliamentary Library, just next to the Prime Minister's office, our little band grew so close that Gyuri Szekeres, through the inscrutable will of fate (and of Vera), took over my role not long after.

Looking out of the Parliamentary Library window, I would spy the philosopher Miklós Krassó, true to form, still blond, not gray as he would be in 1985 just before his death in a London flat, where he was fatally burned by a gas explosion. In the spring of 1956 he was bubbling over with ideas, bounding about, waving his arms, having a grand old time. I would be riveted for hours by our conversations about politics and philosophy. We would go to the Dairy Restaurant, where the bread girl listened to him, fascinated, whenever he stopped her to take packets of sugar for his rice pudding from her wooden tray. He would lunge into copious detail about the madness inspired by Fichte and so transfix her with classical German philosophy that jealous cries of "Bread!" "Sugar!" rose up from all corners of the room.

Flitting past Vera and me on the Kossuth Bridge one day, he apologized for his rush by saying he had to drop Hegel and go back to Kant, because nothing existed outside of Kantian morality, though that wasn't entirely possible, because you can't ignore history and you can't understand history without Hegel. Having spent years with Spinoza's *Ethics* and Hegel's *Phenomenology of Mind*, he was at home with the dilemma. As for myself, I was going on at the time about forked paths of consciousness and the simultaneity of events as an apology for my eclecticism (which I called pluralism). Why choose between Hegel and Kant anyway? There's room on the shelf for both. Vera could not approve of my thinking in such matters, because for her it mirrored an inability to choose in love. This one is beautiful, you say, but so is that one. She noticed that when out walking I couldn't help eyeing a woman if she was the least bit attractive.

How to gain, if not freedom, then at least free time, which is occasionally the same thing? One day István brought me the news that the Debrecen crematorium was looking for professional cremators. The crematorium was in operation only two days a week, but it offered terrific pay in exchange for the repulsion you had to overcome. Should we become professional oven-feeders, corpse-burners? We, of all people? At least in this case the bodies were going to the ovens voluntarily. We talked ourselves into it, fantasizing that we would fly to Debrecen and live in the Golden Bull Hotel, doing the work in white gloves and spending the rest of the week in the Parliamentary Library looking out over the Danube at the Castle in ruins. We wrote a dignified letter of application about how deeply interested we were in the job. We had heard the remuneration was excellent. Was this true? The director gave a polite response. They were indeed looking for employees and were delighted with the sincerity evident in our expression of interest. However, they felt it necessary to clarify one misconception, namely, the salary was one-tenth of the figure we had cited. The thought flashed through my then twenty-year-old mind that we might sell the corpses to the Institute of Anatomy. No need there. "You are a very cynical young man," said Professor Kis, head of the Anatomy Department and coincidentally President of the Council of Free Churches. "Earn your bread by the sweat of your brow!" I could have unloaded freight cars, but instead decided to proofread and translate.

Those were the days of the Twentieth Congress of the Soviet Communist Party and Khrushchev's Secret Speech. After my third expulsion from university I was reinstated thanks to the intervention of György Lukács. A group of friends would congregate at our place to ponder historical portents, certain as we were that we stood at the very center of history: Austria had recently been pronounced neutral, and changes were imminent. István was convinced, citing classified information he had found at the Planning Bureau, that the country was bankrupt. He said he had enough material to depose Rákosi should the opportunity arrive.

On the morning of 23 October 1956, the day the Revolution broke out, I was sitting alone in a sun-drenched corner room of an Andrássy Boulevard mansard that served as the editorial office of the recently founded —and strongly oppositional—journal *Életképek* before an ever-growing pile of awful poems submitted by dilettantes, to whom I, as a neophyte literature teacher and editorial apprentice, should long ago have sent polite rejection letters. Instead I spent my time on the phone with friends and lovers, keeping up with political developments. The student demonstrations were banned at some points and allowed at others. It was all well and good that the students were marching, but demonstrations in and of themselves did not particularly attract me: I had done my share of compulsory marching on May Day with my schoolmates. When we assembled, I always tried to avoid having a flag pressed into my hand and to arrange things so I could slink away inconspicuously and go rowing on the Danube with friends. Foisting the flag off on someone else was a pardonable, if low trick. Things were different on that particular day in 1956, I concede, but even then I grabbed not a flag but the wriggling shoulders of a bright girl I knew from the university. I noticed her in the march, to which I had calmly taken the tram. We crossed the Margaret Bridge together.

Carrying flags along the street had been allowed only on official holidays, while saluting the Party leadership, but what had been forbidden yesterday was now suddenly permitted—simply because we were doing it. I was not so ardent as to cut the insignia of the People's Republic out of the middle of the flag; there were plenty of volunteers for that. There are always plenty for everything. During an uprising they turn up on the perimeter of the march route on motorcycles or elbowing their way along or shouting a slogan or two at the crowd from a car outfitted with a loudspeaker and enthusiastically breaking into song. I knew a few at the *gimnázium*, ready to stir up crowds with forced enthusiasm.

That night, after leading my curious companion past the headquarters of the Hungarian Radio, where we heard shots and shouts ("Jewish murderers!" yelled a man who had carefully withdrawn into a doorway), I returned home and told my wife, as I listened from the balcony to bullets crackling in the distance, that I would not take part in the shooting. But as the government had as yet no halfway measures like rubber clubs and water cannons and the only choice was live ammunition or forbearance, escalation was unusually rapid. So in the end when a young poet ran through the university halls shouting, "Hey! Who wants a machine gun?" I told him I did, and soon I was propped on my elbows on the cabin roof of an open truck as a member of the student-organized national guard.

Together with my fellow writers, all in their twenties, we could have taken over the editorship of our monthly literary-political journal from the old guard, who were in their thirties. My editor-in-chief had traded his post for the mayoralty, and a multiparty system was in place. We had withdrawn from the Warsaw Pact, and the Soviet troops were beginning to withdraw from Budapest.

Then, suddenly, they reentered, four thousand tanks strong, first aiming their cannons at spots where they had spied machine-gun fire, then at spots where no one was shooting at all, just to be on the safe side or because the soldiers felt like it. There was a general strike, a nonstop holiday. The city was one big theater with audience participation. When you found yourself holding a machine gun or a stretcher, you didn't think about the future; you lived a concentrated version of the present with no thought of praise or prison. Bravest among the fighters were the miners, freshly released from jail and sometimes still in their striped uniforms, and wards of the state, boys and girls alike, back in the city from their institutions.

Fifty-six was the most memory-rich year of my youth, the year when unforeseen bravery replaced fear. Furs or jackets with astrakhan collars or gallooned overcoats or old Hussar uniforms—you could see all kinds of outfits in the mayor's antechamber. Loden coats too, of course, which were all the rage at the time. Everyone wanted to meet my editor-in-chief and obtain signed and sealed documents enabling them to found new parties and appropriate state-owned assets for their headquarters. The now armed young editorial colleague stowed his machine gun under his chair and waited patiently to see the official inside to discuss his literary journal. While the men set off with their official stamps, the student noted the brand of rhetoric that went with each style of coat. But without the daring of those young toughs out in the square the gentlemen in the antechamber would have had no hope. The family men setting out for the factories had gone through a lot to join the ranks of street fighters. It was a time when half-naked, brutally bruised or bulleted and spat-upon bodies were hanged by their feet in front of Party Headquarters. The victims of these lynchings came chiefly from the State Security Agency. Such was the price they paid for their terror. But when I looked into the dead men's faces, considerations of that sort seemed senseless. Walking home sporting a National Guard armband and toting a machine gun, I was asked by more than one woman if I would be kind enough to rub out one or another neighbor—you know, the one in the fourth-floor corner flat. I did nothing to appease the popular demand for murder.

It would be a wild exaggeration to say that I was an obsessed freedom fighter. What was I doing with a machine gun? It was an adolescent whim, a remnant of the war. Once in a while I imagined an armed group stomping up the stairs to eliminate us. (What would be the best corner of the front vestibule for me to shoot from?) I was a pretty good shot: I had earned the title of sharpshooter during my brief training as a soldier. I was also a political commissar, because when our commander once asked who knew when *Das Kapital* was published, the student soldiers in our regiment guessed either wrongly or not at all until I chimed in: 1867. At last! He praised me and appointed me commissar for one of the company sections.

At the time we had no live ammo, the First World War–issue bayoneted rifles we carried coming only with five rounds of blanks. The reason, perhaps, was to keep us from using our weapons otherwise than intended. Which is just what happened two years later, late in October 1956, when students in my cohort disarmed the Baja garrison officers and moved on Budapest in army trucks. (I was unable to take part in the operation, having been forcibly removed from the community of officers-in-training.) This was in keeping with the spirit of the times, when the word "revolution" felt good. Every revolution got the highest marks: the French, the Russian, the Hungarian. Our 1848 War of Freedom was the very epitome of all that was beautiful and good: the poet falls in battle for his homeland; only the rootless scoundrel lacks the courage to die when his time comes.

A young painter said she would be ashamed all her life if she did not go out to the garrison at Újpest and get herself shot. We had to go, said the excited envoy who came for us, because people were being shot. Were they shooting back? I asked. No, he said. They were being shot with mortar fire, all the way from Gellért Hill; they couldn't shoot back. "So why go?" "Just to be together." It was all I could do to hold the young painter back, thereby laying her open to a lifetime of shame.

The reason I missed out on my classmates' military operation was that during our theoretical training at the university I had smiled impertinently when a captain was at pains to describe how horrible the enemy was.

"You there!" he bellowed." Yes, you, with the long hair! On your feet! You see, comrades? That's what the enemy looks like! Look at him, grinning at our worldwide struggle for peace. I order you to leave the room!"

I promptly stood and headed out of the classroom, a remnant of the grin still on my lips. Few of my classmates expressed their solidarity. They tended to be "serious" and were therefore inclined to have me expelled from the youth organization of the Communist Party. The majority thus raised their hands in favor of expulsion. A few abstained. Only two protested, but they were on the outs as well.

The most ardent supporter of my expulsion—the gifted recipient of a Soviet scholarship, a member of the board of the Students' Youth Association, and a past master at shaping the general mood ex cathedra (he is today a professor of social science)—established with painful gravity that I was fundamentally alien to the people. As I later learned, his diary exhibited a bloodthirsty animosity to Communists and Jews, though he never took part in the battles when the time came and in fact never left the small room Miklós Krassó provided him as a reward for his inquisitive mind. I am familiar with the contents of his journal because the room's primary tenant—Miklós's grandmother, who was then over ninety but still enjoyed the life-extending properties bestowed by curiosity—had dipped into the notebooks lying there on the table. She was curious about what that odd boy could be writing: not only did he fail to set foot outside the flat during those stirring times; he put his jacket on over his bare skin, because he never washed his shirt.

Miklós's grandmother immediately noticed the frequent appearance of the word "Jew." Though born a Presbyterian, she was perhaps particularly attuned to that sequence of letters since her parents had converted in the nineteenth century, the better to move freely among the other landowners and doctors. Seeing all the filth her lodger appended to that word, she took the first opportunity to turn him out. "Be gone, you miserable Tartuffe! How can you despise me so and live under my roof!"

She still called Russians by their pejorative Hungarian name, *muszkák*, and when she heard Trotsky mentioned in connection with her grandson—Miklós had given a successful lecture on him in London—she kept calling him Tolstoy: Tolstoy meant something to her, Trotsky did not.

Her grandson Miklós, though getting on in years, was constantly on the move, and I could only marvel at the whirlwind of energy that secured him a truck and the papers to carry out his plan. He managed it by making a scene in the chambers of the Revolutionary Council of Intellectuals, which had responded to revolutionary demands rather docilely by collecting information, assembling credible-looking reports, and weighing strategies. The inner sanctum was kept under guard, but Miklós broke through. What moronic impotence, he screamed. The intellectuals' place was in the street, in the armed insurrection! And he explained in detail what needed to be done. After putting up with him for a while, the Revolutionary Council of Intellectuals asked him what he would take in return for leaving them in peace. A truck and driver, replied Miklós, and a document stating they supported his recommendation for consolidating workers' councils.

Was that all? They were happy to get rid of him so cheaply.

So Miklós drove from factory to factory, gathering up emissaries of the workers' councils, and that very day saw the formation of the Greater Budapest Workers' Council in Újpest. At the founding assembly Miklós made liberal references to Marx, Heine, Shelley, and Ady, but before he had finished they thanked him for his efforts and begged him to let them pursue their own ideas. Miklós was not in the least offended.

When, eight years later in Paris, I asked him about those events, he reminisced with amiable humor. After leaving the workers, he tried to bring György Lukács, the philosopher, together with Imre Nagy, the democratic Communist prime minister, hoping the symbolic collocation of their names would be a message in itself. I believe Lukács was named Minister of Culture, and I reminded Miklós about Lukács's previous stint as Minister of Culture during the short-lived Hungarian Soviet Republic. When Lukács held the post in 1919, he ordered the pubs closed, a move that did nothing to increase the popularity of the regime. Another reason the move bewildered me was that the philosopher enjoyed a good tipple.

Rum played the primary role in my consumption of alcohol. I would take it with a double espresso at the Saint Stephen Ring Casino Café, where a full-breasted baroness made the coffee, a former Social Democrat MP recently released from an internment camp let you grab his unusually long earlobes for a forint, and an occasional click of heels came from one of the corner tables (a monarchist message immediately following a Polish émigré's references to Dr. Otto Habsburg, rightful heir to the Hungarian throne).

For a day or two I served as bodyguard to the psychologist Ferenc Mérei, then patrolled the public squares of Budapest with my machine gun at the ready and visited a few editorial offices. I would hang up the long, heavy, dark-blue coat I had bought for a pittance at a consignment shop and use the next hook for the machine gun, as if it were an umbrella. Freed from this double burden, I enthusiastically presented plans for the revitalization of our journal.

Stopping at a café for something strong—the woman at the piano had an absolutely perfect, towering, platinum-dyed hairdo, as if these were the most halcyon of days—I watched a group of people rush past, a man out in front, the others in pursuit. They gunned the man down on some cellar stairs.

Walking through the halls of the university, I ran into Miklós Bélády, a beloved teacher of mine. We stopped for a moment face to face.

"Humanists with machine guns?" he said.

"These are changing times," I responded. "Better to be on the safe side." It was unclear to either of us what I meant. I had read Marx's thoughts on "realistic humanism." One protects one's family and oneself if one must.

I headed home to listen to the radio and read Erasmus and Tolstoy. In front of the Horizont Bookshop I had found a copy of Tolstoy's *Childhood, Boyhood, Youth* in the trash and removed it from the other books, most of which had been burnt to ashes.

It had not taken long for piles of refuse to accumulate in the streets. The streets were also full of posters demanding the immediate withdrawal of Soviet troops in the strongest terms. Nor was it enough for them simply to leave the country: they were to ask the pardon of the heroic Hungarian people, which they had ruthlessly dishonored with their recent invasion and unjustifiably extended stay, recalling in our memory the havoc wreaked by Russians in 1849.

On my way home I stopped off at the Writers' Association, where things were buzzing. You could feel a sense of importance emanating from the directorship as they prepared a public statement. It had to be at once brassy and silky, sonorous and deathly—a masterpiece, in other words.

Trucks coming in from the countryside had brought a bit of nourishment for the intellectual leaders, the conscience of the nation, behatted men who were good at pressing against wall or fence the moment they heard a burst of fire. In any case, a nice little package slid into my bag. Down in the restaurant writers were debating how far back to go: 1949? 1948? 1947? 1945? Even further? The day the Germans marched in? Was there an acceptable starting point? Or perhaps this day of revolution marked the dawn of a new era. This very day, with its giddiness, its swagger, its display of the dead. Liberation goes hand in hand with murder.

A stocky fellow made a triumphant entrance, his face flushed with glory: he had managed to shoot two Soviet soldiers and write two stories. His boyish pride suggested he now considered himself a man: he had gone from student to killer.

A reporter had heard that the Soviet tanks were pulling out. Another had heard precisely the contrary: railway workers had sent word that they were rolling in on wheels. He said the Old Man—meaning Imre Nagy—had just waved his hand at the news.

In the café on the corner of my building I heard a man in a Persian-collared overcoat assuring all and sundry that Konrad Adenauer was on his way, though the bearer of glad tidings had added "on a white horse," which turned them into a moronic fairy tale. The neighborhood's high-class whore, a former language teacher and genuine polyglot, was outraged that the swimming pool she visited daily had been closed. She also asked in stentorian tones whether anyone at the café had read Virginia Woolf's *Orlando*, because she had not yet decided whether she cared for it or not.

Before I could open my door, two other doors popped open, and that era's masters of information retrieval, the concert violinist and the filling station attendant, stormed me with their questions. Theirs was a resplendent new friendship. One moment they would feel the flush of victory, the next they would predict a house-to-house roundup, the men beaten and the women raped. And what would they collect now? Wristwatches again, as during the war?

Late on the evening of 4 November the art student—her name was Éva Barna—and I were standing guard with machine guns at the University's Humanities Division. Once in a while a tank came rumbling down Váci Street. That was the banal part. The important part was Éva's beauty, her striking, deep voice, and, most of all, what she said. She had read Camus' *Mythe de Sisyphe* in the original; I had not. A mean-spirited jealousy moved me to make some ironic remarks about Camus. Éva emigrated that December and eventually met Camus and corresponded with him. Between Éva and Camus stood only travel expenses; between Éva and me the Iron Curtain.

Vera made some phone calls. What she heard was enough for her. She had no desire to see the fallen, burned, or hanged sons of whatever nation; she longed only to leave and live among more reliable peoples: she would go to Paris to teach English and Russian, giving us something to live on; she would rent an apartment, set everything up, and I would follow. She said I should stop being so difficult.

On 11 November, after the defeat, Miklós Krassó and my cousin Pál Zádor told me they were leaving the next day and asked me to go with them. They had assured my passage. They showed me my name on the document. Their story was that we were going to persuade others to return home.

I refused. I said it couldn't be as bad as before. I would hold out. I would outlast the leaders. I had no wish to be swept into the great outflow; I wanted to know what was going on here, in these streets. It was an unfinished story, and I refused to tear myself away from it.

Among Biblical heroes I found Jeremiah particularly appealing: he knew in advance what would be—he prophesied the fall of the Hebrew commonwealth—and all he asked of the victor was that he be allowed to mourn his city and his people on its ruins.

I had no desire to look for clever ways out. I wanted a normal, simple life: the same stairways, the same cafés, things as they had been. Even if hundreds of thousands were leaving, millions stayed, and if I had friends and lovers among those leaving, others would come along. My books were here and the sky and the balcony overlooking the Danube and the hills of Buda across the water.

And if I did go, where would I go to? People were wandering off in different directions, but this was still the place where I'd find the most speakers of Hungarian; I'd have the easiest time finding my way around, around the streets, the words, the customs.

Yet I sanctioned their going because I suspected they would be in greater danger here than I. They would be less able to get on here because they were more active, more inclined to speak out, more lively, more passionate, more important than I. I who was just a kibitzer, an armed onlooker. Besides, my parents were here, and if no uniformed compulsion separated us now should I be the one to separate us just to make the life that was best for me? I did not feel any danger looming here. So what if they locked me up. I had heard plenty of prison stories from former inmates: you can have a life in there too. Behind bars I would still be myself. Or so I thought.

What about taking my parents with me? And be dependent on charities? Start my student career anew, on scholarships? No need for me to waste away in the classroom. Every morning I could sit down to my notebook at any number of tables, since I would still have the money for an espresso at Budapest's myriad coffeehouses. I would always be able to find work to cover the absolute necessities: I could translate, I could edit. I had no desire to be rich. I had been rich once. It was no great shakes.

Looking around me, I saw nothing but strategists. How did they deal with the issues, the obstacles? The patterns they assumed, born of compulsion, appealed to me, comical though they were. Every social type, after all, is a complex of clichés. Caricature needs recurrent elements. Life here abounded in provocations and hardships directly traceable to schematic thought. Psychic sprains were never far from our door.

What interested me was how thinking becomes reality not from habit or sober practicality or tradition but from the exertions of the willful mind, from bold dreams, from seeking the truth and then announcing it—how the noble turn base, ideals become a hell, and how, in the end, we will survive it all anyway because we are stronger, we everyday, pedestrian people capable of work, wonder, and contemplation.

If István had stayed, he might have been sentenced to death. Besides, who was I to judge my friends? Everyone who left was right, as was everyone who stayed. Everyone tried to heed the prompting of fate. My advice to myself was: As long as you are not in mortal danger, sit tight. Keep going, but don't rush. All your problems come from impulsive decisions. Just keep working quietly, steadfastly, inconspicuously, ceaselessly.

They searched Gyuri Krassó's apartment and took in Gyuri, Tamás Lipták, and Ambrus Oltványi. But not me, because, true to form, I was late. We were to meet at ten; I arrived at twelve. Gyuri's mother told me what had happened. They didn't find the mimeograph machine, which had been well tucked away. They let Ambrus and Tamás go, but later took Tamás away again.

That they didn't arrest me was a lucky break, suggesting that they had not found the list containing the signatures of the people who had received machine guns. Besides, I had never been particularly active, never stayed in one place too long. I observed things, but made no speeches, didn't belong to the elite of the youth organization calling for reform (I had long since been expelled), didn't even use its language or style. To my good fortune I was insignificant.

So my concierge did not report me after all, though he had seen me come and go with my machine gun and never displayed signs of sympathy. I buried it in the corner of a then still vacant Pannónia Street lot with Vera, my coconspirator (or rather lookout). Two or three years later a large apartment building went up on that site, and who knows what happened to my well-packed and well-oiled weapon.

One day I ran into my philosophy professor, pacing the Ring in the company of a classical philologist. He had joined the new Sovietophile patrol force and was carrying a machine gun and wearing the requisite gray overcoat. He was extremely well-read and capable of reconciling his professional interest in Kierkegaard with his duties as a Party soldier, which included efforts to re-educate me. He wanted me to eliminate all traces of the bourgeoisie from my person, toss them off like old clothes, to steer clear of my old friends and to marry a woman of working-class extraction, a Party member. He himself had done as much: his stern, solidly built wife was unsparing in her theoretical criticism. When all was going well, she called him comrade, but whenever any ideological tension arose between them she addressed him as sir. (There was an analogous practice in the public sphere: at the workplace we could be comrades, but under police investigation we were inevitably sir.) I merely nodded, seeing from his uniform how far he had gone in his intellectual odyssey, and he merely returned my reserved nod: he had no wish to make friends or trouble, which was fine with me. A weapon makes an eloquent sartorial accessory.

After the second coming of the Soviet tanks—this time in greater numbers and ferocity than on the eve of the uprising—that is, after 4 November, two hundred thousand out of ten million Hungarians left the country, young people for the most part, including half of my classmates, most of my friends and lovers, and my cousins and sister.

Fifty-sixers? After a brief stint of valor they had a choice: to go or to stay. Those who could go did, fleeing either the previous state of things or the future revenge. They trudged through snow and ice over the spottily guarded border. Just before Christmas Vera set off too with my sister Éva. They made it to the border and crossed in a midnight snowstorm, trudging on in the dark along roads marked with Austrian signs. Then they saw Hungarian signs again: they had probably walked around the same hill twice. My sister tried once more the next morning and made it across.

Vera came back on the evening of Christmas day and was a little impatient with me for not having bought a Christmas tree. We went down and managed to find a small one and some decorations. There were gifts and an improvised supper, candlelight and family happiness.

I did not leave in 1956. Every time the opportunity presented itself, I sat down at my desk and wrote. Whenever the time came to make a particularly important decision, I desisted, letting things happen as they would. The more dynamic ones left; the rest of us stuck it out, hardening into shape. When I think of them from a distance, I like them; when I meet up with them, I do my best to slip away.

Though I stayed, I well knew that the dark bell jar of reality and nightmares, the space where anxiety looked itself in the face, would close around me again soon enough. It was time to learn to cohabit with angst, yet ensure that it did not become master of the house. After 1956 people no longer tacked their thoughts up on trees. The spirit of fifty-six turned to the wall and pulled the blanket up over its ears. Most memories died out, there being no profit in keeping them alive.

The furniture in my sister's room had once been my parents' bedroom set. A carpenter at the beginning of the century had replicated Maria Terézia's bedroom, and I had angel faces gazing down on me from the head of the bed and from the wardrobe. Two naked angels held up a mirror that had once stood atop a dressing and makeup table with its many drawers, some locked, others not, depending on their contents. When I was a child, sweets, condoms, and a pistol were locked up, while more boring things like photographs, locks of hair, and milk-teeth were not.

This bedroom set survived the most extreme vicissitudes. In 1944, when both the German and Soviet command posts had abandoned the house, the poor of the village came and took away everything they could carry. The large three-doored wardrobe was the one thing they could not manage; they did not even smash the mirror, though they did their best to destroy all manner of other things. So the wardrobe was the only piece that stood there in one piece, a monument of sorts in the refuse-strewn house, a harbinger of a restorable order.

By 1960 the wardrobe had moved to the inner room of our sixth-floor Vármegye Street apartment with my bicycle on top. The makeup table served as my desk, though the angels holding the mirror had been disposed of by history, which at this point tended to resemble a collective disaster. When you get hit in the head, you stay down for a while before initiating the long struggle for restoration. We should be players in the match, not victims (or so I would tell my friends at our regular coffeehouse table).

In the early morning hours sometime in 1960 a drunk hacks below my window. I am sympathetic: we are the only ones up. We are surrounded by the kind of silence that amplifies snores, angry whispered words, the screeches of distant trains, the moans of trams rolling out of their yards. There is a flood of stimuli in

Budapest, but I can only take in small bits of it. In the hours before dawn we need not contend with the assault of distracting sounds, calls, and obligations that demand attention and dull us into indifference. Perhaps I am not a city person after all.

When I go out to do field evaluations as a children's welfare supervisor, my job requires me to enter the living quarters of complete strangers as if I were in my own home. Within a couple of minutes I discover I am in fact at home.

"It's the man from the Council!"

A kitchen chair is shoved under my behind.

"Well, sir, you see, what happened was . . ."

The words gurgle up like water. I hope I can keep from nodding off.

Rezső Rajnai sleeps in the cellar wrapped in his coat. He sleeps only till dawn, when his drunkenness wears off. The cold wakes him up.

A police officer tries to throw his weight around. I might be able to take him down a peg or two. This I do with a secret passion.

A Jehovah's Witness spends his life being jealous of his wife. She could have him institutionalized permanently, but keeps having him released at her own risk to protect him from the stress. She brings him home; he tortures her some more.

The wife of an obstetrician's best friend gives birth while the friend, a cripple, waits outside in the hallway for the good news. The doctor reaches into the infant's eyes instead of his rectum, blinding it. A surgical error. He goes home and poisons himself.

I have a bad chill. My bones ache. I may have a fever. I had a fish soup at the Golden Pheasant for lunch, which helped me put the "House of Lords"—a rundown vagrant shelter where all my dealings are with toughs—out of my mind. Still, one stern word from me and the beating of sensitive hearts is immediately discernible under the threatening shell.

A woman's husband dies: he was standing on the sidewalk when a bus hit him and killed him on the spot. The woman gets a hefty pension to replace her well-situated husband. A year and a half later, the late husband's best friend leaves his wife and moves in with the widow. They marry. As a result, the widow loses her pension, which was larger than her salary. She has a kindergarten-aged son from her first husband, but finds little time for him. I ask her why they got married. They were already living together, weren't they? The woman smiles and blushes. I blush too, then take my leave.

An old woman who sold newspapers walked into the main distribution center and asked for her quota. In those days people were reading *Népakarat* (The People's Will), but they foisted *Népszabadság* (The People's Freedom) off on her. She went out and sold almost all of them. Three young men, armed, were walking quietly along Rákóczi Street when they spied her with a *Népszabadság*, tore it from her hands, fell upon her, and kicked her as she lay on the ground. As the woman was dragging herself away, one of them said, "Finish her off, why don't you."

"What for?" one of the others said. "She won't dare hawk that trash anymore."

The old woman's skull was fractured. She was blinded in one eye and has had neuritis ever since.

Now on to six more addresses, six new kinds of despair. But first I sit and pray on a bench in Bethlen Square. There is a synagogue nearby.

Now off to the darkest heart of the district. Mrs. Alabárdos and her daughter. She wants the girl to respect her. The girl will not. So she is cruel to her.

Then I grant absolution to a widower who has committed incest. His daughter forgives him as well. If I had him locked up, what would they live on?

I look in on little Lajoska Musztafa. His father, now dead, was Turkish. His mother has remarried. Her husband is a locksmith named Bogyi. The handsome young boy was proud of his Turkish roots and mourned his father. When they studied the Turks in school, however, Lajoska heard bad things about them. His fellow pupils started eying him, so he asked to take Bogyi's name. After which Lajoska Musztafa (or, rather, Bogyi) stopped mourning his father.

A young typist goes out to Óbuda for rowing practice. It is winter. The training grounds are empty, nothing but fields and gardens. Four kids attack her. Screams. All four rape her.

"I know what you look like! I'm going to report you!"

So the boys poke out both her eyes.

An old man sits down next to me on the bench. His face is soft but stubbly; he has few teeth; he wears his winter overcoat even in the sun; he smells. An old woman with a pointy nose sits down with us. Her speech and movements are sprightly, her legs wrapped in bandages under her stockings.

Woman: "What's for lunch?"

Man: "Tea, and bread with lard."

Woman: "Don't you cook?"

Man: "No, I don't."

Woman: "Kids?"

Man: "I had a son. He was executed."

Woman: "So you live all alone?"

Man: "With my bedbugs."

Woman: "But you must have a nice little pension."

Man: "Six hundred forints. I drink it up pretty fast. Then I don't eat, just the leftovers they give me."

Woman: "Where do you live?"

Man: "I've got a nice apartment, two rooms plus kitchen."

Woman: "Why don't you rent out one of your rooms?"

Man: "I did, but my tenant went crazy. He stopped paying."

Woman: "You should get married."

Man: "Yes, but I can't find a woman I like. If she's young, she might not take care of me, and if she's old I'll have to take care of her. So I'm picky."

I stop for a glass of milk. A wheezing old man underpays by twenty fillers. He walks with two canes. When the woman at the counter calls after him, he pretends not to hear. Every day he underpays by twenty fillers.

A woman is called into a police station and asked about a man they have arrested. He abandoned her not long before. She is either afraid or cannot bring herself to lie, and testifies against him. She is the main incriminating witness.

An electrician has recently lost his wife. Every evening he lays out a table setting for her, then eats alone. He can't stand television. He goes over to the wardrobe and takes out his wife's clothes one by one. "She wore this one on such and such a day and that one on another." That is how he spends his evenings.

The welfare officer has grown thick-skinned from his work. The office madness and his wife's nerves box him in. Unable to sleep, overworked, he learns to put a stern face on things.

The heavy iron chairs on the playground are screwed into the ground. In January 1945 I looked into the corner coffeehouse through the broken glass. It was crammed to the ceiling with the bodies of Jews shot dead in the ghetto. That was the day we went looking for Aunt Zsófi's mother in the ghetto hospital and found her alive but with a bullet in her face. Now the new wallpaper has a sunflower pattern. An energetic woman greets all comers, apologetically bemoaning the lack of one or another item on the menu as if conveying the news of a dear one's death.

Little shops are opening in the courtyards of the old apartment buildings, and people are withdrawing into them. Here in Elizabeth Town everything is cavelike. There is no pretense about the place; it is full of life and people-friendly. I am no stranger here; I understand everything muttered in its most distant corners. I know the crocheted cloths under the clay pots with dried flowers, the bursts of cackling women, the heavy clank of the iron doors. That tall, attractive girl reading a magazine has probably knitted her midthigh-length white sweater herself. Comfortable oldies emerge from the depths, the espresso machine clatters, and spoons and saucers clink. The man making the coffee never takes a break. The guests know him and make small talk. "Ate the flowers, dammit!" *Who* ate them?

During my *gimnázium* years Budapest's Elizabeth Town represented the heart of things, a magic place, the place where I could find anything I might wish for. The population density is highest there, and as they used to leave the main gates open I would catch whiffs of the human smells wafting out of open kitchen windows into courtyards. I would walk along the hallway-like balconies lining the courts as if looking for someone.

I used to trade books by weight with the blind antiquarian

bookshop owner on Hársfa Street. All that mattered to him was that what I brought in weigh more than what I took away.

"How is it you never go broke?" I asked him.

"You're still a pipsqueak, young man," he said. "You lack all understanding of the profundities of human stupidity and stochastic processes. You suppose that everyone brings in junk and takes away the good stuff, but the opposite holds just as often. Besides, what constitutes junk is a highly relative issue."

On the way to and from school I did some urban sociological field research, if we accept my friend Iván Szelényi's definition. Years later, when during a trip to Pécs for a study of urban society we spent the first three days simply walking around and I guiltily suggested we were wasting time, he responded no, we were doing genuine fieldwork. This put my concerns to rest. But the only time I did fieldwork in the strict sense of the word was from 1959 to 1965, when I visited Elizabeth Town families as a youth welfare supervisor for the Public Guardianship Council and wrote reports on their living conditions.

All I could do was set down my impressions, but the great consistency of those impressions gave them the weight of objectivity, and the recommendations I made led to measures affecting the lives of children. My beat was the area between the Ring and György Dózsa Street, and I saw six to eight families a day. There was hardly a building I did not pay at least several visits to. Most of the time I spent in apartments facing the inner courtyard rather than the street, so it was the less fortunate aspect of the area I came to know. Sometimes it seemed hard to sink any lower.

What has changed over the past forty years? Poverty is lasting; only the faces change. But poverty is more than a condition;

it is a blow, a disaster, a pit you fall into. How can you expect a person in dire straits to have the patience of a saint? When the well-to-do go off the rails, they may or may not pay a price; the poor have no choice: they kick, they scratch, they torture one another.

Reviewers found the world of my first novel, *The Case Worker*, hellish. I found it quite normal: one's imperfections make one mortal, hence real. Moral philosophy must be built on human frailty, and our acceptance of it. Behave outlandishly and you scare people. They take you for a criminal or a lunatic who belongs in a prison or asylum, as if humans were cars and could be taken to the shop for repairs. Crazy people exist, but most of them get by on the outside; only a few give up and entrust themselves to institutions. Weakness and abandonment require assistance.

The more moneyed and better educated a country, the more it confronts issues of weakness, a condition that fosters a frightened, dependent, and childish relationship with body and mind, with sickness, fear, and sorrow, with intimations of mortality. People are frightened by portents of death, having had no training in dealing with their problems and pain. If something is not entirely as it should be, they are in a bad way. Yet the zone between a perfect state of affairs and a wretched one is where most of life plays itself out.

My workdays were full of decisions, and everyone I met was a challenge. Each of my clients required some kind of action. Some people need more than a cordial nod. But how far are you willing to go when an entirely helpless child enters your charge?

It was worthwhile to spend time in the kitchens of those one- and two-room apartments: each kitchen was interesting in its own way. It is only when you hear a hundred versions of the same story that you begin to understand and feel it. I had a daily wish to combat my overwhelming feeling of superficiality which, even as I flattered it by acknowledging its existence, I found stultifying. "They are all of them just like me," I said to myself every evening on the brightly lit tram after leaving my charges.

A yokel gawking at urban life, I was never blasé. I studied the metropolis, wanting to write about everything, taste everything through my words. Asking my questions and giving my curiosity free rein, I felt an infectious bliss. Budapest was an endlessly juicy tidbit. Even in twenty years a voyeur from the provinces could not get enough of it.

At the time I was also editing Tolstoy's diaries. Tolstoy would begin each morning with a vow and end each evening with a guilty conscience; he broke every vow: he drank, whored, brawled, played cards, and picked fights. I did not brawl or play cards.

One day I got up early, read some Tolstoy proofs, and went to the Magyar Helikon Publishing House where I edited Hungarian translations of Russian and French classics. The head of literature called me in. He wanted to appear in high spirits, but the stories he told were not happy ones.

F. had intended to marry a working-class girl designated by the Party when his "bourgeois" girlfriend informed him she was pregnant. Abortion was out of the question in those days. Socialist morality took the side of the girl; his fallibility took him to his girlfriend, a class enemy. The child would be born, but he could not simply leave his bride-to-be because of an ideologically and otherwise problematic woman. Like the poet Attila József, F. lay down on the train tracks in front of a locomotive. The train sliced off both his legs. The policeman who arrived on the scene established that his nice trousers were salvageable.

His fiancée visited him every day at the hospital. F.'s first question when he came to was: "Did you find my party membership card?" Two weeks later his bourgeois girlfriend came in and confessed that she wasn't pregnant; she had merely wanted him to marry her. In 1956 the miners got word that a Party bigwig lived on the fourth floor. F. was no Party bigwig, but he did happen to live next to the Party's district office. The miners stormed his apartment intending to take him off, then noticed his artificial legs. They knocked them together, enjoying the noise they made.

He was my boss at the publishing house. My fellow proofreader Tamás Katona and I would carry him in the elevator in our intertwined hands. Though somewhat embittered, he was unfailingly alert when it came to ideological matters. Yet by playing on his sentimentality, I managed to trick him: I published Isaac Babel and Bruno Schulz.

I would look at women with the alert hunger of a hunter. In those days I felt there was no simpler way to get to know people than by lying naked with them in the same bed. Conversation is better afterwards; it is permeated with reciprocal gratitude and openness. The girl who sold bread and the hairdresser, the girls studying at the university and the women colleagues teaching there, the soprano who lived across the way, the pediatric nurse—they all were frightfully interesting to me, every one different in her own way, miraculous in her uniqueness.

I would go to the station and pick out a train, then get off at a small-town station, take a room in a hotel, and look out onto the main square. The constricted undulations, the slow passings were all so many offerings of meat, in hiding until they burst into the public eye. I turned around as a woman with a nice body passed by, paused a moment, abandoning my original purpose, and set off after her. We entangled, then fell out of each other. A housewife babbling to her baby was a font as precious as old diaries discovered in the attic or the ferocious rancor of a divorce court.

I phoned a woman at the number she had slipped into my pocket among mutual friends. I canceled all my plans, went to the address she gave me, and tried to guess as I walked up the stairs what she would have on: underwear or armor? How did she arrange to be alone? What would her smell be like from up close? I go and sit down beside her, listen to her talk about all kinds of things. I have never yet heard a story that was entirely dull. And what will be the situation that gives rise to the quick embrace that encounters virtually no resistance? What is the touch that will make her shiver and whimper like a child? And what will happen afterwards? Will she phone me back or show up unexpectedly at impossible moments?

At sixteen we are awkward because our bodies are complete but our understanding still childlike. At twenty-seven we are ill at ease because our minds are adult but our blood still childlike.

I have a job, but a tiresome one. I should be a Confucian at the Guardianship Council and a Taoist at home. I laugh at the thought. Who could pull it off? I have a contract with the publisher for a book on Stendhal, but am not writing it. I have a love, but am nervously repelled by the idea of marrying again. I have friends, but know what they are going to say before they say it. In fact, I sometimes fear I know what I will be thinking the day after tomorrow. I have reached the point where each successive birthday only reminds me of what I have failed to accomplish during the stupid five years since the Revolution.

At our regular coffeehouse table I made some antideterministic remarks, unable to reconcile myself to the idea that I am the way I am as a result of the effect on me of others. I insisted there was someone inside me making complex decisions at every moment, though I didn't know exactly who it was. My decisions were not influenced by my father's wealth or my childhood sexual fantasies, I asserted in opposition to fashionable contemporary views, reverse determinisms I found tasteless and morally questionable. This is a land of sloughed-off responsibility, a land where people justify their acts, whatever they are.

In the library catalogue room a former professor of mine mentioned that he had been hearing identical antigovernment theories from various students of his and that when quizzed they all turned out to have talked to me recently. My teacher, who was in direct contact with the highest echelons, shook his head and said no good would come of this. I should think carefully about what I said. And to whom.

After the fall of the Revolution, in the "consolidated sixties," I encountered the touchiness of tyranny wherever I looked. The police captain and the concierge were the state's patron saints. They were granted practically nothing else but the right to high-minded rage and to vengeance on their fellow citizens in the name of the state. Do not imagine that people who appear intelligent, good-natured, and civilized will not go wild when presented with a chance to take umbrage in the name of the state. And there is no one they despise more than the person who exposes the vanity of their everyday treacheries, for that person denies their very raison d'être. Who is the traitor's most natural enemy if not the non-traitor?

I had a classmate whose mother happened to see her son standing on a chair in his room delivering an address. He was denouncing his friends, one by one, to the General Secretary of the Communist Party of the Soviet Union, Nikolai Sergeevich Khrushchev. On and on he went, his voice rising in intensity, until he fainted and fell off the chair.

It was always cause for celebration when we happened upon islands of terra firma in the ocean of verbiage. Reading substantive works during the years of censorship was a form of refuge, a suspension of the falsities that had elbowed their way into house and home. One good book in my bag was recompense for all the clichés that had to be endured. We can use literature to be hard on our fellow humans, but if we truly learn to read we can use it to forgive them and revel in their beauty. Since my *gimnázium* days I have believed that the constant discussion of substantive texts is what keeps humanity going.

From spring to autumn I sought out garden spots. There were still outdoor restaurants with tables decked in red-checked cloths, and I deemed it a mark of distinction to lunch in the garden of the Fészek Club with writers older than myself, the prize of the day being the chance to measure my mind against theirs and thereby establish I had a rightful place at the table. There would always be someone in the company who had just been abroad—to Paris, naturally—and would speak of it to the provincials, for whom Paris is as far off as the moon. But just as we had no desire to pop up to the moon, we could do without Paris. We had refined the art of determining who all and what all we could do just fine without.

You could still play foot-tennis with a soccer ball in the street. Little girls still chalked hopscotch squares. You could still find mossy ruins and nooks for love trysts. It was still the fashion to carve arrow-pierced hearts and initials into tree trunks. There were still hideaways where a poet and his paramour could settle into a room on the basis of his verses.

The latent elegance of the city transcended all obstacles. You could still find white-haired watchmakers in nineteenth-century workshops and elderly, elegantly dressed Jewish salesmen in state-owned fabric shops. Waiters with prewar manners still served you in restaurants that still featured prewar pianists.

The only people in my neighborhood who could afford a car—a Škoda—were the saucy fashion designer and perhaps a writer or two or film director. The city still belonged to the pedestrians, a fact of which I took free advantage. To this day I have not learned how to drive.

We knew each other's habits in love: our lives were virtually open books. We were shut in together on the same stage, and love was our ethnography. We sought it out, then did what we could to escape its consequences so as to seek it out again. There were no girls in white boots leaning on their cars. Business pleasure and private pleasure were not yet distinct realms. If someone was in pain from, say, the infidelity (or, for that matter, the fidelity) of a partner, the chronicle of their heart's agony was met with sympathy rather than scorn. Everyone had a trusted friend to pour his heart out to; all secrets tended to become public knowledge.

Women in the center of town and at summer houses in the hills, women in every district, in little ground-floor rooms looking onto courtyards, women encountered in the night, women encountered in cafés staring back at you, letting their eyes rest on you, women looking down from the bend in the stairs above, entering a shop and pleasantly surprised to note the loyal perseverance of this still-unknown knight. Girls who hopped onto a tram, girls we hopped on after, and finally the embrace of unanticipated intensity, as if we had set off explosives inside each other.

They were looking for something more, or less, than I was. They were curious, and so was I. The bolder ones took the elevator; the more timid tiptoed up to the sixth floor and hesitated before ringing the bell. Thighs twisted and curled; nails clawed the bed; breasts swayed left and right; labia opened and closed, sopped and dried. You were good if you didn't toss her out, if you were willing to stick around, go for a drink, look at the falling snow, study the veining of a hand, hear out a family saga. They were psychologists and hairstylists, teachers and tapestry-makers, lawyers and medical assistants, opera singers and bookkeepers, ceramicists and bank tellers. What I like about many women is their two-sidedness: a woman without a hidden agenda is like a lily-of-the-valley without a scent. The lady comrade made it clear she disagreed with you in matters ideological, but demonstrated total agreement in matters sexual. Leaning against the banister, the doorjamb, the mirrored bureau, on the ground, in the bathtub, in the pantry, in the most unorthodox places. Sailing over hurdles, getting back at prohibitions, ending up in new beds beside new bodies observed with the exhilaration of a teenager.

The bed is warm, the radiator cold. I can reach the nose of the white Rococo angel with my left hand. I give it a pat. All's well with the world. I have developed a lifestyle not particularly suited to a married man, but permissible for one in the process of divorce. I go to bed early in the evening and get up at three a.m. Then I climb into the bathtub and lie back cross-legged, the cold water splashing over my chest. A goose-down comforter calls me back to its embrace in the unheated room. I deliberate whether to sanctify the day with a glass of tokay. (My sister Éva has had a case of tokay delivered to me from America.) My birthday is coming up, a number substantial if not round: twenty-seven. It is the year of our Lord Nineteen Hundred and Sixty.

I begin my day earlier than the schoolchild, earlier than the factory worker. I go out into the still-dark city, wending my way to the Pipacs Bar. They let me in; they are open until five. The guests are drifting homeward, and the only girls are the ones the taxis have brought back. There I sit by the jukebox, absorbed in the work of Samuel Beckett, engulfed by the smell of dusty curtains, polished shoes, coffee, cigarettes, beer, hairspray, and the body odors of a city where only every other apartment has a bathroom.

"Looking for decadence?" asks the pianist, his hands prancing around the keyboard. Am I looking for decadence? More a state of fallenness, the hour where makeup on wrinkles smudges, when the collar pops open behind the necktie, when the belt gets loosened a notch or two. The Finnish ambassador's son starts dropping glasses, but Gizi comes over and sweeps up the shards. "You just go ahead," she says. She gets a good tip for every sweep-up.

Out to the banks of the Danube, to the Pest abutment of the bombed-out Elizabeth Bridge! The little motorboat is not running yet, but I need to look at the water every morning from the steps that line the riverbank. It is not so long since we set out from here to a still backwater at the Tas locks, where the surface shone black and the waters lapped softly amid perfect silence. A factory owner whose plant had been appropriated by the state had survived the difficult Rákosi era by fishing there for sturgeon every morning and selling the catch to the better restaurants.

Leaving the Pipacs Bar one morning in early summer, I have a few words with the Petőfi statue: "Europe is quiet, Mr. Petőfi, quiet again. We're keeping our mouths shut as we did after 1848, after your revolution, and at least no one is getting shot into the Danube. But as you know, Mr. Petőfi, they hanged our Prime Minister, Imre Nagy, two years back. We were terribly broken up when the news was announced, and could think of nothing to say."

Ambrus Oltványi, our host that evening, made us excellent tea with a series of scything movements, a legacy of polio. Towering above us in bookshelves that reached to the ceiling was the intellectual history of the nineteenth century. We were overcome with the beauty of the view from his windows, but Ambrus tempered our enthusiasm. "Yes, it's beautiful all right, but beauty is a great thief of time."

Ambrus's father, Imre, was a great collector and patron of the arts, a former banker, a retired Minister of Finance, a great believer in civil society, and a translator of composers' biographies. He spent the worst years of communism in his bed in a silk robe, surrounded by teapots and ashtrays, the corner window darkened by a crimson velvet curtain. When his son speculated that the current regime might turn out a bit more liberal, Imre listened to him quietly as if he were a madman.

In 1961 I began a half-time job for Helikon preparing a ten-volume, onion-paper, leather-and-canvas-bound edition of Lev Tolstoy's collected works. My days passed under the sign of Tolstoy. I read *A Confession* sitting on the bank of the Danube by the remains of the Elizabeth Bridge.

It is a work unparalleled in its clarity of vision (particularly the first half), though lacking in personal humility in the face of the universe. It is an honest and passionate compendium of every pessimistic, existentialist, life-denying philosophy. Once the mind breaks away from the superficialities of a mechanical will to live and daily tasks and responsibilities and rejects its identity with its existence in time, in other words, once it begins to question life itself and has a good look at death (which it had previously lacked the imagination and freedom to know), it suddenly feels that mortal existence is distressingly pointless, repellent, and humiliating and that it is pointless to seek a goal or mission or anything higher into which one's individual existence may meld and find peace. Science is valid only when it deals with nature, which has no mind; it loses its validity the moment it tackles the human element. We have no goal, no future other than the pursuit of our own annihilation. The mind is incompatible with life. Consistent and logical thought leads to suicide.

The only way to keep suicide at bay, Tolstoy tells us, is to develop modes of behavior that skirt the issue. The common people, fettered by workaday struggles, are too dull to devote their lives to seeing things as they are. People surprised by death with a blow to the back of the head may be left out the equation. One pure type is the hedonist, who revels in intense pleasure, who does nothing but eat, drink, and make love; another is the scar-picker, who debases life instead of confronting death, who looks towards death half-crazed, with endless whining.

Then what sustains life? asks Tolstoy. What pulls a person through despair? What makes suffering worth the price? What pacifies the soul of the people? What structures our civilization? What in history transcends the personal?

Faith, answers Tolstoy. He first settles on religious faith, then searches for something personal. Faith and intelligence are unrelated. One cannot use the one to verify or support the other. After intelligence has done its work, faith demands its rights at the outer limit of our helplessness. (Faith and not God, Who is a consequence of faith, faith as one of the vital functions.) The concept of infinity does not arise from the circle of the finite. Faith carries us beyond the limits of the finite to a state of humility in the face of the infinite, a humility that releases us by undoing our very selves.

At this point his train of thought gives way to an apostolic brand of speech, which I did not follow in its stark moralizing tendencies, its idealization of the peasants and the poor, its depiction of the landowners' guilt, and its romantic opposition to civilization.

My own experience with the poor—manual laborers, people who have received the short end of the stick—has not borne out Tolstoy's claims. As I see it, we must all pass through the thinking man's stages of development. I can testify that Budapest's Chicago, Elizabeth Town, has developed a kind of raw, barroom variety of existentialism, the lives of its inhabitants subject to the same insoluble questions and same loneliness and consternation affecting those of us who are relatively well educated.

I would like to think I will never curse life, not even if I develop a serious illness. This is something I wrote forty years ago in the Kisposta Café. I prize *what is* with all its fortune and misfortune. I have no desire to break with this world or merge with it. For the time being I hope the world and I will keep staring each other down.

All I can assume about the future is that human life on earth will eventually disappear. This likelihood offers me no moral choice. I have always been amazed at how simpleminded religious concepts of the afterlife and communist-inspired (or other invented) utopias tend to be.

Both earthly and heavenly utopias presuppose a rejection of the world, of the here and the now. Any exaltation of the future entails a vilification of the present. Whatever my present existence may be like, I cannot wish for something radically and elementally different, because I do not believe in the possibility of such a thing. In fact, I find promises of theoretically good alternative states as repulsive as common lies.

Are we capable of living here in our bounded present, rejoicing when we can manage it, suffering when we are in pain, keeping the prospect of death before us, yet rejecting fear of the next time round, the other side?

Human beings are travelers, on their way somewhere. Once there, they are travelers no longer. Amidst all the suffering en route they naturally think of how nice it will be to get there, the way an exhausted person thinks of falling asleep to blank out everything. But it feels good to wake up the next morning too.

We live with three problems: the vexations of our daily existence, the uncertainty of our knowledge of the world, and the certain knowledge of our deaths. The believer says that God, the only truth, compensates for all this. Even the nonbeliever can hope for a friendly obituary or, in rare cases, a memorial tablet on the house where he lived. But some people require no compensation: they accept the problems and are unshaken by the ultimate uncertainty of their knowledge of the universe. How can one have certain knowledge of the universe when one can say nothing certain about one's nearest and dearest?

In this part of the world, people eat and drink a lot, buy ugly clothes off the rack, and watch television nonstop. They don't execute the opposition, because there is no more opposition. There are no happy and unhappy people; there is really nothing and no one at all. Our society is sometimes tedious, sometimes delirious. Having had it with uniformity, it is receptive to disorder of every kind. It is a glutinous heap, incapable of taking things seriously or knowing where to draw the line.

If you are looking for an elaborate, sublime apparition here, you are in for a disappointment. But if you feel you absolutely must have a genuinely local article, then try this: shapeless battles abandoned before they begin. All you can find here are the jumbled by-products of existence. Everyone is a snail, a caterpillar, a worm. We are strong on flesh, weak on spirit. People die of fatty degeneration of the heart. There is no slaughterhouse; it is all do it yourself. Premature debility carries you off.

I have tried to wring the self-pity out of my prose.

When I first met Júlia Lángh, who would be my wife from the autumn of 1960 to the autumn of 1976, she had floated into the Kisposta Café trailing blond hair and a rustling black raincoat and wearing a white blouse with a turned-down collar. She had just come from the university—where she had been accepted thanks to her perfect *gimnázium* record and a captivating articulateness—and entered the café, a first-year student in French and Hungarian, suppressing her timidity and wondering, "My God, what happens now? Who is that old man, that twenty-seven-year old?" She was not quite eighteen.

I would show up at six a.m. with notebook, pen, and ink, as if punching a time clock. It allowed me to watch the rendezvous, generally hurried, that took place before work.

Her overcoat unbuttoned, Juli sweeps in on the wind. It is better not to stand in her way, because she can bowl you over. (This gives a hint of things to come: while you gape at her in wonder, she has put breakfast on the table and talked Miklós into finishing his story some other time and Dorka to stop covering Miklós's mouth with her hand. But that is all a few years down the road. First she had to go through the university.) Her entrance does not go unnoticed. The waitress gives an approving glance to her inky-fingered regular: "Others have been pretty, true, but this one has the energy to match." Juli even has a manuscript in tow. The elderly gentleman emits a satisfied "Hmm." (She wrote well then, as she did forty years later, carrying our youngest grandchild in her arms on her way to the car, where our daughter-in-law sat at the wheel and our son Miklós sat calming his son Jankó, the three-year-old swooping eagle, as he spread a shielding wing over his three-month-old brother, who, he tells all and sundry, "is going bald.")

From that morning on, Juli and I saw each other practically every day for sixteen years. I could always be assured of stories: she is the kind of person whom elaborate things happen to, or who can make them happen. For her part she did not appear to find the stories of the aging welfare officer and part-time proofreader tedious and had no qualms about putting the necktied knight in his place when the stories turned into analyses. She was obviously free of all dishonorable intentions.

It was days before the first kiss, when her head leaned back just a bit. Then lips fused and bodies coupled to the point of exhaustion, leaving not a fingernail-sized patch on the other uncultivated—a mutual cultivation that continued until I checked two fabulous personalities in swaddling clothes out of the hospital across the street and put them in a cab.

Who are you? As we looked at each other, I tried to sail through her eyes to the harbor of the enigma. And who are those two figures in the slatted bed carrying on a mysterious conversation, sister supplying little brother with imaginative stories and he turning to her, the nearest authority, with his questions. Everything a family needed—except that I was not really there. The marriage classifieds of the day used to end: No adventurers need apply! They made me shudder.

During our courtship Juli would tactfully remind me to remove my arm from her shoulder when we neared her home, because the eyes in the windows had known her from earliest childhood and expected of her the sort of behavior befitting a young lady. Juli's grandmother asked her permission to leave the family's title of nobility hanging on the wall when her youngest granddaughter's suitor came to call, though she ultimately resigned herself to the fact that, though a polished gentleman to all appearances, he was (no use mincing words) a Jew. Jews can be decent, can they not?

There followed roughly sixteen years of cohabitation and submission to a common judgment—the children's gaze—confident as we were of the strict but fair verdict of Anna Dóra (1965) and Miklós István (1967) and hopeful as we were of their mercy.

The Case Worker appeared in 1969, the darkest book to come out during those years. I could not believe it was permitted to appear, so strongly did it call the regime's official self-portrait into question. No matter from what angle I read my words, I could find no hint of uplift, the hero and narrator of the novel merely handling his cases as best he can, trudging on, ever downward.

After 1956 many of us were in that situation. Our lives would straighten out only if the regime changed. But that did not seem possible. At best, change would be slow in coming. In the meantime we pulled our hats over our eyes.

In the morning I would report to my new job but soon abandoned it for the café on the corner, the Alkotás (Creation). Even so, I managed to get more done than those poor old fogies who run panting from tram stop to office. Signs of work flourished on my desk—charts, texts, slide rule (it was a planning bureau with liberal pretensions)—but the morning still belonged to me as it had in my earlier days as a welfare officer. I had begun to grow into the city. My person and my name were now recognized here and there.

It was in this context that Iván Szelényi and I did our first extensive urban sociological study in Pécs and Szeged. We used approaches current at the time. Walking into my first computer room I felt I was entering a temple: How does a system of settlement relate to the structure of society as a whole? How do people move in social space? How do they get where they are? I traveled the country using a flexible system of optics: at times a microscope, at times a telescope. I combined close-ups and long-distance shots within a single sentence. I had put politics on the back burner, my concern now being how we might put up with one another in a time that passes slowly.

I roamed about in search of useful conversation partners, walking the streets as if they were the stacks of a library filled with books I had never heard of. I sniffed around doorways and courtyards, copied out stairway and toilet graffiti (both offers and requests), and knocked about as if snuggling up to a woman with a boundless body.

The large hopes had gone up in smoke, but small hopes remained. At the time any celebration of life would have seemed a self-compromising form of kitsch, but love still served to counteract the constrictions of life. Amid so many prohibitions it felt good to eat forbidden fruit, break rules. The one-night stand had its honor.

And there was literature. Literature had remained an adventure. Who can tell what events will filter into our storytelling? The number of tellable tales far exceeds the number that can be put down on paper, and what we choose to put down on paper is arbitrary. You pull something out of the spectrum; you reject the rest. That is the karate of saying no.

The aim of a story is to be hard to forget. We writers take over selves we have never before inhabited. We look into the heads, and beds, of others. Can you be other than what you are? Once the child who needs no stories comes into this world, we must all start to worry.

As a child I would lie on my stomach in the darkness as it rolled in from the window in treacherous waves, pressing my fists into my eyelids to call up unforeseen images, images over which I had no control, withdrawing my will to let them flow where they pleased. Once they begin to flow, I told myself, let them happen, let them follow their own secret logic.

Later I would put off decisions, letting myself be swept into marriages (and jobs) and entrusting the progress of my life to happenstance. I felt that by doing something, I learned more about it than by not doing it. I felt a constant devilish temptation to escape the passage of time.

In 1973 I finished my second novel, *The City Builder*. Although the head of the Magvető Publishing House liked it, he felt he had to reject it because of its dark view of the world. (It was ultimately published in Hungary in 1977, minus certain passages, after it had come out in German and French, without official permission, in violation of the law.) Also in 1973—during a trial for incitement mounted against my friend Miklós Haraszti, the accusation centering on his superb essay "Piece Work"—the political police declared me a suspect and carried out several searches of my apartment, confiscating my diaries, firing me from my job, and depriving me of the right to travel abroad for three years.

In the spring of 1974, Iván Szelényi and I rented a peasant house in Csobánka, a mountain village not far from Budapest. The "sexton's house" was part of the parish priest's residence and led to a friendship with Father Zsigmond, a Benedictine monk. It was in this house that Iván and I wrote *The Intellectuals on the Road to Class Power* in secret. We planned to publish it abroad.

On New Year's Eve in 1974, a large group gathered in the one-and-a-half room studio apartment of the painter Ilona Keserű. We were surrounded by her colored arcs depicting female bodies, birds, and gravestones along with her engraving equipment and other tools. There was a mood of excitement in the air. It was reminiscent of sixty-eight. Our cultural region was preparing for something new. A subculture, in the broadest sense, had formed. There were alliances of friends in every possible field: everybody knew everybody else, and we met regularly. There were rival schools as well, and the tribal chiefs cast jealous glances at one another in the Young Artists' Club. The secret police cast their own glances, so as to prepare a precise description of the age in all its color. The Counterreformation was in full swing.

Having lost my position as urban sociologist the previous year, I was working as an assistant nurse at a work-therapy mental institution in the countryside. I directed story readings and excursions and chatted with the patients. My experience in the mental institution was indispensable for the novel I had just begun, *The Loser*. I learned a lot from both staff and patients. Rationality was part and parcel of our state culture, or had at least come to be absorbed into it, while critical attitudes—dissident attitudes, if you will—depend on *transrational* decisions. They may be matters of faith, they may result from a quick blow, but they are inevitable. You follow the path open to you, risk or no risk. But why? Is it intellectual gratification? A command issued by the hedonism of thought? It was sheer pleasure to think through the possibilities.

Friends of mine, superb minds and personalities, would poke a finger to their foreheads if we met on the street and ask me if I had lost my mind. "Have you no idea where you are living?" they would ask Iván and me. The simplest explanation for our (to them) incomprehensible acts was that we had understood something and written it down just because we felt like it.

Early one summer morning thirty years ago the doorbell rang and five men burst into my apartment brandishing a search warrant.

The Major looked over my papers, sat down at my desk, and said, "I'll crush you like a leaf." He was a nervous, pedantic man who bragged he would clean up the mess I had made in my filing cabinet. He told me that if I kept my keys in a leather pouch as he did they would not pull my jacket pocket out of shape. He instructed my children not to tangle up the tassels on the rugs. (At his house they had a special brush for keeping them straight.) He then informed his wife he would soon have done with the suspect and would hurry home so they would not miss the movie. That was how I found out that I was a suspect.

I asked him how I could have incited anyone to hate the basic institutions of the Hungarian People's Republic with my diary entries, when I kept them locked up in a filing cabinet. Nothing could be simpler, he said. If I had a visitor and went into the kitchen to make coffee, he could hop over to the filing cabinet, take out the diary, and read it. That was all it took, and there you had your criminal act, with me as criminal, my seditious diary as corpus delicti, and as victim—my curious but ideologically innocent guest who, during the time it took me to brew him coffee, had made his move. I always invite my guests to the kitchen when I make coffee, I told him. "The kitchen?" he asked, concerned, as if this would constitute an affront to my guest. Yes, I told him mildly. That's where coffee gets made. I also told him my friends didn't do things like poke through my manuscripts. The only people I knew who engaged in such warped practices were your people. Professionals, in other words, who were not susceptible to being incited to hate the fundamental institutions of the Hungarian People's Republic.

"Your daughter is eight years old. *She* can read her father's notes. The moment she lays eyes on them the conditions for regulation 127/b have been satisfied. In fact, I don't even need to establish the fact of her having seen them, only the possibility that she has. If the key is in the lock, the crime can take place—a *criminal act*, mind you. Because what you think is your own business, but once an enemy thought acquires objective written status, that is no longer a private matter."

I imagine he had just recently learned the phrase "acquires objective status." The Major liked sounding scholarly. "Besides, the key to the file cabinet is not on your key ring." This was hard evidence—of which he was duly proud.

The next day he sent a police car for our son Miklós's nanny. Erzsi had instinctively asserted that the Engineer's filing cabinet was always locked and she had never seen the key. The Major barked at her to stop lying. Erzsi blushed, then rose. A retired textile worker, she was a model proletarian and a member of the Workers' Guard. The young man had no right to call her a liar. She had worked her entire life in the same factory, lived in the same house. He could ask her coworkers or her neighbors whether she was a liar or not. (When she retold the story recently, she gave a little laugh and said, "The fact of the matter is I fibbed a little.")

In any case, the Major was unimpressed. When the Department of the Interior rescinded my right to travel abroad for three years and the Major personally saw to it that I was dismissed from my job (if I insisted on writing something that was bad for me, I must be suffering from a maladaptive disorder), their logic found support with certain friends of mine, all bright, decent people in their own right, who wished me well but took it for granted that challenging authority would elicit a stern response. Some thought me crazy, others devilishly clever—but I was really quite guileless. In any case, I was now a freelancer after eleven years in the employ of the state.

Not that I had ever wished for a public role, a podium under my feet. The Major had saved me from an institutional career. If anything, my goal was internal emigration: a garden I would leave only to satisfy obligations I felt obliged to comply with. I had no desire to win or to lose, just to hold out a while longer. God forbid I should be the carrier of some first person plural. I shun the high ground that inspires envy. Even while under the employ of the state I managed to avoid having a single subordinate. I am at home only in groups where all are equal and speak in their own name—and feel free to tease one another. When required to speak or read on a stage, I slip back down as soon as possible.

After 1973 Iván and I could be sure that every document ultimately reached *them*, that *they* read every sociological interview we made. We wrote; they read. Research became evidence: every fact became part of the case against us; every wiretapped word made it stronger. Words could sweep you away, force you into roles, set traps for you to fall into, turn against you; they could make you do things you never dreamed of.

I first encountered Iván Szelényi at some meeting or other and found him standoffish, but then most of my friends are standoffish. He asked me from behind his pipe, "So you people are doing a survey too?" My answer came out a dilettantish jumble that only reinforced the wearily magnanimous superiority of the fellow, whom I judged to be five years my junior (about twenty-eight to my thirty-three). His jacket and tie were perfect. Everything about him bespoke the civilized young scholar, a rare bird in our context.

I was taken aback by the *you people* as well. So my office and I were a *we*? And he was with the Academy's Sociological Institute. But we soon realized our institutions could pool forces and create a new wave in Hungarian urban sociology. Our incipient friendship provided an added stimulus, but neither mentioned it explicitly: we were too bashful.

Suddenly I was a young Turk reformer in a planning and research institute of the ministry. Iván and I—published professionals from Budapest, presenters at conferences where the most the local eminences could do was make a comment or two—mocked or disparaged things they still found interesting and respectable.

As I have said, Iván taught me that walks are the sociologist's primary modus operandi: If you want to know what a city is like, walk its streets. Observe the rocking chairs along the narrow, sloping sewage gutters that go by the name of thoroughfares in Pécs's poverty-stricken Zidina neighborhood. Watch the grandmother telling stories to her grandchild. Note the mirror up by the window enabling the old woman to follow who is walking along the street, ensuring her a constant flow of fresh information from the outside world.

Iván had an eye for such details along with a propensity for good dinners with our mostly local colleagues, who became our sources for gossip and local folklore. The morning after, they would take us to the Gypsy settlement or to the new row of elegant apartments they dubbed "Cadre Ridge." We also paid visits to any number of locals: council presidents, party secretaries, ancient barons, priests, schoolteachers, blacksmiths, gardeners, merchants, miners.

I would step out of my front door in Budapest at eight a.m., and by ten the propeller plane had me in Széchenyi Square in Pécs, where I began the day at a marble table at the Café Nádor, watching the locals coming and going southern style, in waves. Then Iván and I would set off, exchanging greetings with the people we met—men leaning on shovels in their gardens, women with net shopping bags, short-skirted, ponytailed girls whom we asked for directions.

We were the saccharine-smiled, arrogant sophisticates who had seen so much of the world. I had spent a total of maybe two months in the West; I had written in a café on the Île de la Cité, observed the blue-aproned peasants in a nearby village, and lain at the nearby seashore in Normandy alongside the great *transatlantique*, the *France*. Iván was a hopeless cosmopolitan who had spent a year in America on a Ford Foundation grant. When I asked him to describe New York, he said, "You're in New York and you're tossing and turning with insomnia because you have no lion. So you grab your wallet and out you go and before you know it you've got a lion on a leash."

"Hmm," I said to myself. "Why didn't this man go into literature?"

One night a good ten years later I had trouble sleeping in New York and went into the first grocery store I found to ask where I could get my hands on a lion. "Wouldn't you rather have a nice tongue sandwich?" asked the owner, a strapping fellow with a smile to match.

Which all goes to show that research and a sense of humor are not mutually exclusive and that you could do good work under the old system as well. The orange Volkswagen that was the vehicle for our merry pop-sociology, with our younger colleague Róbert Manchin at the wheel, took us to one after another of the hundred-odd villages we had chosen at random. In a parsonage we devoutly touched the four-hundred-year-old desk on which the Calvinist preacher Gáspár Károlyi had translated the entire Bible from Hebrew and Greek. We would take large bags of children's clothes out to the Gypsy settlements, where kids ran out of their shanties naked through the snow, bombarding us with their "Money, Mister! Give us money!"

Sometimes we thought we would simply observe them and describe their social structures; sometimes we imagined that if we managed to define the situation reforms might come of it. But the system, the ultimate subject of our observations, searched our apartments one day, initiating what would become a long series of unpleasantries, probably under the impression that if they put us on strict notice and isolated us, others would learn from our example and we would either come to our senses or leave the country as our Russian, Czech, and East German dissident colleagues had. We were naive perhaps, but so were the authorities. We persevered.

We persevered with Iván's peripatetic method, lugging the tape recorder up hill and down dale, discussing our subjects while perching on Serbian gravestones in Csobánka or a bench at the base of Oszoly Cliff. Then came the precise formulation beneath old brown rafters and bugging devices. We grew accustomed to passing the narration back and forth, giving signals to one another, rewording sentences that, though perfectly fine to begin with, assumed added luster from an unexpected twist or transition.

Our primary theme was how the regime was being ground down through conflicts among parties of opposing interests. The table of contents was as clear as a Christmas tree; only the ornaments were wanting. But Iván's main concern was the relationship of trunk to branch, while I was more interested in content and improvisation. Every time our exhaustive conversations helped us to make a point more clearly, we earned a refreshing hike up the Oszoly Cliff. We fleshed out my old idea that history was the locus of the intellectual, the knight of totality, the poet of thoughts, explanations, principles, and nightmare scenarios, the elevating force and the force of outrage. Look to the words, for in the beginning was the word. Look to the modelers of sentiment, the confectioners of feeling. Look to their own rhetorical gumbo. Before long it dawned on me that our exchange of ideas was beginning to intrigue me more than socialism's miseries and even socialism's prospects.

One day we heard there had been a search in the Ágnes Heller–Ferenc Fehér household. Their agenda being dissident like ours, we grew more cautious. A few times we wrapped the typescript in a plastic bag, placed it in a box, and buried it, though in less careful moments we simply hid it in the coal bin under the coal. That every room in the bell tower had a bugging device in a saucer-sized porcelain holder recording our every snore or key stroke or love groan—of this we had no inkling. We did not consider ourselves important enough. True, we had heard of Solzhenitsyn's deportation to the West, of exiles domestic and foreign; we had heard that Andropov, the former ambassador to Budapest, was now at the head of the Soviet Secret Police and shaking things down, purging the resistance counterculture, but it never occurred to us that our Hungarian counterpart would resort to similarly coarse measures. Before long we had to accept the fact that they were doing so: I had told my wife that there was a key in the silver sugar-cube container in my mother's glass cabinet, and the next time they raided the house, that was the first place they went.

From then on, whenever we needed to discuss anything to do with writing and manuscripts or politically sensitive encounters, we wrote it out on slips of paper we then flushed down the toilet. It also became second nature to look for nooks and crannies the size of the typescript. What we wanted to conceal most was how far along we were. I was afraid the manuscript would be seized as soon as it was completed, so I always denied any progress. When asked on the phone, "Are you working?" I would answer I was just pottering around.

"You are an intellectual resister," said one of my interrogators. Until then I had not thought of myself as such, but I liked the way the police officer put it. I grew more sensitive to the police lexicon. I spotted the eye watching me from a little hole scratched in the paint of the window of a shop in our building, a shop that was never open. I sensed that two faces were following me from two windows in the building across the street. I started recognizing the men in cars that rolled slowly past me and the old man leaning on his elbows in the courtyard and the people behind me whose footsteps never let up and the car parked by the front gate. I had the clear feeling that the policeman who came to the bell tower to check my papers and ask what I was doing in the town was an integral part of the machinery whose charge was to ensure the survival of the Great Lie.

Since we paid little attention to either communist or anticommunist ideologies, we befouled the self-images of the unofficial and official intelligentsias alike. Feeling insulted in the name of the intelligentsia, even our opposition friends took issue with *Intellectuals on the Road to Class Power*. What had happened, we concluded in the book, was that the intelligentsia was ensuring that the system functioned effectively by refraining from calling the power hierarchy into question, while perceiving itself as an abused victim and thereby absolving itself of responsibility.

One hot Sunday afternoon my friend the film critic Yvette Bíró brought a sad and skeptical Czech film director to the garden at Csobánka. Iván and I felt an immediate intellectual affinity with him and graced him with our most precious thoughts, but all he did was shake his head. "You'll be behind bars before you finish. And such bright people!"

One sunny morning my friends Gabriella Hajós (Zsabó) and György Jovánovics came out to Csobánka with me. While Zsabó stood watch down below, the sculptor took before-and-after photographs: first of what those ugly, old-fashioned bugging devices looked like in situ in the loose clay, then of what the loose clay looked like without them. I had ripped them out like carrots. Not knowing what to do with them, I tossed them into the kitchen cupboard along with the other trash. That evening, as usual, I took the bus and commuter train back to Budapest. The next day, when I reentered the Csobánka house, I noticed that my treasure was no longer in the kitchen cabinet. I was not such a free spirit as Václav Havel, who hawked his bugging devices at the flea market.

We did not intend to publish our book in Hungary; we wanted it to come out in normal countries, that is, in the West. I imagined it my duty as a citizen to see to the publication of the book, after which whatever happened did not much matter. My wife helped us to type it up, and we asked a friend of mine, Tamás Szentjóby, to photograph it page by page, the few photocopy machines in the country being under the supervision of the political police.

Walking along Péterpál Street in Budafok, where a row of houses once belonging to vintners ran up the hill, I was reminded of my hometown. We are so fatefully shaped by the place we lived before the age of ten that only in a similar setting can we feel at one with our perceptions. I kept returning to the second chapter in my novel, the one on childhood and the family. Life, for me, was beautiful, and to the question "How are you?" I generally answered—strange as it might seem to an outsider—"Great." This feeling dates from my days at the *gimnázium*, when all it took to make me happy as I left the house in the morning was the knowledge that I had no obligations for the day and could go off by myself.

One day, out of the blue, another friend, Tibor Hajas, came to say that Tamás had been arrested: searching his apartment for pornographic literature, the authorities had come upon our manuscript. The couple necking constantly by my front gate turned out to be police officers. Ambulances and taxis would follow our steps, as did all sorts of conspicuously average-looking men and women—or odd-looking men and women, if they wanted to be noticed. Since things like this could happen solely with the permission of or on the orders of Party Headquarters, we could only deduce that our own arrests were not far off.

We told each other that come what may our efforts had been worth it, and agreed on a story: we had no idea whose manuscript it was or what it was. Disowning one's work was a remnant of an earlier time, when you could get years for partial authorship of a leaflet.

Iván's wife Kati and I saw him off to the Belgrade train. He still had a valid exit visa for Yugoslavia. Naturally he was taken off the train and sent back. We were green at the game of resistance.

One day two men followed Iván into the sauna at the Csillaghegy pool with orders to arrest him. They sweated it out there on either side of him for three-quarters of an hour, taking his arm only when the three of them stepped out of the pool's main entrance together.

I had a desire, undoubtedly childish, to give them the slip, throw off their calculations, spoil their game. At least I could gain time. Once word got out, the decision-makers might come under pressure from writers or even their children. I asked my first wife Vera to put me up for a while.

I doubt I had been in Vera's seventh-floor apartment for more than two days—reading, watching the birds in the gutter and the slow-working roofers on the building across the street (who were watching me as well, since they were not real roofers) when the officers of state security knocked on the door. It was 23 October 1974. They had first gone for Vera at her school, bringing her with them as a witness, but all they wanted was me. They did not even bother to ransack the place. I thanked Vera, shoved a toothbrush into my pocket, and followed the plainclothesmen out of the house.

Lieutenant Colonel Gyula Fehér, who politely asked me to forgive him for taking up so much room in the back seat, was my interrogator. He told me he had suffered a great deal reading our work, unaccustomed as he was to such vocabulary and train of thought. Despite doses of strong coffee he had fallen asleep more than once over it.

"So the study did not particularly provoke you," I said.

"Not at all," he acknowledged.

"Then why am I here?"

The Lieutenant Colonel lifted his arms skyward.

The handwriting sample established the corrections to the typescript to be in my hand.

"Is this your work?" I said it was, thus breaking the agreement I'd had with Iván, who stuck to the story that we'd had nothing to do with the manuscript. I thought they would be unable to bring formal charges against us, because no one had seen the text besides its authors; in other words, they had jumped the gun. I decided they wanted to annihilate the book by confiscating every copy.

I found confinement tolerable: getting up early, swabbing the floor in the cell, eating bean soup and potatoes with noodles. The prison library supplied readable books, and the authorities allowed me to sign an authorization enabling my wife to pick up the royalties I had received from the American publication of *The Case Worker*. The Lieutenant Colonel regularly recited his favorite scenes from Hašek's *Good Soldier Švejk*. We did not speak about the book itself, only about the other copy. The expert had determined its existence, based on the confiscated copy, whose cover showed the traces of carbon paper.

One morning I woke up sensing I had gained a perspective on the matter. I would suggest they put it out as an in-house publication alongside Trotsky and Djilas. They might think me an idiot, but there was no harm in that. The point was to nip this in the bud or at least before it entangled others. Friends were bound to have their apartments searched and be summoned and questioned as witnesses. We needed to gain time. We would publish the book once things calmed down. (Iván had hidden the "real" second copy and the working manuscript.) I would work on my next novel, *The Loser*, and find a safe place for it.

In the meantime, we would give the authorities the feeling their work was not in vain. I would let them have the third copy, which could not possibly have carbon marks on the cover. They would have obtained a manuscript with some police value and could hope, for the moment at least, that the book existed nowhere else. I decided to let them have it on two conditions: that they release us both immediately and that the person in possession of the manuscript suffer no ill consequences.

Such was the line I gave them the following day. A few hours later the Lieutenant Colonel, acting on the authority of his superiors, accepted my terms. I took a seat with him in the police car, and off we drove to the flat of my sister-in-law, Zsuzsa Lángh, and her husband Ernő Sándor, who had done some fancy driving to ditch the car trailing them, get the manuscript to their place, and hide it in their tile oven. Both were at home. Pale and stunned, they acceded to my request that they turn the manuscript over.

That very afternoon, all three of us—Szelényi, Szentjóby, and I—were released on probation. An official decree forbade us from publishing the hostile document (the book) or even communicating its contents verbally. Any violation would result in criminal prosecution. Should we feel unable to adapt our activities to the laws of the Hungarian People's Republic, the authorities would countenance our emigration. We could even take our families with us. Iván said he would give it some thought, but I told them, "No, I am a Hungarian writer."

Then our case received a bit of attention in the Western press—Kissinger had supposedly asked about us—and we both decided to emigrate together with our families and proceed with our work at a university in the West. We would need job offers and visas and an exit passport, all of which we pursued through official channels.

Although life in the academy abroad seemed feasible, I had trouble picturing myself as a grateful émigré and (if all went well) university professor: I would tire of it; it would seem a waste of time. On days when something kept me from writing, I would be nervous and grumpy and get the urge to escape to a spot where

I could go out into a garden for some air, where no one would bother me.

I was an enthusiast, yet infantile. On my first day in a new city—east or west, large or small—I could imagine spending the rest of my life there. This would be *my* window and so on. Yet walking through town the next day, I had the urge to move on, generally homeward. To Csobánka, perhaps, where, surprisingly, no one searching the house had ever lifted the tabletop in my bell-tower room, where the notes for my novel lay untouched.

I settled back into my routine, writing in small lined notebooks in Budapest cafés. A button-eyed observer often watched me ply my trade. When there is danger, when the crowds stampede, stand still. I would abandon plans to emigrate, I wrote to György Aczél, the Party official in charge of cultural affairs, if they published my novel *The City Builder*, called off the police harassment, and let Szelényi leave. The way I put it, my decision to remain in Hungary was a sacrifice, a gift, though in fact it was the desire to continue the life I had led hitherto, a life I considered neither fruitless nor disagreeable. Aczél replied that no one could prescribe conditions to him but that he did not find my requirements outlandish.

It was painful to both Iván and me when I informed him we would not be a team writing in the West. You could stay too; we'd get by somehow, I thought. And he: You promised to come, and now you're going back on your word. Do you really think you'll be able to write your books, publish them in the West, and continue to take your constitutional through the streets of Budapest? Yes, that's exactly what I thought. And that's what happened. Thus began the decade and a half of my life as a banned, underground writer.

Children are smart. When I was arrested and Juli found her hands full, she took our seven-year-old Miklós to stay overnight with Feri Fehér and Ágnes Heller, who had a son about the same age. Miklós played with him all afternoon, but when evening came he took Feri aside and asked him with a touch of an aristocratic intonation, "Are you a good person?"

Sensing what he meant, Feri answered, "Yes Miklós, I believe I am."

"Good," said Miklós. "Then I'll sleep at your place."

Influenced by tendencies I observed in myself and those around me at the mental institution where I began to work at the time, I tried to view mental illness as a behavioral strategy, an individual concept of the world. The patient may act strange, but he sees himself as an innovator. Such might be well be a description of my type of dissident, I thought. The hero of my novel was committed to an asylum. Confiscated copies of the novel were condemned to destruction by court order as "hostile material." Not me, just a few years of my work.

Ultimately the mental institution is a reflection of state power. The illnesses there are fed by that world, which provides its causes and its symbols. Rationality was part and parcel of our state culture (or at least claimed to be), while critical attitudes—dissident attitudes, if you will—depend on transrational decisions. You follow the path you believe in, risk or no risk. But why? Intellectual gratification? The hedonism of thought? It was sheer pleasure to think through the possibilities.

After being dismissed from everywhere at the age of forty-three, I no long needed to put up with nerve-racking types (though I had always handled them fairly well), so I exiled myself to a garden, where, relaxed, I had plenty of time to sort things out. Enough money had come in from my writings to keep us going for a few more months. But our lives were not without risks—the aforementioned house searches, bugging, surveillance, and the three-year travel restriction—and my wife Juli was banned from the radio, where she had been giving insightful and refreshing book reviews every morning just before eight.

Writing counts as action only in unusual circumstances. Throughout most of the twentieth century writing had a chance to become action here in Hungary. All it had to do was go beyond the norm. Almost any statement was an opportunity for anti-state agitation.

Just after I lost my job a thick-browed colleague stuck his head into my office and whispered, "You sealed your own fate." But I despised the idea of begging my way back into the fold. Officially sanctioned normality contains all the symptoms of neurosis. Only the free are healthy, and the healthy are their own masters. The sick are directed by others: they are dependent, they cannot take care of themselves, stand on their own two feet, make decisions, see things as they are. They see what they want to see—or what they fear.

Excluded from regular employment, I recognized my condition as consistent with the logic of the centralized party state. Hence it did not enter my mind to make the rounds of the editorial offices. I knew they had no choice but to reject my work out of hand. And yet I occasionally experimented with submitting an article. The weak-willed did not even respond, while the stronger wrote something to the effect that they did not dare publish me. Ultimately I let up: I was ashamed to have put them in such a position.

I was now convinced I was not cut out for steady jobs in the East or West. Much as I respected all those who sawed and sanded, taught, or examined patients, I was thrilled to be released from it all, and viewed my life as an endless holiday. Only the typewriter's thump lent a touch of respectability to my activity—after all, typists were considered workers—but in fact, thanks to the generosity of the system, I was a pipe-smoking rocking-chair adventurer.

Too lazy and inept to handle the organization that went with oppositional activities, I did not get much involved, especially since political activism started early in the morning—my best time of day—which I never would have considered giving up. I stuck to formulating and distributing antipolitical texts.

It was hard for insiders in the old system to imagine that anyone would leave their ranks in the state power apparatus for civilian life. But representation, respect, and remuneration I needed like a hole in the head. Some make time to do what they like; others do not. The Gypsy nailsmiths from the outskirts of Csobánka had time to go into the woods and gather mushrooms whenever it rained. If a CEO headed for the woods on a workday morning, people would think him insane. I admired artisans supporting their families from their homes and gardens, oblivious of professions requiring them to report to the boss at a fixed time every day.

But even as I sat in the small Gypsy pub in Csobánka looking deep into my golden-yellow marc, I had to admit it was better to walk in the sun in a foreign city than pace the same five steps up and down in a cell here at home. Why then did I cling to the homeland?

The white walls in the Csobánka sexton's house and the dark wooden cross-beamed ceiling had not changed in over a hundred years. Beyond the grassy area at the kitchen door stinging nettles grew among the fruit trees. To the left of the door stood a marble table, once a tombstone. That is where I worked. The garden produced an abundance of fruit: sour cherries, walnuts, apricots, pears, and endless plums. In fat years a couple of the more tired branches would break under the weight of their yield.

A small lane arched upward past the house. It was called Red Army Boulevard and was sprinkled with white, gravelly sand and an occasional tuft of grass. On Sunday mornings the elderly, black-clad, kerchiefed and bonneted women of the village wended their quiet way up the lane clutching prayer books. Few people used the lane during the week, so I was assured of privacy. Only the parish priest might drop in of an afternoon, but he soon went his way. "Our humble respects for the fever of creativity!" he would say, leaving the memory of many smiles.

If I made a noise stepping out of the house, the deer at the end of the garden would prick up its ears, slink behind my back, and butt me gently with its peach-fuzzed antlers. The dog would bark, then fling himself prostrate while the deer rubbed its belly. But the deer's best friend was a feisty Japanese cock that slept with it, burrowing under its belly to keep warm. The cock's alliance with the deer reinforced its cockiness, and it would bluster like a rowdy and give horrific crows with a voice as thin as its body.

I had set a few stumps in the grass for seating, but they had been taken over by ant colonies. If I gave one of them a kick, it shook their world like an earthquake, sending them pouring to the surface in a frenzy, saving eggs and crumbs and bumping into one another in zigzag paths of panic. Desperate, tens of thousands streamed up from the depths, blackening the stump in a mad society that, seen from above, behaves not a whit more reasonably than our own. Once the danger (during which they occasionally bite off one another's heads in terror) has passed, they will boast of their heroism and the trials they have suffered. I give the trunk one more kick and the ants swirl out in even greater torrents. May they enjoy the shocks of history. After chaos comes peace, when they will have to reorganize and depose the incompetent leaders. In the company of the deer, the dog, and the cock I observe the ants coming to their senses, crawling back into the fissures of their shaken universe. The fickle god's wrath has faded.

Cloaked in my jaded and enigmatic cruelty, I, the Lord, head back to the house. Why should I, incorrigible scoundrel that I am, refrain from exerting my power as long as I have it?

The way I spent my time was my reward and my punishment. I concocted wiles to trick my congenital stupidity. If I was unpleasant, I had to put up with an unpleasant character. *L'enfer, c'est les autres*? What if it's me? Locked in a dark room, the only light from a screen: myself in an endless loop.

I enjoyed going back from Csobánka to the wild chestnuts along the bank of the Danube in Buda. I found something to my liking in almost every café and pub and did not mind the slowness of life. What comes of its own accord is enough.

From age forty to fifty-five I was a nonperson in my country, a person whose very presence violated the regulations. My response to the prohibition against working and publishing? An unchecked, internal, authorial freedom. I distributed my work in samizdat, usually Gábor Demszky's underground press. Not only did I receive no fee, I regularly contributed to the printing expenses, considering the dissemination of my works in Hungary a public service.

I could spend the day at my desk and the evening with people I wanted to see. There were a few I would rather not have seen, the ones who stood around on the corner or sat in a car by the door. They accompanied me everywhere, but kept a respectable distance, not really disrupting my solitude. Blacklisting and internal emigration were not so much blows dealt by fate as the result of a decision on my part, so it was my duty to cope with the vexations that went with them.

It was impossible to be normal here at home, and putting a good face on it was an unpardonable offense. The critical intelligentsia saw itself as a separate camp: us, with the police on our trail, versus them, bearers of the prevailing mindset and therefore police-free. People published all sorts of attacks on me, but I neither responded nor penned any of my own. I could never understand where their hostility came from. It took the utmost self-discipline and sense of humor to keep from going mad.

At eleven I was compelled to accept the reality that the spirit of the age was doing its best to have me shot and tossed into the Danube. Bad experiences made me suspicious earlier than most. Big words? Big words can turn people into child murderers.

As a banned author I had the luxury of being free from the expectations of others: I didn't need to embrace local public prejudices; I didn't need to be confident or outraged or despairing; I didn't need to worry about the authorities taking umbrage at what

I wrote. I required no future different from the present I was living in if for no other reason than that I did not believe in the possibility of a different future.

I am watching the Moscow May Day celebrations on television: a giant soldier extending his arms across the entire facade of a building, tight phalanxes lined up in Red Square. The flag-bearing gymnasts along the edge of each formation are dressed in white. Only the most distinguished—winners of workers' competitions—are allowed to appear in the square. Under the pictures of Marx, Engels, and Lenin there are pictures of the current Party leaders, and beneath those the men themselves.

Every participant at the great assembly holds a little red flag in his hand. Filmed from above, the network of roads stretching through those human colonnades looks geometrically regular. Between the carpet of citizens (the first-string squad, as it were) and the complex of platforms (with Lenin's mausoleum as its center) stands a wall of white-gloved policemen at attention; above them—the marshals, their medal collections clinking and flashing on their chests, along the parapet of the mausoleum—the leaders of the Party and the government, dressed in the state's version of men's fashion: a dark gray overcoat and a dark gray hat pulled down to eyebrow level. Dour old men waving at the crowds there to hail them.

Bugle fanfares. Brezhnev doffs his cap and steps up to the microphone. He struggles with a text written by others and full of long words. A face covered with the wrinkles and bags of arrogance. Behind him, gruff and motionless, the other leaders, their hands behind their backs now, jaded faces sunken inward, obviously heedless to his words. "Warm greetings, the struggle for the workers' happiness." The leaders turn their heads sternly, left, right. When the boss has finished, the two leaders standing next to him initiate the applause. The crowd takes it up. Once in a while the men on the parapet remove their hands from their pockets as if out of a sense of obligation and strike them together a few times. They have absent faces with no curiosity. Athletes on large platforms carry those faces past the parapet.

This is the seventies. I go out onto the highway, where a sign indicates that taking pictures is prohibited. Of what? A missile silo? A radar station? The forest entrance of an underground weapons factory, accessible by a high-quality cement road? The small hill sloping up to it could house a tomb. The miniature bugging devices manufactured there suffice for all Eastern Europe.

The surrounding fields are uncultivated; grazing is prohibited. Through the strips of forest that line the road I catch glimpses of gray concrete buildings, guard towers, targets, bunkers, all ringed by a concrete fence covered with furls of barbed wire. Officers' housing is hidden behind a painted brick wall at the edge of the village. Children play ball behind barbed wire; husbands walk with their wives among the prefabricated apartment buildings; shaven-headed soldiers run back and forth along a beam three meters off the ground wearing full marching gear and carrying machine guns; little flags of indeterminate symbolism flutter atop the dusty hills; a jeep carrying two drums of milk pops out of nowhere.

Soviet troops—temporary guests in the country for thirty years now, athletic, pimpled kids smelling of sweat and foot cloths, staring through the fences of the garrisons where they were confined for months on end—wore the sad looks of sons separated from their mothers combined with a touch of arrogance. Guarding their armored vehicles and rocket launchers, they would gape with wild envy at the natives in colorful clothes walking and driving by. The only time they would be seen individually was on their way to the station for the Moscow express after their one- or two-year stint. Odd occupiers they were. Everything they had was beat up. Even the vehicles looked jerry-built.

A somber procession of trucks has been flowing past in an endless iron stream, each truck towing one out of commission, every second vehicle unusable. Only after two hours does it come to an end and we can go and buy our milk and bread.

I was always a bourgeois by nature and a dissident by compulsion. We inhabited a mad world in which the written word seemed to carry unfathomable weight, when in fact it did not. The most important structural component in the defunct political system was its thought, its texts, its curricula. That being the case, I sat down every morning to produce sentences that could pass for incitement against the state, and a good many people who deserved better dashed around spying to make sure a few warmed-over clichés did not see the light of day. My bag held neither bomb nor revolver; it held only a notebook. Just when I thought I was getting used to the situation, I ran into a young man who was being followed by three cars for having made copies of one of my studies. The cowboy-and-Indian games involved in publishing a few hundred copies of a dissident text unofficially kept both sides busy. No country house containing printer's ink and thinner escaped police surveillance.

Here at home I led a muffled existence. Living in Eastern Europe meant being constantly prepared for defeat and backwardness but also to question what it is to be human. There was no real dictator, only a long line of downtrodden individuals, each imagining that everyone in front of them was an informer and everyone behind them a reckless anarchist. But once informing has become common currency—and the informer the model citizen—what is left to inform about? Where is the truth whereby we can recognize the liar?

"Waiter! The bill, please! And would you be kind enough to tell me where I might find God?"

"I recommend the golden noodles with vanilla sauce, sir."

"In that case, could you tell me when things will improve?"

"Never."

In 1976 I received a fellowship from the DAAD, the German Academic Exchange Service, for a yearlong stay in West Berlin. My three-year travel ban having expired, I wrote a letter to Premier János Kádár requesting permission for a one-year stay abroad. Unusual as it was in those days, not only I but my wife and two children received a passport with the necessary stamp.

Given that Juli was a teacher of French and did not speak German, she decided to take the children to Paris. Nor had she any intention of returning: she had no wish to go on living in a police state. My feeling was that since I had started out as a Hungarian writer I might as well finish as one. This led to a divorce, my wife remaining in Paris with our children, who were entering their teens, and I returning home in 1979 after an extended, two-year stay in the West.

After walking Budapest for five days, I stopped being amazed that people were speaking Hungarian. My nose was no longer struck by the stench of unrefined gasoline. The dark gray buildings, the dusty shopwindows, the electrical wires sticking out near the staircases, the half-finished repairs in the courtyards, the pocks of bullets from the war and 1956—everything looked familiar again. I took down the things my mother had put up on the walls except for a photograph of my children. I bought the books that looked interesting, sat in each of my armchairs in turn, and spent time in apartments whose familiar decay did not surprise me. I took pleasure in the spreading boredom.

I tried to make out what had happened in my absence. A little more was permitted. The long-haired, self-styled avant-garde artists had had haircuts; the young women had learned to cook and were having babies. People who had longed to go abroad had come to grips with the idea of trying to be happy here at home. Young historians were proud to question the Party line about 1956 and surprised that it caused no great stir in the world. Political dissidents were becoming chief architects, theater directors, and editors-in-chief, buying better cars, taking trips abroad. There were jokes they could no longer laugh at.

I made a raw kind of peace with it all and with the somnolent passing of time and things. I shrugged my shoulders. "Everything's fine with me. You're all fine just as you are." The apartment was full of silence and nights that were not always easy.

If I switched on the light and looked around, I was amazed to see where I was. Persian rugs on the floor, a matching (if improvised) set of furniture that had seen better days, an Empire table with copper inlay that bore a tea saucer's marks, and the library, in disarray, with shelves reaching up to the ceiling. The cracks in the once white, now gray walls sketched the face of a camel, which I used to scan to establish where I was. I never had the room replastered. My wish was to leave behind as few traces of myself as I could and intervene as little as possible in the lives of those around me. In spite of everything, this was the only place where I could speak without making grammatical errors, where I did not need to be embarrassed every time I opened my mouth.

I ran into my former boss. Until the authorities ordered him to fire me, he had been kind and called me into his office for chats, but once the political police said the word he had dismissed me on the spot. He had trouble extending his right hand after transferring the dog's leash to the left one. He too had had a stroke. All he remembered was what good friends we had been.

Looking around on the boulevard, I would think that everyone was a Communist, everyone I saw there—not just the Party members or the flag-wavers, everybody. Even people who hated the system, because they could not stop thinking about it. Not just the coachman, the horse too. Everyone who lived here. Including myself.

From my childhood until 1989 I lived with the consciousness that anyone who followed his own path had to reckon with the possibility of ending up between guard towers. By shaping his own life, the iconoclast made it more likely that others—and less likely that his own self-neglect—would kill him. The anxious desire to make life last as long as possible is a form of suicide.

Sitting at the marble gravestone table in Csobánka, I even remembered things that had not happened to me. But whatever you remember did in fact happen to you. Since the life of a mortal lasts no longer than the fall of a raindrop, I cling fast to anything inhabited by time.

Back from my Csobánka hermit's lair to my Buda apartment I receive a telephone call from a friend in telephone code: Had I heard the news? We meet at the Angelika Pastry Shop with its view of the eclectic neo-Gothic Parliament, where representatives approved every single motion submitted. (We recognized the lady and two gentlemen who came in the wake of the phone call for the pleasure of seeing and listening to us.) Had I heard, he asked, that Gábor Demszky had been openly followed for days on end, and when they stopped him for not using his directional signals they found the manuscript of my novel *The Loser*. They'd hauled him into the district police station, confiscated the documents, and taken minutes of the interrogation. Nine miniature bound copies of my novel were confiscated at the publisher's. *That* again?

In idyllic Csobánka one tended to forget where one was living.

In 1982 I entitled an essay I wrote there "Antipolitics," given that everything was political. A few years later a panting Demszky dashed up to my place with a heavy bag over his shoulder—fresh copies of *Antipolitics*. Written and published in secret, it argued that the time had come for a peaceful end to the Iron Curtain and the missile dialogue. The matter should be handed over to the Europeans. After the attempts at freedom in Budapest, Prague, and Warsaw had been quashed and avenged, Moscow and Berlin were next. Send home the Russian troops! Bring on the Russian tourists!

Europe, and particularly Central Europe, has Berlin to thank for so much. Think of the millions of lives lost, think of the decades wasted because of Berlin's arrogance. Had Berlin not instigated a war, there would be no Soviet troops in Budapest shoring up a system in which the publication of an uncensored book turned into a midnight secret, a conspiracy, a criminal act ("the preparation and circulation of materials containing incitement to action against the state") that could get you as much as eight years.

From the armchair I had a view of the top of the cliff, and by standing I could catch a glimpse of Jutka's dark head and long thighs. She was inspecting the fruit trees one by one, while studying a useful little book called *A Small Garden Is a Thing of Great Joy*. She was planning to plant dill, asparagus, bok choy, and eggplant. There would be flowerbeds, a lawn, and perhaps a child as well.

We are both Aries. Once I tossed out an offhand remark, and she answered with something brusque. I left in a huff, and she hurled mugs and spoons and unseemly curses at me from the balcony. She told me to wait, then ran down and tore my shirt to pieces. I went home in tatters. The phone rang. It was the voice of a frightened girl telling me to come back. I changed shirts and returned.

I see you twenty years ago, in a colorless woolen sweater, cotton stockings wearing thin at the heel, and the dark blue, baggy Chinese linen trousers fashionable in the subculture of the time. You are lying in the grass reading Goethe's memoirs when your head drops. A few minutes later, you lift it with a jerk. It is etched with the pattern of grass. You say you've had a good sleep because the book was so nice and boring.

Our daily lives melded, as did our memories. Silently we watched the shadows move. Most of our choices are in fact discoveries. Someone rings our doorbell and slips into our life, leaving the silk nightshirt bought at the flea market on our hook. If I wanted independence, why choose the dependency of family? Such was the question I asked myself before marrying for the third time. The following were my arguments against the move, which I put forth with ever weakening conviction: The man with a family is a prisoner: he can no longer assert he has nothing to lose. The married man is condemned to domesticity, the paterfamilias to simplemindedness. A wife is like the state: she is curious about everything you do and observes you in secret. Isn't it enough to have the state listening in? (True, I do not generally kiss the bugging device.)

The women I stayed with longest were the ones I most feared to upset. The less fear I felt, the sooner I beat a retreat, the sooner I chose another to step into my room without knocking. Mere whim drew me to some, but it was no whim that I was attracted to Jutka's voice, Jutka's touch, smell, movement, speech, and way of thinking, all from the very first night, or that the feeling has stayed with me for some twenty years.

Delicate, restrained, cautious, gently laughing, humming, and proffering considered judgments, Jutka came to West Berlin with me in 1982 for my next stay there, having been my partner in Budapest for three years by then. She proudly announced that she could understand the radio in German and had no trouble with French; English was a foregone conclusion. She loved golden leaves, rye bread with gorgonzola, and a Macon burgundy.

After our return everything was as before. Once, in 1987, the border guard checking my documents at the computer screen disappeared and brought out another guard, who found and confiscated the manuscripts of some talks I was planning to give. The Department of Education would return them to me should it see fit.

"But how can I lecture without them?"

"That's your problem."

"Well, that's the end of my talks," I said.

He liked that.

But it was all just an experiment, a ruse: the text had been smuggled out and the German translation was waiting for me in the West.

Looking out of a car window in Berlin, I see a peaceful, clean, and ordered city. Everything works. Not *almost* everything, *everything*. What you see in the shopwindows is what you see people wearing, which suggests that people change their possessions frequently and hence have no need to grow too fond of them. If I lived here, my wish would be to acquire means with a clean conscience. I would worry about spiritual frigidity, surround myself with prudent formalities, and carefully plan my time.

Back home there is a purple fog in the streets: the exhaust of east-bloc cars. That summer Jutka finished a book on death and funerals in Budapest at the beginning of the twentieth century. Her mood was far from funereal, however: she was more concerned with diapers.

I refuse to cling to situations and refuse to run from them. I have pure chance to thank for every turn in my life, including my three wives. One day I happened to catch a glimpse of Vera's hair in a classroom, though I had seen her a hundred times before. Juli plopped down on the arm of my chair at a happy gathering and stayed for sixteen years and two children. Jutka rang my doorbell one day in Paris—we were compatriots and lived on the same floor—and asked if I would like some coffee. The coffee never materialized, though a marriage and three children did. In the most traditional manner I have discovered the simplest purpose for life in my children and grandchildren, for whom I mean to stick around as long as possible.

Notes to myself: there is no point calling the attention of others to what I do not want or do not know. I have been shameless enough. No one wants to look at my bare chest anymore, so I'll wrap a scarf around my neck instead.

Nothing I come out with is of any use for anyone. It might have been once, but those days are gone. The day is approaching when I shall no longer set my glasses on the nightstand or say good night to my wife before withdrawing to my room. It won't be long now before my eyes are like two glazed chestnuts.

Every life is better than no life; every life, including the pain that goes with it, is good. True, getting through the daily grind is like wading through seaweed, but I can get through all sorts of things, therefore I am. And given the fact that I am alive, the question of why is as inane as fly droppings on a grape.

At twelve I survived National Socialism; at fifteen I saw Communism take over. Communism and I grew old together. Decades passed in active, disciplined resignation. Since I was fifty-six by the time the regime collapsed, I spent the best years of my life in the shadow of its stupidity. Still, I never watched my country from afar. I groped my way around in it.

Life was slow, which I did not regret, because there was so much of it. Humans are made mortal, hence real, by their imperfection; frailty and mortality are synonyms in the moral sense. Moral philosophy can rest only on frailty and our acceptance of it.

If every written description of human reality constitutes literature, then perhaps so does man himself. The novel's main character may be a welfare lawyer or city builder or retired revolutionary, but these are just naive masks, for there are no welfare lawyers or city builders or retired revolutionaries who ponder their lives with such profundity when lying in bed or sitting on the bench of a mental institution. Interior monologue does not occur in complete sentences.

All my life's more important choices have sprung from my decision as an adolescent to become a writer: I refrained from crossing the temporarily open border in 1956, chose jobs that required observation, became interested in people at the lower end of the social ladder (not that I was so high up myself, with my small salary, small apartment, and two or three changes of clothes), accompanying my former fellow student Tamás Csillag to the housing project at the Old Buda Brick Factory and spending the next seven years in Elizabeth Town as a supervisor of children's welfare. Then I grew curious about Hungary as a whole, the outlying cities and villages, and took a position with an institute of urban studies.

It is summer. How little the people of Budapest try to cover up their bodies, whether beautiful or ugly! I put it down to the city's sensuality and the survival of a pre-Christian, pagan lust for life. Budapest always goes whole hog: Stalinism, the Revolution, the compromises of the Kádár regime, you name it. It experiments with strategies of survival, grinding up the system to soften it, reviving old traditions—anything to curb the damage. Remember that Budapest was the first city in Eastern Europe to proclaim its freedom. The city is more enduring than the government; it has never let that pagan lust for life be taken over by ascetic delirium. There are plenty of upstanding cynics around here who do not think suffering is more moral than good cheer.

Even my internal emigration was basically a chance happening: one morning at dawn my doorbell rang, and in they came, picking apart my filing cabinet and dismissing me from all institutions. Then came the changes in 1989, and soon thereafter I had a phone call inviting me to be the president of International PEN. It was a serious offer, and it behooved me to accept it and do a good job.

Some authors love to play it tough; they are not satisfied until they have brushed with mortal danger and can recount it to their readers. I am not that type. I am of a more placid nature. But once in a while I run smack into fate's outstretched palm.

The good things always come on their own, the gifts of fate (or Providence, if you will), but the bad too come randomly, unexpectedly: there it is, and that's that. The ravages of fate are not something we can sense approaching or prevent. We make our way along a stairway of the gifts and accidents that constitute chapter divisions.

I do not like to be engulfed by the situation I happen to be in at a given time; I would rather look at it from the side or from above: I enjoy backing off and moving on. What is this compulsion, this current sweeping me on, this whistling wind, this gentle breath? The wish to slip the traps? To keep from being surrounded?

I was born in 1933. I was six when the Second World War broke out, eleven when survival meant the collaboration between fate and vigilance, particularly for Jewish children from the Hungarian provinces. When my parents were taken away in May 1944, my sister and I received an invitation to move to Budapest. Staying in Berettyóújfalu, waiting it out, would have been the normal thing to do. Had we done it, we would not be alive today. I owe my life to Budapest. It provided refuge for my sister and cousins and me; it kept us out of Auschwitz. All that mattered to me then about Budapest was its size: it let us be needles in a haystack. By May 1944 it was clear that people in the provinces would do nothing to stop the deportations, that they were following the dictates of a government that wanted to make all cities and towns *judenfrei*. The official culture around me has always been deceitful and, except for a few exceptional years, hostile to me. Although I had committed no crimes against it, I would eventually realize the time had come to start.

Every word puts the writer in a new situation. He is carried onward by the throat-tightening intoxication of improvisation. If a person's choices and actions count for anything, then this day, from the rising up unto the going down of the sun, is his constant pilgrimage. There is no line between everyday and holy acts.

The tactful pilgrim recognizes the possibility that dialogue with a saint is forever one-sided. He may spend his whole life speaking to someone who does not exist. Yet even if he never gets an answer, if the saint never reveals himself, he has no trouble addressing him, the eternal *here and now*.

On such secret, private pilgrimages we retrace the steps of a route long since traveled, reliving a past event, leaving the land of servitude and trudging the road of suffering to the cross. Our man brings the lamb, the most valuable offering of all: the son. He gladly offers his neck to the heavy blade. He appears before the godhead-in-hiding to offer It his life. So it is with books: a constant struggle with the angel fate has delivered us to; an eternal plodding, pinning down traces, making stations visible. The writer's path as pilgrimage? The parallel is perhaps justified by the pursuit of the unattainable: writing the book after which no other books need be written, after which there is only the bell, the flash, and loss of consciousness. They put all they've got into that last book, thinking about it during every waking moment, living with it, a lover full of promises, yet ultimately elusive.

I would have liked to write the kind of book I could have been called away from at any moment, one that could never be finished, only stopped. One more glass, one more pipe, and nothing for me to be ashamed of.

Who is observing me? Who is the all-seeing guardian of my fate? Why not just say someone. If He has created me, He can watch me. Our dream is a universe that is made for us and looks after us. If we weave God into a story, He turns out like a person who is ever at our disposal, even if He does occasionally go into hiding. Our Father is a good deal like us. If He is equally Lord of Life and Lord of Death, then he is both good and evil, as we are, and He simply mimics the game being played on earth, uniting the mind and blind happenstance.

I used to hold sin to be fatuous and shallow: the sinful are impatient and scatterbrained, panic-stricken and hysterical. Could they have but imagined the consequences they might never have sinned in the first place. Lately I have been inclined to think that hatred and cruelty are independent passions and can fill a life, be it stupid or intelligent. Even the most determined relativist can distinguish between a decent person and a scoundrel, especially if he is affected by the behavior of the party in question. Our sense of whether a person is good or evil works instinctively, the way we blink when something gets into our eye.

I smile a lot. My father also had the gift of smiling. It stems from our simple natures. The smarter you are, the angrier you are. When asked whether I am happy, I respond: often. When asked whether I am ever unhappy, my answer is: rarely. Which goes to show how simple I am.

While I was studying in Berlin on a German fellowship in 1977, my mother was my main tie to Budapest. She was my only blood relative in Hungary. A terrible correspondent, I phoned her every week. I tried to keep her happy with gifts and alleviate her financial condition, and in the spring I invited her to Berlin for a month: a pair of warm boots is no substitute for a smile and long leisurely talks peppered with *édesanyám*—literally "my sweet mother"—which in its slightly antiquated Hungarian sounds perfectly natural, yet cannot be translated naturally into any other language.

When we part, I kiss her hand. The joints in her fingers have grown a little thicker, and she remarks with humorous regret that light brown spots have appeared on her skin. "Old age is ugly, my boy. Nothing nice about it." By way of consolation I tell her that even an old face can be beautiful if it reveals a good soul. I have refrained from asking myself whether my mother was beautiful. That she never was. But her eyes have an oriental kind of mystery that has grown brighter and more meditative with age.

My mother was happy about my being a writer. She would read reviews of my works in German, French, and English with a dictionary at her side, looking up every word she did not know. She would say a few words of praise, then begin to worry whether the work in question would be published in Budapest and get me into trouble. No need to write about absolutely everything, she said. "You can write something that is good and still not provoke *them*, my boy."

She would have been terribly gratified to see me on Budapest television and have her friends phone her the next day, to be congratulated by her old hairdresser or the young woman caretaker in the building or perhaps the neighbor with the friendly face, whose husband had been a prison guard known for his restrained behavior.

My mother was hardly surprised at my trouble with the state, as she herself had had less than pleasant experiences with the authorities. She felt her modest pension to be insufficient, but would have been perfectly satisfied with half again as much. At midday she ate a little soup with potatoes and an egg or two on the side. Listening to old man Kádár would put her to sleep. "You've had your say," she would tell him, switching off the television.

At six in the morning she would drink a cup of coffee in the kitchen, then go back to bed and read or listen to the radio until eight, then spend an hour exercising and bathing. She never went to a private doctor, not wishing to spend the money; the free clinic doctors suited her just fine. She was overjoyed to get a two-week, union-sponsored pass to a medicinal spa every year. On those occasions she shared a room with her old friend Marika. Marika never married and was a touch crotchety, but Mother was used to her eccentricities. They would have espressos in the café and watch television in the common lounge. They might also indulge in a jigger of brandy of an afternoon (though a bottle of cognac could last half a year in my mother's cabinet despite the fact that she offered it to guests).

I did not stay on in San Francisco in 1978, though I might have chosen to work for any number of causes: the American Indians, or the Catholics of Northern Ireland, or the gays of the Castro district, or tanning-room devotees protesting nuclear energy, or Australian Aborigines. I might have chosen South Korean CEOs, communards from the Pyrenees, instructors of bioenergetic analysis, Sufi gurus, levitating meditators, faith healers, or Jews for Jesus. I might have joined an African resistance movement, offered to help the developing world, or I might simply have stayed on, playing with films, holograms, videos, computers, visiting prisoners in jail, converting to homosexuality, or moving into the pink house where Janis Joplin committed suicide. But I didn't. I could have landed a teaching job in some provincial city, where at this moment I would be walking onto the main quad, past the bank to the café, where I would be ordering apple juice in a paper cup and looking out over the young men and women made angry and headstrong by trying to work their way upward. But I didn't do that either.

The books on my shelf are alive, entreating me to look at them, take them out of the darkness, follow them. Boxes fill and pile up behind me, my abandoned writings pursuing me. I delay opening them and restoring lost time. So many faded pictures, names now just barely familiar. But when the heavens are kind, a chink opens up and something comes out of nothing.

My work goes better in the village than in Budapest or Berlin, where I spend most of my time. Since I live my life in both kinds of place, however, the extremes of pro- or antiurban cultural philosophy are alien to me. In fact, the tension between the two is my domain: I enjoy moving back and forth between density and sparseness, between the natural and the artificial; I have no desire to drop anchor at either end.

I dash out of the house into the meadow. You cannot see this spot from the village. I stop and turn around. The vast emptiness is refreshing—the surrounding hills, the ruins of a castle sacked three hundred years ago, the solitude. There is no one here in the bright noon light. It is no effort at all for me simply to be.

The years have come and gone, and I am still here at the Academy of the Arts in Berlin, stressing the first syllable of German words in my Hungarian way. I give the Germans what advice I have and make my umpteenth introductory speech. I've been reelected president. There were no other candidates.

I support my family as best I can and do my best to stay out of their way. I recognize (and accept) the fact that my wife is boss of the hearth, and I do everything in my power to obey her. I try to provide warmth and encouragement to the family, knowing they will have troubles enough—anxieties, failures, loneliness, sadness, losses—the extent of which a parent can never know. I am content to start each day with the patter of footsteps around me.

I might just as well be a conscientious farm animal, giving regular milk and getting by on modest fodder. For the family I am not Mr. President; I am a simple smile at all the goings-on around the kitchen table. Who can tell how true to life my descriptions are? Even my mother is a product of the imagination when I write of her, as I am myself when I am my subject. Whatever is made of words is narrative, not reality.

In tonight's joint panel discussion of the Berlin Academy of Art and Academy of Science we are to delve into the question of whether science and art are not mere luxuries. Of course they are. Almost everything human is a luxury: morality, religion, conversation, recreation, love, mourning—luxuries all. As it is a luxury whenever a person does not steal or cheat or kill the weak or denounce his competitor with a real or trumped-up accusation. Only in barracks, prisons, and concentration camps are there no luxuries.

I have been informed that I shall not escape the final agony, that I shall not be resurrected, and that on the other side there will be nothing at all. In response to this I shall call for a white horse and, taking a deep breath, a white widow as well, and make cynically merry in the dark of night when the rest of the family is sleeping. I do not acknowledge my sinfulness and expect practically nothing of others.

The narrator prepares: he has taken his medicines, lifted his weights, kept himself alive. If he obediently follows the path of his pen on the paper, he can invent and vicariously experience situations with the aid of his imagination. Today is the novel, the eternal today. The best hours are those in which nothing can happen unless he is the cause. The narrator's freedom means life imprisonment. He even writes when no one encourages him to so do. What is he after? More days, more sentences, and the well-being of his dependents.

He is ignorant, helpless, and perplexed, with no choice but to look his decline in the face. Meanwhile his past, his fortune, has appreciated in value. Old photographs assure us we are the same people we were as children. Tell me a nice, boring story, my friend. We'll fill in the gaps, go round and round, repeat ourselves.

I have been a spy for the writing profession in all my roles: welfare officer, urban researcher, dissident. (The things we get ourselves into!) With the political changes in 1989 I turned oracle for a while, a role that required some reflection. Does this mean I strayed onto the path of sin by selling myself to the devil of worldly vanities?

I get up. There is a cramp in my leg. I stumble, hopping from the table to the armchair and back. I lie down and groan: standing was better. Images from a sleepless night, a night too long. The only remedy is to sit at the desk and do what I usually do.

Every sentence is an independent entity, a freestanding unit, a closed circle, as if internal cohesion were drawing together a fistful of magnesium buckshot. Picture a pile of fish roe or a clump of bees stuck together on a tree branch after you shake it. More than once I have felt like vanishing unnoticed like a drop of water falling from the spout.

A brook is babbling under the wooden bridge. A neighbor's hen has gone mad. It has rained a lot lately after a long drought. The grapes have begun to shrivel: the stalks have sucked them dry. We are sitting out on the terrace. The clouds are shedding tears, and moisture hangs in the air. Birds are chirping lazily, and the elders are blackening. A poplar begins to shimmer in the bloody disc of the sun, as if suffused with glass.

At the end of the dock I am struck by the suspicion that I have reached the very end of the end, that there is nowhere to go from here. As an adolescent I imagined one would have to sit at the end of the dock for hours before profound thoughts would come. Given that no such thoughts come to me now, I trudge up Saint George Hill to the sunlit garden stairway of the crumbling winepress house. There is hang glider floating above, and the heavenly figure speeding in my direction brings a sudden shade and wind.

The woman who lives next door stumbled on her way back from shopping. We helped her home and looked in on her a few times, but after lying down for a while she was back at it: shaping her pretzels, adding a coat of egg white and a sprinkle of grated cheese. I look forward to munching on them and drinking her vintage. I smell ducks roasting behind her: her grandchildren are coming tomorrow.

In the afternoon I go out to where there are people and movement. I stare in wonder at the goods in market stands, holding up a wine goblet, buying a whistle and a string of beads for my daughter Zsuzsi, a jackknife with a carved handle for my son Józsi, and for Áron, the boy poet who disdains possessions, several portions of shish kebab. Jutka buys some red basil for her herb garden.

We visit the artists' festival in the nearby village of Kapolcs. We see a wooden pig with gleaming eyes and a little screen in its mouth showing the slaughter—but in reverse order, from sausage to living animal—in copious detail. We hear its yelps and observe the details of its disembowelment projected large, as the eyes are removed and sliced and the blood stirred. We have the feeling we are eating one another, draining one another's blood into a bowl to make sausages or serve it, steaming fresh, over browned onions.

Then comes a Punch whacking at ghosts, but once he has whacked them aplenty and they have whacked him back, once all those *palacsinta* sticks have been put to good use, the rain, till then only a drizzle, starts coming down hard and the show is stopped. Drums and cymbals fill the street. The bus can't move. A slender girl takes her bows, the grotesque head on a wooden, collar-like apparatus on her shoulders bobbing up and down. A booted actor clacks his booted hands, then splits into a four-legged creature or, rather, two figures that have it out with each other, shaking blood- or flour-speckled skulls over their backs. The eye pops out of one of them like a tomato.

I became part of the cavalcade, standing there with an enormous green-and-white Dutch umbrella in my hand next to my sons as they bolt down one *palacsinta* after the other. The churches, sheds, and pubs all around are full of things to see.

The only sad note is Summer Santa pulling his sleigh, his cotton mustache drooping, melting off his face. He has lost his way and ended up in summer, inconsolable as he drags his empty sled over the gravel in search of a better world. Last year he was the Bad Boy of the Village, slapping the bottoms of the prettier women, tossing a bottle far away when he found he'd been given mineral water for his thirst, and sneezing gargantuan sneezes which fascinated Áron and Józsi. But he's on his good behavior this year: after a few words he moves on, downhearted, never giving up hope of finding a nice world full of snow for himself.

In a pub we find a tableau vivant and *cimbalom* music, outside—trucks with actors jumping and sneering and screeching and stomping something fierce, little children searching for their mothers, balls rolling off, drivers yawning, beer, wine, and *pálinka* flowing. A robust fellow stops the cars asking people to taste his beer, which he has brought in a fire truck.

My sons liked the Summer Santa best of all and then the four-legged, two-headed wonder. Zsuzsi liked both of them best.

It will soon be 2000. I am sorry to trade in all those nines—svelte, swollen heads—for the potbellied zeroes. With its large, backward-looking head, the nine seems so intelligent, while the three zeroes signify self-satisfied achievement.

The millennium is over. It's time to pay the bill. Here comes the waiter.

"I had a twentieth century," I tell him. He pauses. I don't see why. I've made it clear I intend to pay.

"What about the second millennium?" he asks.

"Must I pay for that as well?"

"Who else?"

"Fine. Add it to the bill."

But the waiter shakes his head sadly. "What about the first millennium?"

I am seized with fear. "How far back do you mean to go? You can't hold me responsible for everything, can you?"

"Who else?" he says, shaking his head again sadly.

This time I'm angry. "I want to see the owner, the Lord Himself!"

And what does God do? He appears on the balcony. In person. He points a finger at me. I get up from the table, look Him in the eye, and point my finger at Him. We stand there for quite some time. Host and guest, father and son.

"I shall call for your mother," He finally says.

"And I for your daughter," I finally say.

The women come. The children have not yet had dinner. We are told to wash our hands, take our seats, and stop our bickering. "Stubborn old asses. Still pointing fingers." We sit, nonplussed, the Old Man and I, waiting to be served.

After dinner the Old Man will not give up. "That bill of yours still wants paying." We are about settle on a price. I hold out my hand. The Old Man's hand rises. I wait for it to reach mine. Where does it stop? I do not know.

Where is home? Where I stand, inside a solar system. Where I sit, holding my pen tight. Here in the bed where I awake, where I set off for the bathroom, where I step out of the door and greet whomever I happen to meet.

Home is those few square kilometers where my paths come together. Home is the Jewish cemetery at Berettyóújfalu, unused for fifty years, my grandmother's tall gravestone and my grandfather's, just as tall, in black granite. (My great-grandfather's, in white marble, is less than half their height.) Home is in the classroom I wanted so desperately to escape as I stared at the bakery sign across the way. (My schoolmates were murdered and the school torn down.)

Where is home? Where they don't strike me dead. Where I know my children are safe. Where the individual and the word are held in high regard. Where being who I am and thinking what I think are granted the benefit of respect. Where there is a quiet kitchen nook for postprandial conversations over wine. Where the children play hide-and-seek and build bunkers. Where Jutka sits reading, feet up, in an armchair. Where I can stop for a glass of wine here and there on my way up the hill and, after the friendly invitations, prance my way down again.

Home is in the middle of the Elizabeth Bridge, where, coming home from my travels, I murmur, “How beautiful!” It is a house overgrown with woodbine, where I search for my key, climb panting to the third floor, a bag on each shoulder, and hear sounds within. Lively sounds. I have arrived.

Printed in the United States
by Baker & Taylor Publisher Services